Characterological Transformation

The Hard Work Miracle

Characterological Transformation

The Hard Work Miracle

STEPHEN M. JOHNSON, Ph.D.

W · W · NORTON & COMPANY · *NEW YORK* · *LONDON*

For Margaret and Merle,
Mom and Dad

ACKNOWLEDGMENTS

THE ROAD THAT ends in the publication of this book has been a long one—arduous and rewarding. It has involved many teachers who have been willing to share generously of their knowledge and many clients who have been willing to risk trust in spite of former injuries. Here I want to acknowledge those colleagues who have stood beside me for a good deal of this journey and whose presence is reflected in these pages. First among these must be two psychologists who have been there through it all and unrelentingly encouraged me to stay on the path and trust my own judgment. They have given me the safety to be and the support to be myself. Thanks to Peter Alevezos, Ph.D., and Larry King, Ph.D.

The other companions on this journey are the leaders and members of a supervision/training group. Edward Muller, Ph.D., has been the guest leader of this group for many years, and has been my mentor for much of the work included here. Ed introduced me to the possibility of the integration of characterological, object relations, and ego psychology theories which provides the underpinning for this volume. G. Timothy Scott, Ph.D., has provided years of training, particularly in bioenergetic therapy, both in and out of this supervision/training group. Finally, the other long-term members of this group have seen me through. Thanks to Susan Rutherford, M.S.W., co-leader, Gypsy Frankl-Podolsky, M.S.W., Debra Jackson, M.A., Pollyann Jamison, Ph.D., Richard Klotz, M.A., Judith Lindsay, M.A., and Georgene Ollerenshaw, M.A.

Two people have made the production of this volume possible. Jane Gantor typed the manuscript and contributed helpful criticism and encouragement. Susan Barrows, my editor, recognized the value of the work, edited it, and shepherded it through each phase to completion. Her competence and support have considerably eased the task of producing this book.

CONTENTS

Characterological Transformation

The Hard Work Miracle

INTRODUCTION

CHARACTEROLOGICAL TRANSFORMATION suggests the union of two approaches to human problems which are generally regarded as separate if not antithetical. Characterological theories are basically psychoanalytic, classical, and usually within the purview of the psychiatric literature. Transformational psychology, on the other hand, is largely derived from the human potential movement, popular, and often associated with nonprofessionally led movements. Where characterological theories focus on rather basic immutable characteristics, transformation suggests the possibility of immediate and profound change. While psychoanalytic therapists generally use more passive therapeutic methods, transformers are usually highly active. *The Hard Work Miracle* mirrors this multifaceted polarity and suggests again an integration of opposites. Such is the purpose of this book, though the integration reaches between and beyond these two poles—to other forms of conventional and unconventional healing. Essential in this integration, however, is the affirmation of the hope that we can transmute the immutable and the reassertion of the fact that this miracle usually involves some pretty hard work.

This book is the first of a series integrating a number of theoretical and practical approaches to psychotherapy. It is the result of my search for the psychic origins of human pain and the potentials of human expression. As a psychologist, I have chosen this search as my life's work, and as a person with my share of pain and potential, I have found it to be a personal necessity. The search has involved contact with many forms of therapeutic thought and practice, both as a recipient and practitioner. In every case, I have found something of value. Each major school of thought and practice has something to offer—an insight, a technique, a useful theoretical point of view. At the same time, each field seems to miss a great deal about the condition and cure of human pain. Moreover, those who have the most to say about that pain often have the least to say about the other side—the wonder and joy and peace that are possible for people. Each field seems blindfolded to the value of the others, each touching a different part of the elephant and taking it for the whole.

Those of us who appreciate the value of at least two different approaches are often hard pressed to formulate, much less articulate, an integration yielding a whole view of psychopathology, therapy, and health. Through a unique and fortunate set of circumstances, I believe I have developed a theoretical and applied view of psychotherapy which uses the wisdom of many therapeutic schools, while at the same time providing a solid grounding in the principles of characterological development and change.

Like many therapists of my generation, I prematurely gave psychoanalytic psychotherapy short shrift and moved on to almost everything else before returning to find the great wisdom of that basic theoretical structure. My early frustrations and disappointments with psychoanalytic thought and practice were not unwarranted. Large portions of analytic writing are unnecessarily obscure, dominated by an imprecise and often archaic jargon, and full of unsubstantiated dogma.

In contrast, a number of the newer therapies, including but not limited to transformational psychology, behavior modification, rational-emotive therapy, neurolinguistic programming, Gestalt therapy, hypnosis, family and strategic therapies, are far more accessible, sensible, and productive of therapeutic results in a reasonable length of time. Yet, the theory of each of these newer approaches is incomplete and unsatisfying and the result of the work done by each is often limited, one-sided, and even short-lived. None really provides a holistic view of what human pathology is all about. They provide no owner's manual for mental, emotional, and behavioral health and well-being. So, for the most part, each offers only a narrow view of a life process of awe-inspiring complexity and beauty.

Those who have taught me psychoanalysis in more human and comprehensible ways have helped me to see the core human issues with which we all must deal and to appreciate the ecstasy that's possible when those issues are no longer at issue. The ego psychologists and particularly those working in object relations theory have provided a very useful sequential outline of these core issues. Though evolving from a somewhat different orientation, those who have delineated characterological theory have developed a typology involving archetypal expressions of roughly the same core issues. The understanding of these issues which persist throughout and rule adult life offers great potential for a very deep appreciation of the tragedy, irony, and pathos of existence. At the same time, this knowledge sows the seeds for appreciating how life can be full, relaxed and joyous.

Contemporary psychoanalytic thought also highlights the central role of feeling and emotion in understanding human pathology and health. Our primitive sensory system is absolutely central in the development of human problems. People do, in the layman's words, "have emotional problems." Though they are not the only type of mental health problem, one cannot hope to begin to understand the human condition without understanding feelings and emotionality.

Analytic developmental psychology provides its richest gift by giving us an understanding of the *origins* of the core human issues. These issues come from the interaction of the young child's basic needs with his environment's ability to adequately fulfill them. The tragic disappointments which often come out of that interaction provide the crucible in which the issue is formed. When the child's basic needs are not met, rage, terror, and grief are the ultimate affective responses to that reality. Because the child cannot live in such a state of chronic negative emotion, a defensive structure will be created to ward off these incapacitating feelings. The particular defenses used will be a function of the severity of the trauma, the developmental level of the child, and his genetic strength or weakness. The child of five, for example, has many cognitive, behavioral and affective resources which the infant of six months does not. That difference will largely determine the defenses he chooses to avoid the affect and cope with the environment. Similarly, the development of the ego, of the self, and of the living sense will be retarded at the point at which these defenses are chosen and cemented into the character. This is the very valuable concept of *developmental arrest*, which will be outlined much further in this text. This is the essential analytic perspective which I find gives an understanding of life and human pathology missing almost everywhere else.

If one reads between the lines or is taught by more evolved analytic therapists, one can derive a model of positive mental health from this theory. Yet, the psychoanalytic and particularly characterological labels for characteristic adaptations are singularly negative and pathological; there is relatively little emphasis on where the absence of pathology will lead. There is little attention paid to what we really could be, and none to what this melodrama of life is all about. In traditional characterological terms, one has the choice of being one of the following or something equally horrible: oral, schizoid, masochistic, psychopathic, narcissistic, rigid, hysterical, obsessive-compulsive, etc. While, of course, we need to label psychopathology to communicate and think about it in a systematic way, these labels are, unfortunately, often powerful negative suggestions that convey judgmental attitudes and further separation between those whom one considers healthy and those whom one considers sick. By now, we have enough research on the effects of negative labeling to be very concerned about the effect on ourselves and others of using these pejorative words. While I feel I must use them here because it seems necessary to relate this book of integration to the larger field to which it owes so much, I do so reluctantly. I will attempt to develop a more sympathetic and communicative orientation to the labeling process. As a beginning, I will focus labeling on the etiological traumas which caused the core issues. I hope this will stimulate more sympathy for our own and others' problems than do the labels based on the typical consequences of these etiological factors. Orality, for example, is developed as a response to neglect, abandonment, and the demand, either implicit or explicit, that the infant grow up too soon. To see a person as one dealing with the consequences of that history will do more, I think, to stimulate a healing response in another than will a focus on the often-demanding, whining, sucking, and placating behavior associated with one possible adaptation to such a history.

Finally, we all need to pay more attention to what is possible for people. Do even the classically trained analysts have a deep understanding of what a genital character with firm object constancy acts like? And even if they do, does this explain all of the richness and complexity and beauty that is possible for people? Perhaps if we pay more attention to where we are going we might have a better chance of getting there.

Many of the newer approaches to psychological healing have even less to say about this than do the psychoanalytic schools. The behaviorists and the cognitive therapists have, it seems, almost nothing to say about it. Primarily, one must turn to the "third force"—the humanists and the experiential therapists—to find someone giving attention to this question. Many therapists, especially those trained in the scientific, hard-nosed tradition, find a great deal of writing in this area to be so much cotton candy—nonspecific, unsubstantiated, and romantic. I have had this experience on many occasions and have sought to find another way. I believe that object relations theory and character analysis can help with this, in that they give us a greater appreciation of what our innate human needs are. Thus, they suggest more specifically what the person whose needs have been and are being met will look like. In addition, the joys of the schizoid's evolution will differ from the joys of the rigid's growth in ways that can be concretely described. Explication at this level will be largely the focus of my discussion of that issue. In this way, I hope to escape glowing descriptions of human nirvana while still attending to the objective of positive human health.

In the first chapter, I will present the basic theoretical integration of object relations theory, ego psychology, and character analysis. This will be a brief summary of psychoanalytic developmental theory derived primarily from the work of Mahler, Spitz and others in the object relations and ego psychology schools and of characterological theory which derives primarily from Reich, Lowen, and the other bioenergetic theorists. In this chapter, I will also define a number of terms which will be used throughout this and the coming volumes, including such key concepts as the *ego*, the *self*, the *schemas of ego organization*, etc. The remainder of the book will be organized around the presentation of each archetypal character structure as understood through an integration of character analytic and object relations theory. The outline for the presentation of each character structure is as follows:

- Etiology
- Affect, behavior, cognition
- Energetic expression
- Therapeutic objectives
- Therapeutic techniques

Thus, for any given characterological classification, we will explore the etiology in terms of child development and the concept of developmental arrest. This will be followed by elucidating the characteristic affective problems and assets, behaviors, social functioning, and cognitive abilities to be found in the type in question. In discussing the energetic expression of a character type, I will rely largely on the Reichian and bioenergetic experience to present the bodily expressions of character defenses and set the stage for therapeutic interventions at a body level. This will be followed by an exposition and listing of therapeutic objectives for the archetypal structure in question. Finally, a major portion of the text will be devoted to therapeutic techniques from all major contemporary schools of psychotherapeutic thought, including psychoanalysis, transactional analysis, bioenergetics, ego psychology, Gestalt therapy, hypnosis, client-centered therapy, behavior modification, strategic therapy, rational-emotive therapy, family therapy, and neurolinguistic programming. I highlight this organization here because I think that it is a heuristic device for use in thinking about any case study. I have found it a useful outline for case presentations in supervisory and other contexts and recommend it for the reader's consideration beyond whatever specific content may be found here.

A final outline which permeates this book has already been mentioned. It is the concentration on *affect*, *behavior*, and *cognition*. A character type can be described by outlining the characteristic feelings, behaviors, and thought processes which define it. The major schools of psychotherapeutic thought may also be simply classified in these areas. Techniques from any school can obviously affect experience in any or all of these categories, but it is certainly the case that psychoanalytic and Gestalt work, for example, are more directed at affective experience, while behavior modification and strategic therapy are more directed at the alteration of behavior. Similarly, neurolinguistic programming and rational-emotive therapy tend to be directed more exclusively at the cognitive or thinking processes. Integrating these approaches offers advantages; the recommended approach is to use them to selectively heal and repair developmental lesions in each area. So, this is a book of integration of theory and practice with the presentation of a form for structuring one's thought to be used in the understanding and treatment of the individual person.

This work is devoted to models of character and models of therapeutic techniques. All models are oversimplified and incomplete representations of what is—useful but not true. In discussing characterological types we are really discussing archetypal human issues. Any individual will present a unique configuration of the resolution of these issues, as well as much, much more. So there are really no schizoid characters in the world, but a knowledge of the schizoid issue will help us detect and treat it in a person in pain. This same person will probably also benefit from some work on other issues as well in healing his own unique configuration of character.

In the presentation of techniques, I have often deliberately outlined procedures in the most succinct and programmed way possible. The procedures can be learned most easily in this way, and their essential ingredients are thereby highlighted. Ultimately, however, it is the familiar and fluid use of the basic principles underlying each technique which is the goal of the practicing clinician. Therapy by cookbook instruction won't work. Yet, by following standard procedures, the therapist can begin to integrate the principles and procedures and ultimately use them, rather than the outline, to guide his work. Whether the therapist is using an outline or not, it will always be the client's response which will dictate the therapist's action. Therapy is a dynamic interaction between people only somewhat influenced by the models which guide its comprehension.

Korzypski has written, "The map is not the territory." When doing psychotherapy we may add, "Keep your eyes on the road, not on the map."

CHAPTER I

OBJECT RELATIONS AND CHARACTER ANALYSIS

A psychoanalyst is one who pretends he doesn't know everything.

— Anonymous

THIS CHAPTER WILL present and begin integration of two areas of psychoanalytic thought that are essentially compatible but have developed independently. The object relations school is made up of those child development researchers who have observed the developmental process and those analysts who have incorporated these theories into their understanding of adult psychopathology (e.g., Horner, 1979; Jacobson, 1964; Kernberg, 1976; Kohut, 1971; Mahler, 1968; Masterson, 1976; Spitz, 1965; Winnicott, 1965). These theorists focus on the natural evolution of ego development and the effects of trauma on ego functioning. Too, they have emphasized the *object*, and more particularly the *human*, relations impact of trauma during early childhood and extended these observations to valuable insights concerning the nature of transference in therapy.

The character analytic school was originated by Wilhelm Reich (1949) and its more contemporary writers include Alexander Lowen (1958), Stanley Keleman (1981), and David Boadella (1977). This school has focused on various forms of environmental trauma and the results of such trauma on character development. It is one of the very few schools of thought focusing on the energetic or bodily consequences of trauma and the associated arrest in development.

Though coming out of a similar analytic tradition, these schools of thought have focused on different psychopathological entities, which makes their integration somewhat difficult. The object relations theorists have concentrated heavily on the etiology, characteristics, and treatment of the borderline and narcissistic character disorders. The character analytic theorists have focused on five basic character structures: schizoid, oral, psychopathic, masochistic, and rigid. Where the issue has been addressed, there has been theoretical controversy as to where the borderline and narcissistic characters fit into other frameworks (Horner, 1979; Muller, 1982). The integration is made more difficult by the fact that borderline means different things to different people and reviews of the literature have discovered quite a bit of inconsistency in the use of this label(Perry & Klerman, 1978). An integration of these characterological entities will be offered in this chapter and elaborated on in all that follows.

Apart from the confusion or controversy engendered by the differences in characterological labeling, these two schools of thought do integrate nicely. Though character analytic theorists emphasize the nature of environmental trauma and the consequent energetic or body armoring, their theory acknowledges developmental factors in character formation. The object relations theorists add a good deal to a comprehensive understanding of character by their emphasis on the evolution of ego abilities, particularly defense mechanisms and the evolving complexities of cognitive representations of self, others, and the object world. Their evolutionary outline of ego development helps explain pathological functioning and suggests treatment strategies for ego deficiencies, not only for narcissism and borderline functioning but for other diagnostic entities as well.

In the present chapter I will first summarize the developmental paradigm, which comes primarily from the observers of early child development—Mahler, Spitz, and Bowlby. Then, I will present the overall structure of the character analytic approach, which emphasizes the universal nature of the young human's response to the frustration of his natural needs and evolutionary processes. Following this general outline of character formation, I will outline particular character structures resulting from the integration of character analysis and object relations theory. Finally, I will offer an overview of the potential of this integrated understanding for diagnosing and repairing areas of developmental arrest in the psychotherapeutic context. In this third section, labeled "Ego Psychology Perspective," I will concentrate particularly on the potential of diagnosing by ego functioning and treatment oriented to ego repair. In all that follows, the specific character structures will represent the underlying organization of the book with an extensive analysis of each structure and recommended treatment procedures for each in the affective, behavioral and cognitive arenas.

OBJECT RELATIONS PERSPECTIVE

There are two primary contributions of object relations theory to a comprehensive understanding of human process and pathology. First, this body of literature offers an outline of the phases of early childhood development, with particular emphasis on cognitive and social relations development. As such, it provides a sequential unfolding of developmental tasks and an understanding of pathology as those tasks incompletely accomplished. The concept of developmental arrest within this theory offers an analogue explanation for many adult problems. While the "separation anxiety" of the adult is not precisely like that of the infant who first encounters it at about seven months, the similarities can prove instructive. To study basic human issues in their first expressions and resolutions makes a good deal of sense. When such issues are unresolved in the adult, object relations theory would suggest that they were never really resolved by the child at the appropriate developmental period. Further, the theory asserts that knowing how the child typically resolves a particular issue would help in treating the adult who still needs to acomplish such resolution.

In these ways, object relations theory offers both clinician and client a plausible and useful structure from which to view any number of cognitive and emotional difficulties. In my practice, I generously use the theory in an explanatory fashion with clients and find it extraordinarily useful in this way. Typically, the client is relieved to have some explanation for his difficulty. This often results in his greater self-compassion for the problems he faces. The explanation orients the client to the problem on which he needs to work and introduces him to the fact that, in a sense, he is dealing with a very young and often very frightened "child" when it comes to his core issue. This understanding increases patience and self-nurturing in dealing with the "irrational" and "childish" reactions which so often bring him to therapy.

A related use of the theory is the description it gives of how the infant, as an emerging human being, masters each developmental task.

It is valuable to know, for example, that the nine-month-old child will use "transitional objects" (e.g., a blanket or teddy bear) for soothing and comfort when mother is away. Further, the infant learns to tolerate the separation anxiety and repeatedly experiences that mother comes back. Eventually, the child internalizes the nurturing functions of the transitional objects. Further, he develops a solid internal representation of the mother, internalizing many of her caregiving functions. In general, the adult who has "missed a stitch" in this process needs to return and repair it in the therapeutic context. Thus, object relations theory is valuable for presenting a sequential and detailed understanding of child development — a valuable analogue for understanding and treating lapses in that development for the general and specific case.

The second and very related value of the theory exists in the even more detailed analysis that it can offer regarding the assessment and repair of certain cognitive or ego functions. Blanck and Blanck (1974) have recommended what they term "descriptive developmental diagnosis" in clinical treatment. By this they mean a broad span diagnosis of ego functioning in view of developmental knowledge about these functions. In other words, one may assess the developmental level of such things as reality-testing, decision-making, ability to delay gratification, self- or object-representation, characteristic defense mechanisms, etc. With this as a diagnostic base, one can then set about to repair these functions.

It is in this area where I believe object relations theory, or more broadly ego psychology, offers a very important bridge between psychoanalytic theory and contemporary cognitive and behavioral approaches to treatment. The cognitive strategies of neurolinguistic programming, for example, or the active techniques of behavior modification seem to have a good deal to offer concerning the repair of adaptive functions. The current focus on borderline pathologies in the analytic literature emphasizes the very real need for a reparative and reeducative therapeutic process. This has been the essential position of the behaviorists and the cognitivists for a long time, and they have developed some very effective methods for that purpose.

The first contribution of object relations theory will be presented now in an overview of the developmental theory. After this is integrated with the insights of character analysis, I will present an overview of developmental diagnosis by character structure under the heading, "Ego Psychology Perspective."

Autism

The autistic stage of early development is generally considered to encompass the first two months of life. This period is so named because the infant is characterized by his relative unresponsiveness to the stimuli around him, as if taking refuge behind a "stimulus barrier." He is urgently responsive to his own inner needs and frustrations, and appears to operate on an instinctive basis. He will root for the breast but not recognize it or the bottle when they are presented. The function of memory is not operative during this early period, so the infant cannot associate need gratification with its source and there is no specific attachment to the source. This stage has been labeled undifferentiated, meaning that the infant not only fails to differentiate between himself and the rest of the world, but also does not behave so as to suggest that he perceives any difference between any objects in the world. It is hypothesized that the infant in this stage experiences need satisfaction as existing within his own "omnipotent autistic orbit." He wishes principally to gratify hunger or other need states and then returns to a sleep or quiet half-awakened state when needs are met.

Pearce (1977) argues that this early autistic stage is really not innate at all, but rather the result of trauma engendered by typical birthing procedures in Western culture. He argues this rather persuasively, in part by citing the work of Gerber (1958), who studied natural childbirthing practices in Africa, where children were generally born at home, never separated from their mothers, and given continual loving attention during their first days of life. These infants displayed the smile response at the latest in their fourth day of life and were upright and responsive almost from birth. Pearce reports that Fredrick LeBoyer, who devised a more naturalistic and gentle form of childbirth, observes his babies to smile from only 12 hours after birth.

Whether induced or innate, this autistic state is, nevertheless, still the observed norm in our culture and will be the typical pattern for those raised in it. And, though the infant may appear autistic, important learning occurs during this period. Physical contact between the infant and caretaker appears to be very important. Stimuli which might startle or prompt the baby to cry under ordinary circumstances will have little or no effect if he is in physical contact with a caretaker. She can tolerate greater physical discomfort or pain if given such contact and, as every parent knows, digestive and other upsets are relieved by holding or rocking. Though the baby may not be able to discriminate the source of human contact, studies show that babies deprived of maternal care are less secure and more easily irritated throughout infancy than are those who have received more normal, nurturing attention. Though it may not appear that a great deal is going on during this period, apparently real learning is occurring because suddenly, one day, the infant smiles in *recognition* of the human face, indicating that he has begun to differentiate this object from others.

Autism to Symbiosis

This smile response, which occurs at about two months, represents a developmental landmark and the beginnings of human, psychological relations. This smile is not by any means his first, but it is different in that it is a smile of recognition or discrimination. Presumably, the repeated satisfactions which have been associated with the human face determine not only its early recognition among other objects, but also the nature of that reaction, a smile. At this two-month point, the infant cannot discriminate between the face of his primary caretaker and any other human face. And by his behavior over this symbiotic period, we assume that he *begins to develop* a merged representation of himself and whomever cares for him. Mahler, Pine, and Bergman (1975, p. 44) write " . . . the infant behaves and functions as though he and his mother were an omnipotent system—a dual unity with one common boundary." The merged representation is presumably being worked on in this period, just as the differentiation of the human face from other objects was being worked on in the autistic period. In each stage of learning, the infant is very much like a student with a difficult theoretical or mathematical problem. Every day there are lessons or repetitions of the basic notion to be learned. One day, it all may fall into place or "click" and there is recognition, insight, or discrimination. Yet, the complete consolidation of the concept comes gradually with accumulated experiences.

Critical to the establishment of sound symbiosis, which begins at two months and is consolidated at around five to six months, is the nonverbal cuing which the infant presents to indicate needs, tension, pleasure, etc. The more demonstrative and clear the baby can be in giving these cues, and the more sensitive and responsive the mother is to them, the firmer the symbiotic attachment. Among analytic developmental theorists, a sound symbiosis is universally believed to be necessary for the healthy development of all that is to come. Mahler, Pine, and Bergman (1975, p. 47) liken the two partners in symbiosis to two poles structuring the organizing properties of the ego. The solid connection of the poles provides a double frame of reference within which the child's experiences may eventually be formed into "clear and whole representations." Spitz (1965) has called the mother the auxiliary ego of the infant, her role being to ground the infant in a secure reality from which a solid sense of self, other, and the object world can eventually be built. In firm symbiosis the child develops a "confident expectation" (Mahler, Pine, & Bergman, 1975) of the world as represented by mother. The maternal holding and stabilizing provide "the symbiotic organizer — the midwife of individuation, of psychological birth" (Mahler, Pine, & Bergman, 1975, p. 47).

While the infant does not appear to give a great deal of evidence that she discriminates the caretaker from others, she is obviously building that discrimination during symbiosis. At about the same time that the symbiosis is consolidated (five to six months), the child begins to show efforts at discrimination and is less a passive lap-baby. She will explore and probe the mother's face and begin to push off against her chest, appearing to study her as if working on the discrimination puzzle.

Differentiation

The period of differentiation as the first stage of separation-individuation begins at approximately six months of age with the infant's first attempts to push off from the mother and perceive her more clearly. The developmental processes involved in developing an entirely separate identity continue from this point until about two-and-one-half years of age and, for many, well beyond that. But it is here in differentiation when the child begins to focus his attention outward. This shift of attention may occur more smoothly if the symbiosis has been secure, establishing a "safe anchorage" from which the infant can embrace the "expansion beyond the symbiotic orbit" (Mahler, 1968). During this differentiation period, the self-representation is still merged with the object-representation but the infant begins to discriminate the specific identity of the other part of the symbiotic unit. During this period, a *specific* smile of recognition will develop for the mothering figure, indicating that a specific bonding has taken place. This discrimination is the essential "seed" of the separation from symbiosis. Another marker event of this period involves responses which indicate that the child discriminates strangers from the mothering person. Children who have experienced optimal symbiotic attachment tend to show curiosity and wonderment at strangers while checking back visually to the mother. Children who have established less basic trust due to a less secure symbiosis show anxiety or even grave distress at being handled or approached by a stranger (Mahler, Pine, & Bergman, 1975). This response tends to occur at about eight months and has been termed the "eighth–month anxiety." Prior to this time, any warm body would do for holding or rocking, but at about eight months, the infant discriminates differences and prefers the mother for soothing. At this point, the gratifications he seeks are more than the material ones of warmth or nourishment. He is "attached" to a particular source of these supplies.

It is at about this time that he begins to show separation anxiety and begins to form attachments to such objects as teddy bears or blankets. These "transitional objects" seem to serve the function of allaying anxiety at separation from the primary attachment figure. This fear of separation signals the beginning of individuation because it signals a dim awareness that the child and his caretaker are separable and therefore separate. With separation anxiety, the infant may experience a panic, tantamount to the dissolution of self, when the symbiotic unity is threatened. Trouble can begin during this period if the symbiotic unit has not been sufficiently strong or gratifying or if the child is, for whatever reason, required to "hatch" and then move toward separation prematurely or abruptly (Mahler, 1968). As indicated in detail later, the schizoid and oral character structures are hypothesized to be a function of disruptions in these early peroids from birth through differentiation. Integrating object relations theory and character analysis suggests that these two pathologies come out of failures in the early symbiotic attachment and its graceful and gradual dissolution into individuation.

Practicing

The practicing subphase occurs between about the 10th and 18th months of development, when the child becomes increasingly absorbed with the growth of his autonomous functions and the consequent mastery of the world that these abilities permit. He is increasingly able to learn, perceive, and discriminate, but perhaps even more profoundly for him, he attains upright locomotion during this time. At the beginning of the practicing subphase, the infant will usually still be crawling about not far from the safety of his parents, but he is beginning to explore both his own abilities and the world around him. Eventually, through the magic of maturation and the perseverance of trial and error, he will learn to walk. With this new ability comes an entirely new view of the world. These are particularly high times in which the child has been observed to have a "love affair with the world" (Greenacre, 1957) and "seems to be intoxicated with his own faculties and with the greatness of his world" (Mahler, 1972, p. 7). As he explores, he demonstrates great imperviousness to knocks, falls, or frustrations, showing an unbridled spirit for life and an exhilaration in his own capacities and discoveries. During the practicing period, he can become so engrossed in all of this that he appears to be oblivious to the mother's presence. Still, he will return periodically to her, apparently needing her physical proximity from time to time, as if for recharging. Generally active, he may slow down and appear to concentrate inwardly when parental figures are absent.

From experimental evidence, it appears that the toddler begins, during this period, to imagine objects which he cannot see and thus build representations which will over the entire course of individuation eventually consolidate into solid and separate representations of self and others. The child's grandiosity and belief in his own magic omnipotence are "still to a considerable extent derived from his sense of sharing in his mother's magic powers" (Mahler, 1968, p. 20). There is, at this time, in Mahler's words still a "symbiotic dual unity" and "an inflated sense of omnipotence" which come from the child's own emerging autonomous functions merged with the mother's magic powers in the self-representation. At this point, the world is his oyster.

Rapprochement

The period of rapprochement is roughly 15 to 24 months. At about 15 months, the child begins to wish to share her discoveries with the mothering person and relates to her somewhat more as an independent entity rather than just a self-extension "home base" for need gratification. The primary sign of this change is the child's new habit of continually bringing things to her parent, often filling her lap with her world discoveries. The child's requirement shifts somewhat from need for "refueling" to need for parental interest and participation in the discovery process. On the heels of this shift comes greater awareness of the separateness of others in the world and greater interest in social interaction. At about 18 months of age, the child masters upright locomotion and, as she does, becomes somewhat less absorbed with this and other autonomous functions. She is now more independent of parents than ever before and, with her cognitive faculties developing, she becomes ever more aware of the separateness. In spite of increased and increasing cognitive and motor abilities, she begins to appear more vulnerable. She is no longer impervious to frustration and injury and may repeatedly appear very disappointed that her mother is not instantly at her side to reassure her when she falls or bumps into something. She will tend to show increased anxiety at separation, and she is no longer oblivious to her mother's presence or absence. She may develop a more or less constant concern about her mother's whereabouts and engage in a good deal of following and active approach behavior, showing her things and trying to attract her attention. As she begins to really experience life's frustrations, it is as if she has to face the fact that she has overestimated herself in the omnipotent elation of the practicing period. She becomes aware that she is not all powerful and that she is not fused with mother and in possession of her magic powers. The awareness of separation further confronts her with her helplessness. Mahler (1972, p. 9) writes,

At the very height of mastery . . . it has already begun to dawn on the junior toddler that the world is *not* his oyster; that he must cope with it more or less "on his own," very often as a relatively helpless, small, and separate individual, unable to command relief or assistance merely by feeling the need for them, or giving voice to that need.

The child is vulnerable during this period, vulnerable to separation anxiety and the frustration of his dependency needs as well as to further erosion of his autonomy and self-esteem. Dependence and independence needs are deeply in conflict, as the child's primary anxiety gradually shifts from fear of object loss to fear of the loss of the object's love. Helping the child negotiate this time of internal conflict and increasing awareness can be difficult, since he is at once more independent yet more invested in parental participation in his world and gratification of his needs. Some parents will most naturally insist that he continue to "grow up already," while others will welcome his return to dependency and infantilize him. The misunderstandings and conflict inherent in this time will enhance the perception of separateness, as will the necessity for language to communicate and resolve more complex matters. The child requires continued and predictable emotional involvement from the parent, together with her willingness to let go and encourage independent development. This is probably the most crucial phase of individuation because of the child's sensitivity, emerging consciousness, contradictory demands, and the critical lessons of this time. At this time the psychological defense of "splitting" is evident, with the child seeming to hold two polar, unintegrated views of the same object, particularly the mother. She is perceived either as the "good" nurturing and fulfilling one *or* as the "bad" frustrating one — but not as one unitary object, both "good" and "bad."

During this period some painful realities become inescapable. The parent and child are not one, but separate; the child does not own the parent's magical powers but may be unwillingly subjected to them. The parent is not all good and all powerful; the child is not omnipotent and his ability to control the world is very limited. The painful working-through of these realities is termed the "rapprochement crisis" (Mahler, 1972) spanning the 18- to 21-month period. This is the most dramatic phase of rapprochement, when most children exhibit more temper tantrums, splitting, adverse reations to separations and limitations, and open conflict between autonomy and dependence. These conflicts are often acted out in dramatic fights with the parents, the outcome of which may shape the child's character. For the delusions of grandeur and fusion to be relinquished, the child must lose some of these battles, but the "good enough parent" (Winnicott, 1965) will allow the child to move from delusion to reality without undue anxiety or shame. For healthy development, the child must be allowed to oppose without losing the support, love, and approval of the parents. And, while he must lose some battles of will, it is important that he not be overpowered in his attempts at individuation. It is during rapprochement that the press of culture in the form of toilet training, eating behavior, and other culturally demanded behaviors offer great challenges to both the child and the parent.

The child will be particularly prone to idealize the parent, initially seeing her as having the power to protect him from the painful vulnerabilities which he must face. Yet, one of the emerging insights of this period is that the parent is not omnipotent and cannot always protect one from life's slings and arrows. As long as the parental figure is perceived more from the point of view of the child's needs and delusional system, the parent is a "self object" rather than a "real object." One of the primary tasks of this period is to begin the shift from viewing the other only in reference to one's own needs (self object) to viewing the other as an individual apart with his own needs and limitations (real object).

Toward the end of rapprochement there is usually a diminishing of the struggle and a locking in of the solutions to the many developmental tasks presented in this phase and before. With the further development of language and other abilities, which contribute to a sense of mastery, the child appears to come to terms with many of the rapprochement issues. At this point he is said to establish an "optimal distance" from the mother — a distance with affords the optimum in security and freedom.

Identity and Object Constancy

The fourth stage of separation-individuation has been labeled *the child on the way to object constancy* (Mahler, 1972) and spans the period of 22 to 30 months. During this stage the child achieves a realistic and unified internal representation of the love object, who becomes available *internally* for sustenance, comfort, and love as the actual parent was previously available externally. Prior to the realization of object constancy, the child may engage in the defensive maneuvering called "splitting," in which he is able to hold only one-sided internal representations of the parent: either the "good parent" who nurtures, supports, and loves him *or* the "bad parent" who rejects, punishes, or disappoints him. Both the "good" representation and the "bad" representation will be held by the child, but they will be "split" or mutually exclusive such that they cannot be held simultaneously. With object constancy, the child can integrate these polar representations into a unified, realistic, ambivalently experienced construct — the parent. With the attainment of this solid representation, the child can begin to retain feelings of attachment and love even when the object is unsatisfying and value the object for things other than its function as a satisfier. Indeed, object constancy is generally understood to provide the basis for a real love between people, in that the other is not valued only as a source of "narcissistic supplies," but is seen as a unique individual in her own right for whom one can have feelings of empathic concern. As this capacity to love develops, the child also presumably begins to comprehend being loved. The object relations theorists suggest that the primary anxiety then has completely shifted from the fear of *loss of the object* to the fear of *loss of the love of the object* (Blanck & Blanck, 1974).

Oedipal Period

From the psychoanalytic point of view, the child enters the oedipal situation at about three years of age at which point a true triangle is possible. With a solid differentiated representation of self, mother and father, there is the possibility of real object love and object rivalry. The object relations theorists make their unique contributions only up to this watershed point, at which time the essential psychoanalytic understanding of the oedipal situation is the same for both object relations theorists and character analytic theorists. Thus, the initial outline of the oedipal period will be presented in the context of character analysis.

CHARACTER ANALYTIC PERSPECTIVE

The study of character is as old as modern psychiatry because it is devoted to the delineation of constellations of consistent human behavior over time and situation (e.g., Freud, 1913; Jones, 1919; Abraham, 1921). Indeed, all clinical work of whatever stripe is devoted to problems which are persistent and characteristic. Except for crisis intervention and those isolated cases of pathology of sudden onset, most people seek out or are assigned to therapeutic intervention because of affects, behaviors, and cognitive patterns which are unwanted, but nevertheless persist.

Those involved in the study of character typically study the most basic underlying or meta-traits, usually assuming that all other traits, both symptomatic and ego-syntonic, derive from these underlying structures. Characterological theorists typically assert that unless the underlying structures are in some way affected, the derivative structures will either persist or change form. In psychoanalytic terms, character consists of the stable ways in which the ego reconciles the inevitable conflicts among the internal psychic structures and between those structures and the demands of the environment. Because these ways of coping have some history of success and are typically long-standing, there is a resulting resistance to changing them. Particularly when they have been forged in the crucible of extreme threat, they have been associated with the alleviation of that threat and are, as a consequence, extremely resistant to change.

The Reichian and bioenergetic schools have become the most active in pursuing characterological notions, and I believe they provide the richest contemporary exposition of this focus. Both because of the unusual ideas embraced by Reich in his later life, and the unusual techniques of Reichian and bioenergetic therapy, the valuable contributions of these characterological views have often been written off or ignored in more "traditional" or "respectable" circles. I think this is extremely unfortunate because in all my explorations and meanderings through everything from classical analysis to "radical" transformational movements, I have found nothing of more value.

One can dismiss all of Reichian and bioenergetic technique and still learn from the rich theoretical structure, which offers an understanding of the underlying human conflicts in their typical characterological resolution. Where object relations theory offers much in understanding the natural ego evolution of the human being, contemporary characterological theory offers an equally powerful understanding of the evolution of basic human needs and the core affective consequences involved when those needs are frustrated or unmet. By combining these insights concerning cognitive development and affective experience, a more holistic and structural understanding of human functioning and pathology becomes possible. Through this, I have come to a much fuller grasp of what is essentially going on with any individual client than ever before. It is this deep and increasingly calm knowledge of the human condition which I wish to share.

Robert Hilton has offered a most eloquent and concise overview of the characterological position emphasizing innate human needs, characteristic forms of their frustration and the consequent characterological solutions. Here is the "short story" or character development from Hilton (1980, pp. 178–9).

The original organismic self-expression (OOSE) is a pulsatory movement of expansion and contraction. It involves reaching out and taking in; contracting and incorporating through digestion. Studied under a microscope, protoplasm exemplifies this process. So does an amoeba.

This basic life movement directs the human organism in the environment toward meeting its needs, and through this contact with the environment, it builds a structure wherein an increasing amount of independence and self-determination are evident. A human being begins in birth with an organismic declaration of right to exist and proceeds to express his needs, affirm his independence, and eventually reproduce himself through expressions of love and sexuality. The strength of these core expressions varies with the growth and development of the organism and the degree to which each core need has been met by the environment. When the right to exist is challenged from the beginning, a human being may spend the rest of his life in a struggle to affirm this basic core expression. All subsequent core expressions become minimized or distorted in an attempt to fill the pre-existing deficiency.

Parental and environmental frustration may block attempts of the organism to fulfill itself. This negativity may be directed more against the expanding-contracting impulses (such as in the oral structure), or it may be directed more against contracting-independence needs of the organism (as in the masochistic structures).

When the frustration persists, the organism, in an attempt to survive, begins to inhibit the impulses which are causing the negative reaction in the environment. This inhibition is structured in the organism in the form of a muscular contraction which says *no* to the impulses.

Through use of the voluntary musculature, the ego inhibits the impulses and thereby identifies with the parental or environmental prohibition. Through this process, the ego creates a pattern of behavior which brings about survival at the cost of spontaneous organismic aliveness. This imposition divides the unitary function of the organism and man becomes at war with himself. The environmental struggle has now become an internalized struggle between the basic rhythms of the organism and its attempts to survive. This survival behavior pattern becomes an ideal of the ego and part of a character attitude which is threatened by an alive body. To reduce the threat to survival, the body's rhythms and pulsation must be kept in check through reduced respiration and restricted awareness.

This survival attitude toward reality is developed according to the ideals and blocked impulses. The illusion of security is maintained through ego control. For the oral character, the block is mainly toward reaching. The block says, "Don't reach; you will be abandoned." So, of course, he sees the world depriving him, and his quest is to find someone to take care of him. However, his ego ideal of independence and self-sufficiency refuses to allow him to surrender to his needs. He is thereby in a constant state of frustration. The masochist blocks his independent self-expression. He finds the price of independence too costly in terms of guilt, so he sees the world as oppressing and burdening him. At the same time, his ego ideal leads him to seek the responsibility of caring for others.

Since the security of the organism depends on parental and environmental approval, the self-expressive function must be kept under control. The feeling is: "If I express myself, I will lose my security," or "When I let spontaneous movement through, I feel frightened and anxious." This happens when the oral person reaches for help and says, "I need you," or when the masochist rejects someone's request for help and says, "I don't need you." . . .

Anxiety develops when a person is caught between security and self-expression. Anxiety emerges when the form of the organism does not permit expansion with the available energy. When an emerging impulse meets a "security" block in the organism, an organismic need is being blocked by an ego ideal or character attitude.

Character formation can be reduced from this exposition to a five-stage process.

1. Self-affirmation. The organism asserts its natural organismic right to expand or contract. The form of this self-affirmation, in other words, is instinctive or built into the human organism. These include the right to exist, the right to need, the right to separate and become independent, the right to be assertive, and the right to love and love sexually.

2. Negative environmental response. For many, these basic human needs or rights are negated, and negated repeatedly. The parents or parent substitutes meet the infant's existence with hostility or coldness. His needs are undernourished; his autonomy unsupported, manipulated, and threatened; his assertiveness crushed; and his love rejected. The original core expression of the life force is blocked. This leads to a second level of instinctive or built-in organismic reaction.

3. Organismic reaction. When the natural life force expressed in the infant organism is blocked, inevitable reactions occur. These reactions are essentially affective and behavioral—nearly reflexive in their nature. Essentially, these negative organismic reactions may be boiled down to the three essential negative affective states with their behavioral expressions: *rage, terror*, and *grief*. These organismic reactions are extremely powerful and provide the "good enough" parent a clear signal to modify her response to her offspring. When the parental response is modified, nature is served and the healthy development of the organism may proceed. When, however, the parent does not take the feedback given, the child is forced to live with unrelenting internal turmoil. When this becomes overwhelming to the young person who is either unorganized in ego functioning or establishing that organization, she is forced to turn against herself and negate her life expression.

4. *Self-negation.* When the negative environmental response is chronic and the organismic reaction protracted and overwhelming, the individual joins the environment to negate the self-expression. To stop the frustration and punishment from the outside as well as the pain of the affective eruptions from the inside, the young human being will finally give up and suppress his life force, choke off his need, stifle his autonomy, deny his need for support, and hold back his love. In addition to negating the original organismic expression, he will also negate this secondary organismic reaction to frustration. The defensive maneuvers that he will use in this self-negation will depend upon the level of ego organization achieved at the time that he turns against himself. Thus, the self-negation process may be very primitive in basic defensive structure or more elaborate and complex. He may, for example, simply deny his rage or sublimate it in some culturally approved fashion. Whatever the defensive strategy, the intolerable negative affects of rage, terror, and grief will be negated.

5. *Adjustment process.* Using whatever resources and defenses are available, the person must now adjust to the profound negation of self, as well as any continuing environmental frustration that persists. However this is done, it must be a compromise because, though the human is the most plastic of organisms, it can never satisfactorily adjust to the negation of the basic human rights and needs. Withdrawing investment in the natural or real self, the individual must reinvest in what has been termed the "false self" (Winnicott, 1965) or the "ego ideal." In this adjustment, the individual attempts to "rise above" his natural self, his human needs, and his overwhelming emotions. He seeks then

to live up to an *ideal* which will be acceptable, eliminate the external frustration and internal turmoil, and even, dare he hope, fulfill the original organismic self-expression. All his energies will be devoted to developing a set of attitudes, behaviors, and strategies to live with the frustrating environment and the self-negation. These maneuvers, designed to minimize the loss and maximize the gains of the compromise position, will tend to become more successful as they are accomplished later in life, when the organism possesses greater self-cohesion and more behavioral and cognitive alternatives. To the extent that the individual can fool the world and himself by his compromises, he displays ego-syntonic character. To the extent that he is unable to fool either himself or others, he displays ego-dystonic, pain-inducing symtomatology. In either case, he is denied his birthright of the real satisfaction of the natural life process. His choice from that point on is failure of the compromise or the attainment of false success. This universal double-bind is the essential human tragedy.

A person rises above her natural or real self through adopting illusions. The ego ideal is an illusion to be lived up to and there are corresponding illusions concerning what one can believe as long as the natural life forces are blocked and what one will experience if the natural life forces are released. These have been termed the *illusion of contraction* and the *illusion of release*. Thus, for example, I may be able to sustain the illusion that I can be satisfied, loved, and supported as long as I am special, nurturing, or accomplished. Alternatively, in my illusion of release, I will tend to believe that the trauma that led me to contract in the first place will recur if I release, live, and let go. If I give in to my natural human need, for example, and experience the natural rage at having been deprived, I will be abandoned or annihilated. Only with repeated failure of the characterological compromise or with the repeated failure of the success of that compromise to give me what I really need will I be able to challenge the illusion of contraction and risk the expected trauma in the illusion of release.

The False Self

From the object relations perspective, the "false self" is Winnicott's (1965) very useful term for that structure formed in response to frustration of the "real self." This is the self presented to the world and used to procure the environmental rewards which might be withheld from the more natural, spontaneous real self. In this sense, the ego ideal represents ideal "false" functioning. The ego's best shot at compromise solutions to all conflicting demands of personal needs and environmental demands and blocks is represented in the false self. The adaptiveness of the false self depends on the severity of the blocks that form it and the developmental level of the ego which exists at the time of its formation.

Winnicott suggests a continuum for understanding the false self based on the ego mechanisms used for its initial creation and the level of its awareness in the person who possesses it. Some people know little of a self reality apart from that "false" presentation which is the mask to the world. With nothing behind the mask, there is tremendous investment in it and any threat to the mask is experienced as a threat to the integrity of the self. With more evolved or conscious individuals, the false self may be used protectively to seek out settings where real self expression is possible. In the healthiest of us, there is a social politeness which is consciously chosen to ease interaction and establish trust before more spontaneous or "real" behavior is manifested.

To the extent that *narcissism* is understood as the false self constructed out of defense against injury to the real self, it is more or less universal in character formation. In this broad sense, narcissism does occur in all character types. I find it useful, however, to consider it also in its more specific expression, wherein the narcissistic character is the result of a particular type of injury at a particular period in development, as will be outlined later in this chapter.

In this volume and those which follow in this series, each character structure will provide the linchpin which holds together the presentation of therapeutic techniques to which these volumes will be devoted. Each character structure will be developed in detail, outlining the insights of both object relations and character analytic theory. In this chapter, I wish only to present a brief overview of the structure to orient you to the underlying schema of this work. In studying each character structure it will be important to remember that the character structures are archetypes. Any individual can best be understood as a melding of the issues and adaptations presented here, as well as much, much more.

Schizoid Character

The schizoid character develops from the environment's negation of the organism's right to be. This negation of the infant's very right to live is believed to occur before or shortly after birth. As a result, the child cannot achieve an adequate symbiotic attachment and, overwhelmed by this environmental response and his organismic reaction to it, he develops a characterological adaptation on the basis of extremely primitive ego abilities and defenses.

The self-negation in this case takes place before the person even has any notion of separation between himself and the other. As a consequence, he can only introject whole and unassimilated this rejection of his own life force and self-expression. As a result, the schizoid often feels possessed by an alien demon who hates him and feels he has no right to exist in the world. Thus, his self-negation is more pervasive than that of any other character structure. His initial trauma is more literally life-threatening and more overwhelming because it occurs prior to any real organization of the ego.

Physically, the schizoid has more or less cut off his life. Typically, his breathing is very shallow and there is pervasive tension, tightness, and stiffness throughout his body. The body appears wooden, mechanical, and dissociated from his cognitive or intellectual life. It seems dead, colorless, and tightly held together, particularly at the joints, with fear or defensive blankness in the eyes.

The schizoid typically does not live in his body, but lives in his head, with intellectual activity highly valued and a tendency toward constant cognitive processing. The schizoid tends to contact the world through his ideas, intellectualizing the content of his life and spiritualizing its purpose. For the schizoid, people were originally not a source of comfort and caring. So he tends to withdraw rather than approach and is usually aware of anxiety in social relations and performance situations. The schizoid attempts to rise above the tragedy of this existence by being special, usually in an intellectual or spiritual way. As the schizoid issues tend to be more severe, and the compensations less effective, these persons tend toward borderline and even schizophrenic adjustment. In spite of common appearances to the contrary, the basic underlying ego structure is primitive and relatively easily overwhelmed.

My associate, G. Timothy Scott (1976), has provided an outline of the characterological view using the five steps of character develop-

SCHIZOID

Self-affirmation: I have a right to be.

Negative environmental response: Hostility or coldness.

Organismic reaction: Terror and destructive rage.
   Chronic environmental frustration impels a squelching of the
   organismic reaction.

Self-negation process:
   —Retroflective attitude: I have no right to exist.
   —Muscular holding pattern: Holding together in the joints,
    neck, and diaphragm, spinal twisting, and frightened or split
    eyes.

Adjustment process:
   —Ego compromise: I'll live without feeling my body and con-
    tact the world through my ideas.
   —Characteristic behavior: Intellectualizing, spiritualizing, with-
    drawal.
   —Ego ideal: I will be special.
   —Illusion of contraction: My life is my mind, my thought, and
    my specialness. I can live through them.
   —Illusion of release: I will be annihilated.

ment outlined earlier. This outline is ideal for an initial, though over-simplified, understanding of the characterological position. For each character structure, I will provide this outline with some modifications made due to the additions and revisions in the model made through the incorporation of object relations theory.

Oral Character

   The oral character is formed when the need for symbiotic attunement and nourishment is given up and denied before it is satisfied. The oral character is abandoned either literally or emotionally. Her needs arc left chronically unmet, and she eventually gives up protesting this and denies her needs. The oral is also severely traumatized and, though in the period of symbiosis and beginning individuation she may have more resources than the schizoid, the trauma is severely disorganizing. She anticipates abandonment again and might be likened to an undernourished and exhausted baby who has given up and stopped crying because her cries have had no effect.

There is an underlying element of learned helplessness in the oral. Aggression and assertiveness are weak and she is unable to reach out or make a sustained effort to arrange her life so that it will work. The oral's energy charge is typically weak and she has difficulty "standing on her own two feet."

ORAL

Self-affirmation: I have a right to need.

Negative environmental response: Deprivation.

Organismic reaction: Voracious rage.
   Chronic environmental frustration impels a squelching of the organismic reaction.

Self-negation process:
   —Retroflective attitude: I don't need.
   —Muscular holding pattern: Holding on with the jaw, throat, and arms with longing betrayed in the eyes.

Adjustment process:
   —Ego compromise: I'll live without reaching and contact the world by giving and waiting.
   —Characteristic behavior: Romanticizing, longing, clinging, collapse.
   —Ego ideal: I will be loving and giving.
   —Illusion of contraction: I am not needy; I am giving and needed.
   —Illusion of release: I will be abandoned and helpless.

This weakness is mirrored in the body, which appears undercharged and unable to sustain prolonged exertion. Typically, the legs and feet are not experienced as stable supports for the body on which she can firmly stand or with which she can confidently jump. The oral's inhibition to reaching out in order to have her needs met is literally represented in the body by a strong tension in the shoulder girdle and at the root of the neck. The natural rage at deprivation is held back, literally in the jaw, throat and arms, while the eyes often betray the very real longing which the person experiences unconsciously.

Because the trauma of the oral character occurs later than that of the schizoid, she typically is able to do more than deny her need and her negative reactions to deprivation. She has developed primitive forms of more elaborate defenses such as identification and reversal, enabling her to vicariously meet her needs by giving and transform her longing into nurturance. Thus, the oral typically compromises by becoming loving and giving, but often does so in ways which demand this in return. She may often commit to responsibilities which she cannot sustain and fail to realize dreams of independence which are beyond her limited energetic capacities. Finally, there is often a manic-depressive or cyclothymic quality to the oral's functioning. She has grandiose plans and makes exhilarated commitments in periods of elation but will typically collapse into depression, illness, or clinging when her limited supplies run out.

Symbiotic Character

Up to this point in the developmental sequence, I have held with the classically outlined character structures as presented originally by Lowen (1958). My clinical experience, however, demands that I make a departure at this point to acknowledge the existence of a characterological adaptation which is not sufficiently covered by the five character types formerly delineated.

Repeatedly in my practice, I have seen patients who present a complex of presenting complaints which overlap with the oral and masochistic structures, but in which the history and nature of symptoms do not jibe with these classically identified patterns. My ability to understand and help these patients was considerably enhanced upon reading the theoretical and practical notions of Masterson concern-

---

SYMBIOTIC

Self-affirmation: I have the right to separate and be myself.

Negative environmental response: Withdrawal, panic.

Organismic reaction: Panic.
   Chronic environmental frustration impels a squelching of the organismic reaction.

Self-negation process:
   —Retroflective attitude: I don't want to separate.
   —Muscular holding pattern: Holding still, holding breath, maintaining an undeveloped, undercharged body.

Adjustment process:
   —Ego compromise: I will live through another.
   —Characteristic behavior: Dependent, clinging, complaining, afraid of separation.
   —Ego ideal: I will be loyal.
   —Illusion of contraction: I am safe as long as I hold on to you.
   —Illusion of release: I will be abandoned and helpless.

---

ing the borderline adult. Masterson (1976) asserts that the etiology of the borderline syndrome occurs when the mothering parent withdraws her attention, support, and approval when the child begins to separate or individuate. According to Masterson, this withdrawal occurs or at least has its greatest impact in the vulnerable rapprochement subphase of individuation. This withdrawal is traumatic and particularly terrifying to the child in this sensitive period. As a result, she decides to give up autonomy and individuation and clings to the symbiotic fusion. This regression is approved by the parent and individuation is aborted. The symbiotic attachment is thereby maintained, perhaps throughout life, or it is transferred to another primary attachment figure. The symbiotic character has a history of difficulty with separation and may, for example, have had considerable difficulty in going to school, or moving from primary school to high school, or from high school to college or work. Continued separation anxiety is the most common and obvious complaint in this structure and the individual may be prone to develop symbiotic attachments to other objects or persons, experiencing a good deal of anxiety when any separation is threatened.

The contemporary book entitled *Do I Have to Give Up Me to Be Loved By You?* (Paul & Paul, 1983) most succinctly states the symbiotic dilemma. The symbiotic person shares with the oral a tendency toward dependence but it is more ego-syntonic in this structure. The desired compensation is to hold onto the primary attachment figure and all other tertiary attachment objects. The withdrawal of the primary attachment figure or the loss of any object viewed as transitional reactivates the rapprochement panic. When this disorganization becomes overwhelming and the individual acts out expressing that panic, one is confronted with behavior which typically is labeled borderline. Personally, I agree with Giovacchini (1975) and Horner (1979) that borderline functioning per se is often the result of more schizoid and oral etiological factors.

The body of the symbiotic character tends toward underdevelopment and low charge, though there can be a tremendous energy in the blow-off which accompanies the panic occasioned by perceived abandonment or object loss. In general, the symbiotic's body is characterized more by lack of development than it is by the kind of chronic holding seen in the oral and schizoid structures. Essentially, the symbiotic has struck a deal with the primary attachment figure, "I won't individuate and make you uncomfortable if you won't individuate and make me uncomfortable." When this deal becomes threatened, as it usually does with the vicissitudes of life, the original panic breaks through until symbiosis is regained or the structure becomes reorganized. The table presents the symbiotic character's outline in the traditional form originally created by Scott (1976).

Narcissistic Character

This structure also represents a departure from the classic characterological format of Lowen (1958) in two respects. First, I have subsumed Lowen's psychopathic character under this heading, as has Lowen (1983), because the label is more consistent with all the rest of the psychiatric and analytic literature, as well as with the lay per-

---

NARCISSISTIC

Self-affirmation: I have a right to be autonomous.

Negative environmental response: Humiliation, using or both.

Organismic reaction: Impotent fury.
   Chronic environmental frustration impels a squelching of the organismic reaction.

Self-negation process:
   — Retroflective attitude: I don't need support.
   — Muscular holding pattern: Holding up with shoulders, chest, abdominal pinching, and wary eyes.

Adjustment process:
   — Ego compromise: I'll live without feeling helpless and contact the world through controlling helpfulness.
   — Characteristic behavior: Maneuvering, scheming, dodging, performing.
   — Ego ideal: I want to be on top.
   — Illusion of contraction: I can do anything myself if I so will it.
   — Illusion of release: I will be used, manipulated, humiliated, and helpless.

---

son's common understanding of these labels. For me, a truly psychopathic individual can be better understood as a complete or almost-complete failure in achieving any attachment whatsoever, so that the arrest is essentially in the period of autism represented by the first two months of life. The character structure which Lowen originally presented as psychopathic is, for me, really a variation or type of narcissistic character, with its origins in the practicing to rapprochement subphases of individuation. The present delineation of the narcissistic character comes from an integration of the character analytic notions of Lowen and others in the bioenergetic movement with the insights of Kernberg (1975), Masterson (1981), and others in the ego psychology school.

The narcissistic character develops out of the frustration *or* manipulation of the normal secondary narcissistic grandiosity of the practicing subphase, which is typically worked through and gently deflated
during the rapprochement subphase. Narcissism develops when this
crucial transition is inadequately managed in one of two ways. The
first mismanagement of this crisis involves the failure of the primary
parental figures to appreciate, support, and participate in the truly
remarkable achievements of the quickly developing autonomous functions. In the most serious narcissistic injury, the parent, rather than
rejoicing in these accomplishments, is somehow seriously threatened
by them and slaps down, humiliates, and sadistically exploits the
emerging person's real weaknesses. Rather than escort the child through
his emerging awareness of vulnerability, the sadistic parent rubs his
nose in his weakness. From our understanding of child development,
we know that the infant will be particularly sensitive to this sadism
or humiliation in the rapprochement period.

The second and more common form of mismanagement of the narcissistic crisis occurs when the child is prevented from confronting his
own weakness. In this variation, more adequately described by Lowen
and his associates, the child is consistently reinforced in his narcissistic
self-appraisal by the parent, who needs him to be "mama's little man"
or "daddy's little princess." In short, the child is expected to be more
than he or she is, to live up to the parents' exaggerated and often nar-
cissistically projected images. In many cases this extends to satisfying
the parent's need for a partner. Thus, the child is used rather than
realistically supported by the parent.

In the first case the narcissistic injury means being confronted with
one's weakness prematurely, abruptly, and harshly; in the second case
it means not being allowed to confront and work through that weakness and being asked to deny it in favor of an exaggerated false self.
A particularly insidious but not unusual form of narcissism occurs when
these injuries are combined. One parent, for example, may injure the
child through abuse while the other uses the child for his own ends.
Alternatively, one or both parents may communicate unrealistic expectations and then reject or humiliate the child when they are not met.

In response to either injury, the narcissist puffs himself up, denies
his helplessness and need for support, and tries to create a life in which
he never again will be humiliated or manipulated. He will himself

become manipulative—promising to empower others, but eventually overpowering or using them. There will be tremendous investment in the presentation of a powerful false self. Frequently, the narcissist is unable to take any real pleasure in his accomplishments, yet is extraordinarily invested in getting everyone else to buy the package he is selling.

On a body level, there is frequently a puffed-up quality, such that the head and upper body are disproportionately large when compared to the lower body. The *wariness* of the character is often revealed in the expression of the eyes. In other cases there is little obvious body distortion but a great investment in making the body live up to the false self-image in musculature, posture, etc.

As with every other character structure, the effectiveness of the compromise varies considerably. The well-compensated narcissist may be extremely successful and popular, while the more seriously injured narcissist may be continually protesting and boasting in an extraordinarily transparent way and not influencing anyone. The revised outline of the narcissistic character incorporates both etiological forms.

Masochistic Character

The masochistic character structure develops in that period when the child identifies with her own ability to say "no" as a way of differentiating herself from the parent and establishing an independent identity. The power struggles of the "terrible twos" are the crucible in which this characterological structure is formed. The parent of the masochist forcibly wins the power struggle and persistently invades the emerging individuated person, refusing to allow her to be self-determining. Developing at a slightly later stage in individuation than the aforementioned structures, the masochist is able to hold out against this pressure and put up a considerable struggle in the battle of wills. Eventually, however, she too succumbs to the greater pressure which can be exerted by the adult parent whom she still needs for survival.

The issue of individuation is similar to that outlined in the symbiotic case, but in this situation the parent is not threatened and prone to withdrawal at the independent adventures of the child; rather, she needs to maintain control or dominance and hence overpowers the child. On the surface, the masochist does give in and allow the domination, but beneath the conscious surface she harbors extreme spitefulness and

---

MASOCHISTIC

Self-affirmation: I have a right to be assertive.

Negative environmental response: Crushing, invasion.

Organismic reaction: Defiant anger.
   Chronic environmental frustration impels a squelching of the
   organismic reaction.

Self-negation process:
   —Retroflective attitude: I am yours.
   —Muscular holding pattern: Holding in with thighs, pelvic
    floor, throat, neck, face (smile), with suffering eyes.

Adjustment process:
   —Ego compromise: I'll live without asserting my independence
    and contact the world through overcompliance.
   —Characteristic behavior: Pleasing, self-sacrificing, self-depre-
    ciating, ambivalence, whining, passive provocation.
   —Ego ideal: I want to be good.
   —Illusion of contraction: I'll be loved as long as I'm good.
   —Illusion of release: I will be crushed and humiliated.

---

hostility. The masochistic body is often noted to be thick, with powerful muscles which are believed to restrain the direct assertion and block the powerful underlying negativity. Characteristically, the masochistic character is overly pleasing and self-sacrificing while at the same time evidencing passive-aggressive behavior. The masochist is a "good" boy or girl harboring resentment at having to be that way in order to maintain contact and not be crushed.

Rigid Character

   The rigid character develops out of the frustrations of the oedipal period. As object constancy is established, the child realizes his own separateness at a deep level and begins to reach out in a loving and infantilely sexual way toward the parent of the opposite sex. He may meet various combinations of frustration in response to this sexual and loving reach. The opposite sex parent may be threatened and withdraw, threatened not only by the child's emerging sexuality but also by his or her own sexual responsiveness to the offspring. A parent who is sexually frustrated may be seductive, using the child for sexual gratification. This is a particularly common pattern in the future development of the used narcissistic child. Alternatively, the child may be seduced and then, when the threat of sexuality is too much for the parent, rejected. Finally, the child may be seduced by one parent and rejected for the sexual response by the other parent.

With the exception of straight seduction, very harmful in its own way, all of these alternatives involve rejection of the loving sexual

---

RIGID

Self-affirmation: I have a right to love sexually.

Negative environmental response: Rejection *or* seduction and rejection.

Organismic reaction: Deep hurt.
   Chronic environmental frustration impels a squelching of the organismic reaction.

Self-negation process:
   —Retroflective attitude: I can't love.
   —Muscular holding pattern: Holding back with surface armor, pelvis, determined jaw, and sad eyes.

Adjustment process:
   —Ego compromise: I'll live without love and contact the world by making myself attractive.
   —Characteristic behavior: Achieving, attracting, self-sufficiency.
   —Ego ideal: I want to be more accomplished and attractive.
   —Illusion of contraction: I will be loved if I am attractive and accomplished.
   —Illusion of release: I will be rejected if I fully open my heart.

response. As a consequence, the child self-negates, cutting off his sexuality, his love, or splitting the loving response from the sexual response. Wherever sexuality is cut off or split from the loving response, some of the natural human loving is lost. In this sense, the rigid cannot truly love.

In self-negation, the rigid holds back her love with a bodily armor and determined jaw, moving into the world to avoid future rejection through accomplishment and attractiveness. Because of the relatively developed ego structure at this etiological point, she is more able than any other character to attract, achieve, and be self-sufficient. Her illusion is that she can buy love with this accomplishment but, because she cannot let true love in, all she really gets is attention.

Love-sex relationships are the most consistently troubled parts of life. She may, for example, find she can be sexually attracted to but not love one man while she can love another but experience no sexual arousal with him. Or, she may find herself sexually attracted to unavailable men but lose interest when these same men become available. Alternatively, she may be very skilled, satisfying and satisfied in the initial seductive phases of love relationships, but unable to sustain any of that as the relationship becomes more intimate.

Typically, the rigid compromise is the most effective, best defended, and culturally most approved. The purely rigid character is unlikely to seek therapy until later in life when the compromise begins to fail in terms of her relationships with others. As a general rule, the more purely rigid people in our culture seek psychotherapy only when their spouse threatens to leave, their children begin to act out, or a heart attack or other illness threatens the workability of the compromise. More commonly, those individuals who do seek therapy displaying rigid characteristics are demonstrating a "rigid overlay" to preoedipal characterological issues. This is not to say that the oedipal issue is not critical for them, but it accompanies other more primitive organizational issues. Any preexisting characterological problems will influence the course of the oedipal issue, including the nature and degree of oedipal charge, the ego organization available to deal with it, and the consequent defenses employed in response to it. Because of the variety of etiological frustrations in this structure and the triadic nature of the issue itself, this is the most complex expression of characterological functioning. Nevertheless, for the sake of completion and simplicity, the most basic, albeit oversimplified, presentation of the rigid etiological process is outlined in the table.

EGO PSYCHOLOGY PERSPECTIVE

Ego psychology refers to that rather large body of psychoanalytic literature relating to the functioning of the ego. Anna Freud's *The Ego and the Mechanisms of Defense* (1936) and Hartmann's *Ego Psychology and the Problem of Adaptation* (1958) are two classics of this school. Object relations theory and ego psychology are parallel, interrelated developments, and the terms are often used interchangeably. Blanck and Blanck's (1974, 1979) two volumes on ego psychology rely more heavily on Mahler's work than on that of any other single theorist. I find it most useful to think of object relations theory as a subset of ego psychology. Object relations theorists tend to focus somewhat more on their developmental theory and self-other relations, whereas ego psychologists tend to focus more on the delineation and assessment of ego functions per se. Thus, for me, all object relations theorists are ego psychologists, but not all ego psychologists are object relations theorists.

The advantage of the ego psychology perspective in the present context is in its focus on ego functioning. In one sense, the study of the ego is the study of almost everything in human functioning. From a psychoanalytic perspective, the "ego" is in charge of everything but instinctual impulse and the eventually internalized rules of culture embodied in the "superego." Even the processes of internalization which create the superego are ego functions. So, in simple language, ego is everything in human functioning but impulse and conscience. Thus, any listing of ego function is bound to be fairly general and the result of rather arbitrary decisions in chunking the data. A synthesis of Hartmann (1964), Beres (1956), and Blanck and Blanck (1974) suggests the following outline of ego functions:

1) Object representations and relations
2) Reality adaptation
3) Defensive functions

4) Identity formation (self-representation)
5) Processes of internalization
6) Regulation of instinctual drives
7) Thought processes
8) Synthetic function

Object representation and relations and *identity formation* provide the organizing focus for the object relations theory we have briefly reviewed. These functions refer to the human's evolving ability to form the representation of self and object and relate one to the other. This involves the processes of identifying and then discriminating "me" from "not me," mother object from other object, etc. The functions of *reality adaptation* include such things as reality testing, judgment, etc. The *defensive functions* of the ego refer to the defense mechanisms, such as denial, displacement, identification, isolation, projection, repression, etc. The *processes of internalization* refer to the mechanisms by which the individual takes in the characteristics and demands of the environment and makes them his own. In other words, this refers to the mechanisms of acculturation which are eventually represented in the hypothetical structure called "superego." The *regulation of instinctual drives* refers to the ways in which such drives are managed. *Thought processes* refer to the mechanisms involved in memory, reasoning, etc. Finally, the *synthetic function* refers to the capacity of the human being to take in, organize, and integrate input. Synthetic refers to the ability to synthesize and as such could be considered basic to the process of forming representations and other functions in adapting to reality or thinking. Indeed, the above listing of ego functions includes several overlapping distinctions. It is so outlined in order to highlight the oft-studied ego abilities within the literature of ego psychology generally.

Horner (1979) has suggested that an understanding of Piaget's findings concerning cognitive development can assist us in better comprehending the ability of the human being to synthesize, thereby forming and refining representations. In particular, Horner (1979, pp. 9–11) highlights Piaget's notions of assimilation and accommodation.

Horner (1979, p. 10) defines assimilation as "the process through which new experiences are taken into and modified to fit with the pre-existing mental organization." Thus, in perceiving reality we frequently take in new information and incorporate it with reference to how we already conceptualize the world. We use our existing classifications in order to categorize or make sense of new input. When a perception is assimilated, it is made part of an existing structure, generalization, or world view. As Horner points out, this is the rationale for projective tests. Ambiguous stimuli are interpreted within one's frame of reference, and their interpretation is intended to reveal that underlying structure. When something is unassimilated, it is not incorporated within the existing structures owned by the person. For example, a schizoid person may experience an alien force within her which is self-hating and self-depreciating. This may be termed an unassimilated introject, meaning that a very rejecting parent figure was essentially imitated in a very early developmental phase before the infant had the ability to take in and *own* or identify with that input. In this case, the rejecting parent is introjected but not assimilated.

Accommodation refers to the process by which we are able to learn and adjust our perceptions and constructs to fit reality. When we are able to accommodate, we can change the map when the map does not fit the territory we experience. Failures in accommodation occur when our constructs do not fit reality but we are unable to modify those constructs. The processes of generalization, differentiation, and integration may be subsumed under the general heading accommodation. When, for example, the young child begins to get that the human face is different from all other objects, he is beginning to differentiate faces from other objects. At the same time, he is generalizing in that he has not differentiated one face from another. At the point of the "eighth-month anxiety," he begins to differentiate his mother's face from the faces of others. At the age where splitting occurs, we infer from his behavior that he is able to develop a construct of good mother and a separate construct of bad mother but is as yet unable to *integrate* these two constructs into a superordinate one, "mother." When this integration is performed, the child can begin to assimilate both good and bad "data" on the mother under this superordinate construct.

These concepts are very useful in the descriptive developmental diagnosis of cognitive function, particularly as it relates to object- and self-representations. We may ask if the deficit is in assimilation or accommodation. If it is in accommodation, is the problem one in differentiation-generalization or is the problem one of integrating lower level constructs into a necessary higher level construct to best map reality?

With the very general overview of object relations, character analytic, and ego psychology theories presented thus far, we can make a beginning formulation of the ego functioning to be represented within each character structure. To do this, we examine the level of ego functioning in the areas outlined above and determine the extent to which this "fits" for the general schizoid or oral case, for example, or the specific case which we encounter in clinical practice.

Schizoid Character

In general, we have asserted that the schizoid character has at least some meaningful developmental arrest in the normal autistic period and into the early period of symbiosis. As a consequence, we expect him to be withdrawn in general and to withdraw in a more severe fashion under stress. As with every character structure, there will be some adaptation through the "false self" which he has been able to construct, but if that structure is threatened or failing, the consequent breakdown can be very severe, resulting in serious withdrawal or even psychotic symptoms. With an unconscious or emotional arrest in this early period, there will be a difficulty in separating self from other. This characteristic will tend to express itself in introjecting, or swallowing whole, the belief systems and characteristics of others or in projecting internal states or their cause on the environment. Thus, there is in the schizoid character little real sense of self and a great deal of propensity to self-other confusion.

As indicated earlier, the negativism of the caretaking parent may have been introjected in this early period; however, it has not been assimilated. Thus, it is not experienced as a part of the self, rendering the ground even more fertile for paranoid projection. The punitive parental figures of the past are not well discriminated from figures in the present, leaving more opportunity for continuing introjection and projection.

There is at this earliest developmental juncture very little in the way of ego mediation of any kind, and in this relatively undifferentiated state the organism is prone to direct impulse discharge. Thus, the oft-stated schizoid's concern about complete emotional breakdown or uncontrollable expression of rage is not ill-founded. These individuals are among those who are damaged by techniques and group processes which overwhelm the defensive structure.

The basic failure to make a satisfying attachment will lead the schizoid to disruptions in attachment throughout life. It is the initial attachment to the mothering figure which creates the matrix in which the organizational processes of the ego develop. It is from the symbiosis that the infant derives her initial identity and "confident expectation" from which she can differentiate, practice, and eventually fully separate. Where the basic symbiosis has been severely disrupted, all the organizing processes of the ego will be at least somewhat affected.

This knowledge provides the central most useful prescription for the treatment of the schizoid character. In her case, the reparative work will require the provision of a symbiotic-like interpersonal matrix which can then be worked through to separation. That this requirement is very different from that needed by the rigid or neurotic character, for example, has been perhaps the most valuable contribution of those working on the treatment of the borderline adult.

Oral Character

In considering the ego development of the oral character, we can presume to be dealing with a development emotionally or unconsciously fixated in the periods of late symbiosis through differentiation. In this structure an attachment was formed but the parental sustenance was insufficient or withdrawn. The child was forced to move up the developmental ladder prematurely. The child's primary anxiety at this point in time is presumed to be the fear of the loss of the attachment object (Blanck & Blanck, 1974). For the oral character, this fear was realized.

The self versus other differentiation is just barely in process at that time. As a result, this differentiation is unstable at best in the oral character. As a consequence, the oral person may be prone to displace and identify. He may, for example, find others who are needy and identify with them, caring for them and then identifying with their gratification. Alternatively, he may displace his need for meaningful attachment to the need for things, acquiring but never finding satisfaction with physical possessions. Not having a solid sense of self, he will tend to need another to define him, yet harbor a profound reluctance to get too close and thereby stimulate his fear of abandonment. With an undeveloped sense of self, yet a beginning ability to identify, he will be inclined to build a self-representation through identification. In building the construct of himself or of the other, the person arrested at this level of development can assimilate but cannot accommodate. Others are seen primarily from the point of view of need gratification, idealized in this respect but not seen clearly for themselves. The powerful effect of identification may often lead to pathological reactions in these individuals, because any threat to another who is the object of attachment or identification will be experienced as a threat to oneself. On several occasions, I have seen the situation in which an oral person is suicidally depressed by a failure or a threat to the integrity of a child or spouse.

In the oral case, the therapeutic task from this ego psychology perspective is to renew the attachment in the interpersonal matrix of therapy and to then complete the differentiation, encourage the practicing, cushion the rapprochement, and begin the cementing of identity and object constancy. The oral character requires a good deal of patience in therapy because she was rushed on before and does not want to be rushed on again. When, however, the dyadic security is well-established and secure, she may begin to really differentiate and reach out to the differentiated other for the help she needs. Additionally, she will learn to soothe and take care of herself, rather than waiting for soothing and care to come from outside. With differentiation, she will learn to tend to her own needs first and others second, firmly knowing who is who. A good deal of practical autonomy work needs to be done with the typical oral character and she will typically appreciate the opportunity to come back and report on the results of her adventures. The therapist or some significant other can play this role, thereby helping her through the rapprochement phase of this maturation.

Symbiotic Character

As indicated earlier, there is a good deal of overlap in the characteristics of the oral and what I've termed the symbiotic character. Essentially, these two structures represent two sides of the same coin. The oral was forced to separate too soon, while the symbiotic was not allowed to separate when the time was right. In both cases, then, separation is the key issue but the etiological circumstances are opposite.

Theoretically, the mother of the symbiotic character does just fine until the child begins to separate. At that point, she is threatened and may panic or withdraw the needed supplies from the child. This panic or withdrawal, contingent upon the child's attempts to separate, naturally creates panic in the still dependent infant. The child chooses to give up individuating in order to keep the supplies coming and to avoid the panic engendered by the parent's panic or withdrawal. Thus, this character structure is formulated during practicing and rapprochement, though the evidence would suggest that the child would be most responsive to such contingencies during rapprochement.

The contributions of the object relations theorists in general, and of Masterson (1976) in particular, are most useful in describing the pathology arising out of arrest in this period. With this problem, there is a persistent concern with boundaries between self and others. On the one hand, there is a tendency to collapse into boundary-less identification with another, absorbing oneself in the symbiotic union. On the other hand, however, there is often a need to rigidly construct boundaries between the self and others in order to bolster a very weak sense of identity. A given symbiotic individual may display one of these tendencies or the other, though more commonly he will display a tendency to flip-flop between them. This alternation may be explained by the fact that boundary-less fusion will tend to produce a fear of engulfment, whereas establishing one's boundaries will tend to elicit the fear of abandonment. So, in terms of self- and other-representations, the symbiotic character is further along than either the schizoid or the oral in this process of differentiation leading to individuation. However, the process is still very much in process and the initial trauma has the effect of freezing it in motion.

The defense labeled isolation or splitting develops during the rapprochement period and may be characteristic of the symbiotic individual. The use of this defense is demonstrated by the person's simple and unipolar affects "for" or "against" something, or the perception of others as either all good or all bad. The same person may be seen as all good at one point and all bad at another. Depending on the individual's ability to further differentiate, he may see this tendency in himself as odd or irrational or he may view it as ego-syntonic. The failure here is in that part of accommodation which deals with integration and the formulation of higher level constructs.

Another vicissitude of fixation in this period is the tendency to idealize others, which creates the necessary condition for the common disillusionment with them. The idealized other may be seen as having the power to protect one, while at the same time the other is envied and feared. When the protection is not forthcoming, as must be the case in most adult living, the individual can be seriously disillusioned and even lose control of aggressive, retaliatory impulses. Particularly where there has been earlier structural damage, this disillusionment and the associated awareness of separation and vulnerability can lead to real panic and disorganization, prompting the psychotic-like symptoms seen in the classic borderline pathology.

From the ego psychology perspective, the therapist's role is to help the client work through his own individuation. In the context of a supportive matrix, the therapist encourages the individuation and supportively discourages the client's attempts to fuse symbiotically with the continuing pattern of idealization and disillusionment. The symbiotic character is notorious for pulling the therapist into an extratherapy union with symbiotic fusion, therapist idealization, and eventual disillusionment. These are the clients with whom inexperienced or needy therapists may foster dependency by involving themselves in this symbiotic "game." Strategies from any school of thought which assist the client in becoming independent and tolerating the anxiety of separateness will be useful, as will cognitive and behavioral strategies which assist him in establishing autonomy in the world. Gently and supportively helping the symbiotic grow up is the essence of the therapeutic task.

Narcissistic Character

The grandiosity of the practicing subphase provides the clearest developmental analog of the narcissistic character. It is, however, in the next phase, rapprochement, in which this grandiosity is usually resolved. Thus, it appears to me that the ego psychology perspective places these pathologies developmentally within the rapprochement period, though descriptively some narcissistic behaviors are most clearly evident in the preceding, practicing period.

In the narcissist, the development of a true or real self-concept has been aborted to defend against the blow of the narcissistic injury. There is in the narcissist a tremendous investment in the false self, particularly where the issue of self-esteem is concerned. More often than with the other character structures, this false self is consciously seen to be the bulwark of self-worth. The false self is isolated from any input which would threaten its grandiosity. Thus, the narcissistic character is typically prone to a very real learning disability when such learning would in any way require accommodation of the false self concept. The narcissist sees himself in relation to the world through rigidly held constructs and assimilates new information into those constructs or ignores it. This tendency, plus the narcissist's failure to complete the discrimination between self and other, renders him particularly prone to paranoia when self-esteem is threatened.

Due to the failure in individuation, the narcissistic character is prone to the same kinds of idealization-disillusionment transference reactions as the symbiotic character. Additionally, the narcissistic character is prone to "twinship" transference in which he sees the good other as "just like me" in defense of both the grandiosity and the need to emotionally individuate. Similarly, others, when viewed positively, are seen more as the source of supplies than as the people they really are.

There is splitting evident in most narcissistic characters, such that others are viewed in one of two distinct categories: the good people and the bad people. A typical narcissist will take great pains to be identified with the good people and shun the bad. He will be particularly sensitive to the symbols of goodness and make extraordinary efforts to possess and display such symbols. Along with this object splitting, the narcissist frequently has a very well-honed perception of who is above and beneath him by social, intellectual, or physical criteria.

The narcissist will take great pains to identify himself with the aggrandized false self, but during times of crisis or failure he is apt to fall into rather catastrophic depression when he experiences himself as abhorrent and unworthy in the extreme. This polarity of self-esteem is definitional of the narcissistic character, though the more solid his defenses the more infrequent will be his drop to the unworthy pole. Others are related to as a source of aggrandizement or gratification. Those who are close or those encountered in a service capacity are often expected to read his mind and provide gratification without being asked.

Because of the arrest at the point of union between the grandiose self and the idealized object, there is a very serious arrest in the development of an internalized superego. While there may be some rules of behavior assimilated within the false self, there is often a serious deficit in conscience and social empathy.

A primary anxiety for the narcissistic character is the fear of humiliation or slight; as one of my clients put it, "Above all else, I don't want to be chumped." It is as if the false self is built up and armored against ever confronting the illusion of grandiosity. There is in this structure a good deal of overlap in ego functioning with that of the symbiotic character. Each is driven by the failure to resolve one of the two primary tasks of the rapprochement subphase. In the symbiotic character, the most obvious failure is in the resolution of symbiosis to individuation. In the narcissistic character, the most obvious failure is in the resolution of grandiosity to real self. So, while there may be a good deal of difference in external behavior and presentation, there is a good deal of overlap in the underlying ego structure of the symbiotic and narcissistic characters.

While the narcissist invites confrontation, he responds best to nurturance in therapy. The therapist's objective is to build trust and support the real self. While this will usually involve some frustration of the false self, the "good enough" therapist will not repeat the narcissistic injury by humiliating or using the client.

More than most patients, the narcissistic client will be prone to offer some service to the therapist to prove his status, attain a one-up position in the relationship, and compromise the therapy. The therapist's necessary refusal of this service, inevitably coming from the client's brittlely defended false self, provides a therapeutic challenge and opportunity symbolic of the central therapeutic task. That task is to do what the parent did not—accept and nurture the real and vulnerable person, allowing the grandiose and now false self to dwindle and disappear. The "good enough" therapist does not need the client to be less or more than he is, to keep him down by humiliation or make him special for his own gratification. Rather, he encourages the expression of the true self, which must involve working through the grandiosity and the injury which made it necessary.

Masochistic Character

The masochistic development is similar to the symbiotic and narcissistic cases, in that it is basically a pathology of individuation. The etiology is hypothesized to be somewhat different, in that it involves a crushing of the will at that point when the child begins to really assert her will and claim her right to be independent. In general, this forceful assertion of will comes somewhat later than that individuation which is derailed in the symbiotic and narcissistic cases. The individual is, at that point, somewhat more herself and there is somewhat greater strength available to sustain the resistance. Though the will of the oppressive parent turns out to be stronger than the will of the oppressed masochistic child, one usually finds, not far below the surface, a seething resentment for having to give in. Typically, the masochistic character shows no twinship or idealization transference, little or no splitting, and more genuine superego development than the other two character structures forged earlier in the individuation process. In short, the ego of the masochist is typically better developed than in the other two cases.

There is in these masochistic cases a continuing dependence on the maternal or love object yet a resistance to this dependency and a resistance to identification with that object. This ambivalence, as opposed to splitting, suggests some movement into the stage of object constancy and identity formation. Because of the failure to fully internalize the mothering functions of the love object, the masochistic character is still quite dependent. She is still subject to anxiety and even depression over the loss of the love object on the one hand; yet, at least at an unconscious level, she is still unwilling to give herself up entirely. Though it may be fairly protracted, the task of her therapy is to complete the working through of identity and object constancy such that she will learn that she can be herself and still have adult love.

Oedipal Issues

The contribution of the ego psychology perspective to the oedipal issues is this: It permits us to catalog the defensive mechanisms used to deal with oedipal problems. Lowen's (1958) observation, for example, that rigid characters frequently separate those whom they love romantically or protectively from those whom they love sexually is clearly an example of object splitting. Appreciating the more primitive nature of this defense could assist greatly in its eventual resolution through therapy. Another unique contribution of the object relations perspective is the view of oedipal or sexual issues as not isolated but layered upon the earlier preoedipal issues. Thus, while there may be in a given case any number of the etiological factors leading to rigidity, there may be previously unresolved issues and fixated abilities for defense which affect the oedipal adaptation. Thus, a descriptive developmental diagnosis may be necessary to deal not only with preoedipal issues but also with the overlaid oedipal issues. Because of the complexities of such layering, as well as the triadic etiological complexities outlined earlier, I believe the whole issue of difficulties variously labeled "neurotic," "rigid," or "oedipal" requires extensive reexamination.

In my experience, individuals experiencing exclusively "oedipal," "neurotic," or "rigid" issues are rare in therapy today. In part this appears cultural/historical, in that we no longer have the kind of widespread sexual repression which produced the kind of cases about which Freud, Reich, and even Lowen have written. Without such severe sexual repression, one who negotiates a "good enough" course through individuation will possess an ego structure resilient enough to handle the oedipal demands ordinarily confronted in this culture. Even when these demands produce less than full and spontaneous living, the rigid adaptation of achievement is very highly prized in the culture. So, contemporary "rigids" may be out there but disinclined to seek help because their compromises are working. While there are undoubtedly still pockets of the kind of culture that produces such classic "rigid" pathology, our culture is now more inclined to produce the pathologies of attachment and individuation addressed here.*

CONFLICT VERSUS DEFICITS IN EXPLAINING HUMAN PATHOLOGY

The ego psychology perspective makes its greatest theoretical contribution, particularly to psychoanalytic theory, in adding a *deficit model* for explaining human psychopathology. The classic analytic position explains human pathology as arising out of conflict between intrapsychic structures as well as conflict between those structures and the external environment. This *conflict model* tends to assume a rather uniform level of ego development for dealing with and resolving these inevitable conflicts. The ego psychology perspective, on the other hand, posits that ego abilities evolve over time and that trauma can arrest this development at various points, thereby creating a deficit in ego functioning. As a result, some pathology may be the result only of the lack of further ego development in a given area. Additionally, what initially appears to be a classic defense of conflict may really be the ego's best possible adaptation to dealing with reality or conflict. When this is the case, an unrelenting attack on that "defense" can lead to a decompensation of ego functioning rather than a more mature level of conflict resolution or reality adaptation.

When dealing with ego deficits, a therapist will generally have to direct attention toward ego repair. Thus, the *deficit model*, as suggested by the ego psychology perspective, puts "resistance" in an entirely new light. Where there is ego deficit, resistance to the breakdown of preoedipal adjustment may be necessary for the literal survival of the organism or its current level of compensated functioning. A diagnosis, therefore, of a patient's level of ego functioning is absolutely essential for the direction of treatment.

Throughout this volume, I will argue that in most cases therapists need to apply both the conflict and deficit models to understand and

---

*I want to credit Ed Muller for helping me clarify these observations.

remedy the human problems typically faced in outpatient care. The recommended approach is typically a combination of ego-building techniques with the working through of resistance to changing archaic forms of adaptation. The rest of this book—and the others in the series—are essentially about when to do what to whom in this process and why.

CHAPTER II

THE HATED CHILD:
THE SCHIZOID EXPERIENCE

Jeanine: You don't want to talk about it?
Conrad: I don't know, I've never really talked about it. To doctors, but not
    to anyone else; you're the first person who's asked.
Jeanine: Why'd you do it?
Conrad: I don't know. It was like falling into a hole. It was like falling in-
    to a hole and it keeps getting bigger and bigger and you can't get out
    and then all of a sudden it's inside and you're the hole and you're trapped
    and it's all over—something like that. And it's not really scary except
    it is when you look back on it because you know what you were feeling,
    strange and new . . .

                       — *Ordinary People*

ETIOLOGY

AS THE HUMAN infant emerges out of the state of primary autism
around three to five weeks of age, the "sensory barrier" slowly dissolves
and the child develops an increasing awareness of the caretaker. The
person met in this initial contact with the world may or may not be
welcoming, contactful, and responsive to this totally dependent being.
Indeed, the parents may be cold, harsh, rejecting, and full of hate,
resenting the infant's very existence. The parental reaction may, of
course, not be that extreme and it may not be consistent. But we know
that many human infants have been unwanted, and those who have
been wanted on a conscious level are not always wanted on a less conscious level. Furthermore, many parents who think they want children
find out differently when the full impact of the totally dependent human
being is thrust upon them, when circumstances change, and when their
resources to deal with the reality of an infant are much less than
expected.

Perhaps even more common is the situation in which parents think they want a child but what they really want is an ideal reflection of their own idealized self. They want a "perfect baby" instead of an alive human being with elements of animal nature. Every infant will sooner or later and repeatedly disappoint this ideal and the parental rejection and rage which that elicits can be shocking. In every case, it is the real, spontaneous *life* in the child which provokes the parental rejection and hatred.

When one couples the common reality of the hated child with the understanding that the newly "hatched" human being has no clear discrimination of the difference between self and caretaker, one can begin to speculate on the nature of the unfortunate result. One can imagine that when the caretaker is sufficiently harsh, the infant may simply choose to go back where he came from—to the detached world of autism. The cold or hateful treatment of the caretaker may be total or partial, continuous or periodic. The infant's defensive retreat will be more profound as a result of repeated child abuse, for example, than as a response to occasional outbursts or periodic coldness on the part of the caretaker.

Winnicott (1953) refers to the concept of "good enough mothering" to describe the requisite empathic caretaking ability which will usher a newborn into the state of symbiosis and keep her there until the process of differentiation leading to individuation begins. Where mothering is not "good enough"—and indeed where it is abusive and punishing—distancing, detachment, and literal turning away from social contact result. Because of the very primitive nature of the neonate's cognitive processes at this point in development, it is difficult to understand exactly how this chain of events is interpreted at any mental level. Nevertheless, we may surmise that at a very primitive level of awareness, and then at increasingly complex levels of understanding, the infant experiences an intense fear, which some have labeled the fear of annihilation (Blanck & Blanck, 1974; Lowen, 1967).

The infant's natural initial response to a cold, hostile, and threatening environment is terror and rage. Yet, chronic terror is an untenable position from which to lead a life, as is chronic rage. Furthermore, such rage invites retaliation, which is experienced as life-threatening and terrorizing. So, the infant turns against herself, suppresses the natural feeling responses, and uses the very primitive ego defenses available in the symbiotic period to deal with a hostile world. In addition to, or as part of, the retreat to autism, the organism essentially stops living in order to preserve its life. The ability to do that is limited by the ego development of the infant in this period. However, through the months of symbiosis she can regress to the previous developmental period and in that deny the reality of her existence. The hatred of the caretaking parent will be introjected and will begin to suppress the life force of the organism, such that movement and breathing are inhibited and there develops an involuntary tightening of the musculature to restrain the life force.

Therapeutic experience with clients who share this type of history suggests that, sooner or later, they make two core feeling decisions: 1) "There is something wrong with me," and 2) "I have no right to exist." These cognitive representations may, of course, be conscious or denied, but at a core level of existence the individual has taken the environmental response personally and has incorporated it into her self-concept. Enhancing this effect is the fact that at this symbiotic point in development there is no real differentiation between oneself and one's caretaker. This factor is the central defining characteristic of symbiosis in the human infant, and it is the preverbal assimilation of this damning "script decision" which renders it so insidious and difficult to change.

One way to gain an appreciation for the initial dilemma of the schizoid person is to remember those times when in a supermarket, laundromat, or other public place you have witnessed the explosion of a mother or father at a young child. This often alarming public example of child abuse demonstrates the not uncommon loss of parental control and one cannot help but wonder about the limits of this kind of outburst. Presumably, the infant herself is not sure of those limits either and on occasion the parent may have gone well beyond mere yelling or minor corporal punishment. In these public circumstances, you may have witnessed the child herself taking on the maternal role and doing whatever was necessary to get the parent to pull himself together and leave the situation. In parents with marginal emotional stability, these abusive outbursts often have very little to do with what the child has or has not done. As a result, the child will often develop rather profound vigilance, as well as the ability to parent her parents when loss of control is imminent or realized.

As will be outlined in greater detail with the exploration of the behavior, attitudes, and feelings of this character structure, the hated child begins to find a safe haven in withdrawal into cognitive and spiritual endeavors. "If mother doesn't love me, then God will," and if the world on face appears to be hostile, it is really a beneficent unity in which one's current life is a mere flash in the eternal pan and "life on this physical plane is really irrelevant." In these ways, life is spiritualized instead of lived. The hated child may be one who loves mankind but twists away almost automatically from the closeness required in an ongoing love relationship.

As the person matures, the sophistication and complexity of the defenses increase, yet at a core emotional level the defensive structure is very primitive and essentially reflects *denial* of what really happened in relation to the mothering person. That denial freezes the situation present in symbiosis—an unfulfilled wish for intimate union on the one hand and an automatic refusal to merge on the other. The frozen symbiotic condition yields a continuing propensity to *introject* whole the ideas, characteristics, and feelings of others, as well as a tendency to *project* both good and bad feelings and motivations onto others. In this character structure there essentially was never a completed symbiotic attachment leading to a later individuation with autonomous functioning. The hated child's experience is: "My life threatens my life." The seeming independence and detachment of this basically frightened and angry person are purely defensive, and there is developmental arrest in the humanizing process and an arrest of life before it really began.

EXTERNAL CIRCUMSTANCES AND GENETIC ENDOWMENT

Some element of the schizoid structure seems apparent in many patients who present themselves for treatment. In understanding the prevalence of these failures in attachment and the associated results, it may be well to consider the effects of particular external circumstances during the symbiotic period that may have put considerable strain on the mothering figure and thereby further diminished her ability to be contactful and accepting. For example, a mother who may have been "good enough" under ordinary circumstances may not be if she loses her husband to divorce, death, or military service. The experience of early serious childhood illness and particularly early hospitalization can also severely disrupt the symbiotic attachment. The child may experience the disruption of object impermanence during this sensitive period, together with agonizing and severe pain associated with the treatment administered by the caretaker or others. Similarly, war, economic depression, or environmental catastrophe may be involved in diminishing the parents' ability to be contactful and loving in the symbiotic period. Obviously, there are levels of hateful or contactless environments, and environmental events can either enhance or detract from the quality of life in symbiosis.

There is also considerable individual variation in the ability of infants to sustain a human relationship. The innate ability of the child to provide the mothering person with the nonverbal signals on which she bases her responses will differ. Some infants will seek to maintain proximity to a greater extent than others or be more motorically responsive to contact. Individual differences which affect the attachment process have been noted by those who have systematically observed these child-caretaker interactions (e.g., Bowlby, 1969; Murphy & Moriarty, 1976). It seems clear now that a good deal of serious infantile autism is the result of some processes internal to the child and not primarily the function of environmental influence (Judd & Mandell, 1968). While the focus of the present work will be on environmental influences, the effects of early external circumstances and genetic endowment should be taken into consideration in each individual case.

AFFECT, BEHAVIOR, COGNITION

Affect

The psychoanalytic concept of developmental arrest assumes that cognitive and behavioral resources, as well as the form of affective expressions, are in some very meaningful way *frozen* at the point of serious environmental frustration. Thus, in the classic case of the hated infant, there is an arrest in the symbiotic period, and in some cases even in the autistic period, to which the infant may regress in defense. Thus, in the area of affect or feeling, the classic schizoid character can be characterized most meaningfully by underlying, often unconscious, feelings of terror and rage in response to a life-threatening environment. The terror may be expressed in a variety of symptoms, including anxiety or panic attacks in response to situations which are perceived as threatening. Such threatening stimuli may not necessarily be consciously experienced as threatening and the individual may be totally unaware of the nature of the triggering stimuli. But, at an unconscious level at least, the stimuli release the terror response. The terror may be circumscribed in phobias; in more conscious individuals it may be perceived as generalized anxiety or tension specific to social situations or intimacy. There may be a general expression of discomfort or lack of belonging in the world and even a sense of unreality about one's connection with it all.

In those who share this schizoid condition, yet defend against it more completely, absence of any real spontaneous affect and a machine-like manner of self-expression will be characteristic. There may be a hyper-rationality and a tendency to see those who are emotional as irrational, out-of-control, or crazy. There may be a concomitant "as if" quality in the expression of feelings, almost as if the person were badly acting an expected role. In some cases the person may express concern about what he or she "should feel" under certain circumstances.

In the widely acclaimed film, "Ordinary People," Conrad enters psychotherapy under the strain of no longer being able to control powerful negative affective states in his adolescent years. In the initiation of that treatment he asks for more emotional control and in the course of it relates an incident after the funeral of his brother in which he does not know what to say or how to feel and wonders how the TV personality "John-Boy" would feel and what he would say in that situation. Timothy Hutton's portrayal of Conrad in this film is one of the best current exemplifications of a person with this character structure. And, Mary Tyler Moore renders a good portrayal of one type of "schizoid-genic" mothering.

In sum, the hated child's most basic underlying feeling is that of terror associated with annihilation or, on an adult level, with failure to make it in the world. All defenses are marshaled to stave off rejection and failure. The more complete the defense against this fear, the more extreme the withdrawal into machine-like behavior and total absence of any apparent feeling.

To an even greater extent than with the terror, there is usually a denial and avoidance of the emotion of anger or rage. In infancy, the destructive rage would risk the destruction of the caretaker and therefore the infant himself and could provoke the caretaker's destructive retaliation. Thus, the repression of this emotion is life-preserving. What is encountered, then, in the adult patient, is typically an avoidance or withdrawal from conflict, an inability to get angry or to face anger in others, and the propensity to express it, if at all, in passive-aggressive withdrawal. The hated child has learned to leave rather than fight back and feels that anger is useless and accomplishes nothing. Very often the hated child denies completely his own anger and idealizes and spiritualizes his own loving nature.

As these individuals become more aware of the deep levels of rage in them, they often express considerable fear of their own destructive power. The fantasy is that they may let go suddenly and destroy everyone and everything in their path. The sudden explosions which result, for example, in that quiet, withdrawn, unassuming boy shooting down innocent people at random from the top of a building suggest that this fantasy is occasionally realized. In the course of a well-engineered therapy, however, where the capacity to tolerate feeling is systematically developed, the existing defenses are made conscious, fortified, and then gradually melted, there is little danger of anything so dramatic. It is not uncommon, however, for some socially inappropriate anger to spill over in the course of treatment; in fact, it is often useful for schizoid individuals to experience loss of control which, while regrettable, is usually nowhere near the feared fantasy. Similarly, it is useful for these people to achieve a rapprochement with those to whom they have expressed the anger and experience that loss of control of this emotion does not result in anybody's annihilation and usually not even in prolonged disaffection.

The therapeutic context is particularly valuable, I think, in providing an atmosphere in which a good deal of this rageful affect can be literally dumped with no negative environmental consequences. It is important to caution, however, that this should not be done prematurely, before the capacity to tolerate this affective experience and self-observe its release is developed.

Whenever there is a death in the family there is sorrow and grief. When there is a death of the self, as in the schizoid experience, there is similarly a mourning for the self that could have been and for the loving relationship that was instinctively expected but not forthcoming. As a consequence, the affect of sorrow, grief, or depression is common in individuals with this characterological makeup. It is usually the least suppressed affect, though its active expression in deep crying or sobbing may be partially or totally absent. As with the other affects, it is not fully and deeply experienced by the organism; rather, it may be experienced as a long-standing or periodic chronic depressive state, characterized more by withdrawal and whining discomfort than by deeply felt grief. In order to get on with life, the hated child also had to deny this feeling and persevere in spite of a chronic underlying depressive condition. Such depression, particularly accompanied by suicidal ideation, the termination of self-caring functions, and the self-recognized inability to feel anything else, may well be the referral complaints of those with this general history and character structure.

Just as there is very little negative affect in this structure, there is a concomitant absence of positive affect. Possible exceptions to this include a not-uncommon ungrounded euphoria triggered by some philosophical or religious idea or artificially induced by drugs. In these situations, there may be a euphoria which is fleeting and artificial in connection with a briefly experienced realization of some of the symbiotic illusion—that is, when *the* religion, idea, mate, or drug state which answers all prayers is briefly found. The high always ends of course, and the person always returns to the essential affective state that characterized him prior to the illusory high.

Behavior

The behavior of the unloved child will vary on several basic dimensions. He or she will be able to function in the world based on how well the underlying powerful affects are controlled or held in. While the holding in may have other detrimental effects, such as psychosomatic illness, to be discussed later, or the diminished capacity for any kind of close relationship, it does allow the person to function. To the extent that this is unaccomplished, one is dealing with an individual who is extremely sensitive to any harshness in the environment, who has difficulty maintaining a sustained commitment to any work activity or relationship, and who will flee, often in a more or less dissociated state, from one thing to another. So, to the extent that the underlying affects are available, one may be faced with an individual who appears quite fragile and susceptible to breakdown into emotional states, confusion, and even loss of contact with reality. This tenuous reality relatedness may be expressed in fairly mild forms of being "spaced out" to more profound fugue states or periods of psychotic-like behaviors.

Where the individual's defenses allow her to be more effective in the external world, one is more apt to find an individual who withdraws into those activities which offer some worldly accomplishment while avoiding other areas of involvement. For instance, one might be a computer whiz, a renowned ballet dancer or a workaholic attorney with a conspicuously absent, late, or damaged history of intimate relationships. In those less damaged, there may be a sustained relationship with a spouse or family but with little emotional contact or intimacy. There may even be the ability for the person to play the role of an assertive or dominant individual in a certain isolated context (e.g., in the classroom or courtroom), in striking contrast to shyness and ineptitude in other social settings.

The key to understanding the schizoid structure is the disconnection of the individual from life processes — from the body, from feelings, from intimate others, from community, and often even from inanimate objects such as food, nature, etc. Except in those areas where an individual may have attained exceptional achievement, there is a universal tendency to avoid meeting life head-on — to look away, to twist out of confrontation or closeness, to "space out" or migrate internally away from contact. The person himself may be unaware of that tendency, since it is often an automatic, unconscious response to threat. Even in areas of great accomplishment, there is almost always the existence of severe and often debilitating performance anxiety, in that the person's identity is so invested in that achievement that any hint of failure is tantamount to annihilation of the self. It is not uncommon for these tendencies to also be expressed in perfectionism and procrastination. As stated earlier, the schizoid person often discovers that the pursuit of mental processes and achievement is a safe haven from life. Since the schizoid character cannot identify with life in the body and develop a solid sense from that biological core, he needs to find that somewhere else. The defensive attempt to earn external approval and self-acceptance through achievement, often involving mental abilities, is common in this structure. This is often the only way in which he contacts the world, expresses himself, gains acceptance or recognition, and senses who he is and what his place is in the world. Failure in this area of endeavor can precipitate serious depression and suicidal thinking and behavior.

Concomitant with all of this, there is often the need, usually conscious, to be special. As a way of denying the reality of being unloved, even hated, rejected, and abused, there is the compensatory ideal of specialness, which is often realized one way or another. This may be through real achievement in science or art or through the delusional achievement of the kind so well portrayed in Robert De Niro's more narcissistic character (Rupert Pupkin) in the film "King of Comedy." When the specialness, real or delusional, is threatened, there results a tightening of the defense and eventually a breakdown in the structure.

I am reminded of one of my clients, a successful 40-year-old doctor, who remarked poignantly, "I think I have worked so hard all my life in order to forget that I don't have the right to exist." The schizoid issue is literally existence and those who have to deal with this issue will try to find something which will justify their existence. Their right to exist is always on the line, and there is extraordinary anxiety in case the justification should fail.

Cognition

As indicated in the last chapter, any of the adaptive or cognitive ego functions which are developing in the symbiotic period may be seriously weakened or retarded by trauma during that period. The extent and duration of the trauma, the genetic strengths of the organism, the availability of alternative resources such as extended family, and the nature of the available defenses or compensations will determine the extent to which adaptive functions or ego abilities are over- or underdeveloped. For these reasons, it is probably more instructive to list the cognitive abilities which the clinician should assess than to describe any fixed way in which they may be represented in people with this character structure.

It is possible, however, to outline a number of internal belief structure, ego ideals, and "script decisions" which are usually operative in people with this kind of history. In this latter area, there will always, for example, be the underlying sense that "there is something wrong with me." And, there will always be the belief that the world is dangerous, hard, or cold. To the extent that the person has compensated or defended against this, these ideas will be denied and there will be a cognitive structure or belief system supporting that denial. The denial may well break down under stress, however, and this breakdown may be accompanied by suicidal ideation or behavior, depression, panic attacks, and other symptoms. The more frequent and florid that breakdown, the more one is dealing with a person whose ego defenses are fragile and whose diagnosis would most likely be borderline or schizophrenic. The more a person is able to intellectualize or otherwise defend against these cognitions and their associated feelings, and the more intact the other ego functions, the more one is dealing with a more reliably functioning person who can tolerate more stress. The underlying dynamic, however, is similar in spite of these very important differences, and it is this core issue which must sooner or later be addressed for the person to realize her potential.

Because the issue of existence is critical in this structure, there will likely be some expression of this in a person's day-to-day life. For instance, the issue of security may be particularly important or obviously denied. Having enough money, holding on to one's job—in short, "making it" in life—may be a persistent concern. Alternatively, in an attempt to escape the anxiety associated with survival, the person may simply look the other way regarding these adult responsibilities and be defensively oblivious to security issues. There will be the polar opposite defensive idea or belief that "I am special." Similarly, there will often be the associated belief of a philosophical or religious nature asserting that the universe is benevolent, a unity, and supremely meaningful. In both cases, these beliefs will not be particularly well integrated or digested within the person. The specialness may be grandiose, at least at times, and the philosophical or religious beliefs may be such a part of the self-concept that contrary beliefs are experienced as threatening. Because these ideas maintain the denial of the original position, they may be held very tenaciously.

Whatever the quality of the schizoid cognitive functioning, one common characteristic is the dissociation of thinking and feeling. It is with these people that one can most readily realize the limitations of pure intellectual, affectless insight. It is perhaps this ability to dissociate, however, which is responsible for the fact that many with this kind of problem have been able to develop cognitive abilities to a highly sophisticated level, though often within a narrow range. It is as if the dissociation of feeling and thinking protects these intellectual functions from contamination. It is as if the intellectual functions are walled off from upsetting affects and thoughts and therefore protected. Like so many other defensive or compensatory moves, this one has its cost, but it also has obvious survival value for the organism, not only in childhood but throughout life.

Further in the service of denying the hatred or coldness which he experienced, the schizoid character typically offers to others what he did not receive himself. That is, his ego ideal is characteristically very accepting and understanding of others—he believes in letting others be as they are. If the hostility toward himself or others begins to emerge, it is experienced as very threatening and cannot usually be acted out unless there is an ego-syntonic excuse for that expression.

In terms of an object relations view of the developmental arrest in the early symbiotic period, it is useful to note that the salient features of symbiosis are the merged representations of self and other. In the first eight months of life, the infant allegedly is unable to differentiate herself from her mother, or her mother from other adults. There is in this period, however, the ability to imitate and the ability to engage in the primitive defensive functions of denial, introjection, and projection. There also is the ability to retreat to the autistic or primary narcissism of the first few weeks of life. The development here is from 1) an undifferentiated state (autism) to 2) a state of undifferentiated symbiosis to 3) a phase in which the mothering person is differentiated from others but not from the self. All through the symbiotic phases there is a merging of the self and the other and a fusion of "good" and "bad" object representations. Thus, during this period, the schizoid infant must introject the hostile, cold, and punitive parent in a fused and diffuse representation with the "good" parent. While there will later develop other ways to defend against the schizoid's reality, in the early period all that appears to be available is direct denial of that reality, as well as the mechanisms of projection and identification. In other words, all the individual can do is to primitively block out the reality of his existence, while introjecting it and then projecting aspects of it outward. This is obviously a highly split and "crazy" internal reality.

As the ultimate result of all the schizoid trauma and these early developmental limitations, the individual will freeze in his body in order to control the powerful negative feelings. He then can move on to develop, in relative isolation, the cognitive adaptive functions which will, as a function of his natural growth, begin to emerge. Because of the disruptions in this early period, there may be a continuing failure of the powers of discrimination, particularly in social contexts, and, at the deepest level, problems with differentiating between his own thoughts and feelings and those of others.

As opposed to those characterological problems to be discussed in later chapters, the hated child is really faced with a choice between autism and symbiosis. Developmentally, individuation is not even an option at this early stage. And, symbiosis is not a very viable option. To the extent that it is perceived as being life-threatening, it is to be avoided at all costs; consequently, the withdrawal and autism of the schizoid character are understandable. The naturally desired attachment is foregone in the interest of survival. In reviewing the research of Harlow et al. (e.g., Harlow & Harlow, 1966), we may remember that while the monkeys raised by artificial mothers were generally not very happy, social, or well adjusted, they did, by and large, survive.

In every schizoid personality I have treated it has eventually been necessary to face the destructive, demonic force. This is typically experienced as completely alien and often completely beyond the control of the individual. Structurally, I believe it is useful to understand this as an unassimilated introject of the mothering figure, as well as the natural response of rage to this rejecting or cold figure. If this destructive force is experienced prematurely, before sufficient grounding, understanding, and the building of security in therapy, it can lead to a disintegration or decompensation. Where the process of differentiation has been weak or incomplete, this disintegration can result in paranoid pathology. These signs of disintegration are most obvious not in the chronically mentally ill but in those persons who disintegrate in response to mind-altering drugs, encounter marathons, or psychotherapeutic techniques which prematurely overwhelm the defenses.

Summary

The schizoid experience basically involves a failure in the attachment process at or near the beginning of this form of relatedness. This failure occurs when the cognitive and ego resources of the organism

are minimal. As a consequence, the defense mechanisms which the individual must use to deal with this fundamental assault are primitive —
primarily denial, introjection, and projection. These mechanisms will
be called upon again and again to deal with the persistent issue of existence and survival, as well as with any subsequent situation which
in any way triggers these more basic issues. So, while the autonomous
functions and other cognitive and ego abilities may very well develop,
often to an extraordinary degree, there exists this basic structural
vulnerability in the organism. In short, it is critical not to underestimate
the degree of damage and consequent vulnerability in this character
structure.

In spite of apparent strength, individuals with an essentially schizoid
character structure must, at core, deal with the issue of survival and
the terror and rage around the threat to existence. It is important that
they not be overwhelmed by powerful therapeutic technique. It is essential to develop their tolerance for aliveness in the body, to solidify their
trust in the therapeutic relationship, and to build a well-grounded ego
strength before they are asked to face this ultimate issue that will emerge
when they melt their defenses and touch the feelings that exist within
them.

ENERGETIC EXPRESSION

Those who emphasize the physical dynamics of character structure
simply assert that the organism will respond to environmental frustration not only with a change of attitude and behavior but also with
responses in the voluntary and even involuntary musculature. When
the young organism comes up against continual and seemingly im-
movable negativity and frustration, it will, in an attempt to survive,
begin to inhibit or contract against the impulses which seem to produce that negativity. This inhibition is represented in the organism by
contraction of those muscles which inhibit the impulses. The contractions become chronic and as a result can produce rather dramatic
changes in posture and even in the functioning of bodily organs.

The muscular inhibition of impulse is a concrete and visible manifestation of the parental or environmental prohibition. It is the physical
manifestation of the process of introjection. This assumption of the
prohibition or negativity initiates the loss of spontaneous movement,

feeling, and behavior. It is chosen only because it is preferable to the pain involved in continuing the natural, spontaneous reactions to the chronic frustration. The decision to inhibit is experienced as a choice of survival over expression. The dependent infant cannot exist in a chronic state of war with the environment and the internal states of chronic rage, terror, and despair which accompany the rejection of spontaneity. So, the organism turns against itself, restricts its impulses, and internalizes that battle between its innate needs and the prohibitions of the environment.

If we accept the proposition that the ego functions to promote the survival of the organism in negotiating the demands of the environment and the organism itself, we can appreciate how the ego becomes identified with the inhibiting process as a survival mechanism. The inhibiting pattern becomes a survival pattern, which in turn becomes a part of the individual's ego ideal. The ego ideal is, from that point on, threatened by an alive, spontaneous self-expression and maintained by control of those impulses. Thus, cognitive self-statements in the form of "script decisions" (e.g., "I am an understanding, giving, peaceful person," etc.) reinforce the muscular blocks.

There is the corresponding illusion that the release of the blocks will yield to catastrophe, often both personal and environmental. In the case of schizoid character, the illusion of release is annihilation—often not only the annihilation of oneself but also the annihilation of others as the uncontrollable rage is let go on the environment. The essential schizoid experience is, "My life threatens my life." So, what is ultimately blocked is the life force itself. The organism freezes, stiffens, or clenches in tension, and twists away from the threatening environment. All of the bodily consequences which the bioenergetic therapists have noted in this character structure are a result of this process.

In listing the body characteristics of the schizoid, it must be kept in mind that they represent the observations of a number of bioenergetic therapists who have treated a variety of clients with, presumably, various mixtures of schizoid and other characteristics. The listing is more of what one may look for rather than an exhaustive or exclusive list of what will always be present. Furthermore, where these chronic muscular contractions have characteristic postural consequences, it must also be remembered that characteristics of posture, as well as other physical dimensions, can also be the result of genetic endowment.

A well-trained bioenergetic therapist does not typically look at the body to classify the pathology; rather, he looks to see where and how the natural flow of the organism has been restricted by chronic contraction.

Perhaps the most salient thing to look for in a schizoid personality is the virtual cutting off of life in the body. Movements tend to be restricted, often mechanical, and lacking in natural spontaneity and flow. Cutting off the life flow is particularly accomplished through restricting the breathing and in this personality structure that is often done by a constriction of the diaphragm and shallow breathing in the chest. This may be accompanied by raised shoulders and a concomitant contraction of the chest. This breathing constriction obviously can affect the voice and accompanying constriction in the throat may yield a high-pitched and often young-sounding voice, due to the narrowing in the throat. Correlated with this, one often finds that the choke response is easily elicited if the person is asked to breathe deeply. It is thought that the schizoid's split in thinking and feeling is literally represented in this chronic tension in the neck—the area separating the head and the trunk. It is as if the natural instinctual impulses are blocked off there and not allowed to register in the head.

Together with this characteristic contraction in the upper chest and neck, there is typically severe tension at the base of the skull corresponding to the characteristic block in the ocular segment of the head. This ocular block may also be observed in the appearance of the eyes, which may, especially under circumstances of stress, appear disconnected or unresponsive. It has been hypothesized that this ocular block results from the attempt on the part of the organism not to see the painful truth of his state of existence. Under stress, the schizoid individual may literally go away from the current circumstances and that escape may be perceived in the eyes, which appear to be looking but not seeing, disconnected from the present reality. Occasionally, the experience of frozen terror may also be seen in the eyes of the schizoid individual, a terror which is not consistent with the rest of the facial expression and which does not systematically vary with the situation but is fixed or frozen.

The early twisting away from the threatening environment may be chronically represented in a twisting of the body, which may be represented literally in a chronic spinal scoliosis. Again, there are many causes of spinal scoliosis but the schizoid experience is hypothesized to be one of them, a function of a chronically frozen twisting-away. The freezing or stiffening of the body is believed to typically result in difficulty in the joints. To understand this, one can imagine the chronic tension which would result in the joints from a response of chronic stiffening of the body. To illustrate this, I often ask my students to assume a posture of complete stiffening, locking the knees, elbows, and lower back while opening the eyes and mouth wide in an expression of terror. I then ask them to imagine themselves going through life in that position, bracing against the threat of life.

Many bioenergetic therapists have also noted a number of characteristics in schizoid patients which could be summarized under the heading of "disproportionment in the body." That is, the body does not present itself as a unitary whole, as certain parts do not fit with the whole. For example, the head may not seem to fit the body or the arms may not be proportional to the trunk. Bilateral asymmetry has also been noted, such that the left side of the body is larger or smaller than the right.

Finally, a general deadness of the schizoid body has often been observed and reflected in the lack of color in the body, particularly a lack of color or even coldness to the touch at the points of chronic constriction—the joints, diaphragm, and points where the body narrows (i.e., ankles, wrists, and neck). The lack of aliveness in the body is also often seen in a thin, narrow physique with limited bodily movement. Personally, I have seen a number of schizoid personalities where the body is more developed than in this classic type, though some of the energetic blocks are still present.

While I have sometimes found my students to scoff and dismiss the bodily implications of characterological theory, I have continued to find the insights delivered by body observation extremely useful. Where the underlying characterological problems are well hidden and well defended, the individual may often be unable to report the reality of his etiological history. In this not uncommon situation, it will be the individual's characteristic behavior and the language of the body which will more reliably indicate the basic issues with which he is dealing. This is particularly true in the schizoid situation, wherein denial is the primary mechanism of defense and where the historical events may have occurred so early and been so traumatic that their remembrance is both less possible and more debilitating.

As is probably obvious, the combination of extreme bodily distortions and lack of bodily and emotional awareness makes the schizoid a natural for the development of psychosomatic illness. The chronic tension in the upper body, neck, and ocular segment translates readily to the susceptibility to headache and difficulty with the eyes. The constriction in respiration results in a susceptibility to respiratory illness, just as the chronic tension in the joints produces a susceptibility to illness and injury there. The chronic but usually repressed anxiety and resulting twisting and holding in the body can render the normal organic processes, particularly digestion, susceptible to difficulty. Further, the generalized diminution of life's energetic properties can render the organism generally susceptible to infection and injury. Indeed, it has been my experience that the better defended the character, the more likely the presence of illness.

THERAPEUTIC OBJECTIVES

In every case, the therapeutic objectives are to repair the deficiencies in ego functioning, to restore the flow of instinctual self-expression, and to integrate these behavioral and cognitive abilities into a life-supporting system which is able to adapt to or modify the external environment. I see psychotherapy as beginning a process which can last a lifetime. As life is a race between maturity and senility, effective psychotherapy is designed to aid the former and retard the latter.

The provision of a trusting and safe environment is, of course, necessary in all psychotherapy, but in the treatment of the schizoid patient its importance is enhanced. Essentially, the schizoid person was scared out of his body and cannot be frightened or confronted back into it. It is essential, therefore, that the therapeutic setting be safe, congruent, and human. Because of the history, the sensitivity, and extraordinary perceptiveness of the typical schizoid client, it is even more crucial that the therapist realize Carl Rogers' three prerequisites for an enhancing therapeutic relationship — accurate empathy, unconditional positive regard, and congruence. In short, the first objective with this patient is to restore trust — trust in the self, trust in the significant other, trust in the community at large, and trust in the life process itself. Once this therapeutic environment is achieved, the other objectives are possible.

Affective Objectives

Perhaps most basic to the schizoid problem is the need to reconnect the person with himself. Without this there can be no essential change in his relationship with the world. This may be begun by helping him regain a greater feeling sense of himself. An increase in the depth, range, and realness of one's feeling is an objective which can be accomplished by many therapeutic techniques, including movement, internal focusing, and physical expression. Along with this increased feeling and an enhanced identification with that feeling, we also wish to increase the individual's physical relationship to objects in the world. That is, the schizoid person needs an increased felt relatedness to reality—to food, work, nature, home, etc. Next, that reality relatedness needs to be expanded to the human world—to the therapist, loved ones, coworkers, and friends.

As a central part of increasing the client's sensory contact with the environment, it is particularly crucial to build the sense of stability or *grounding* in the world. This refers to the felt sense that one's feet are planted firmly on the ground and that one can stand one's ground in circumstances where it may be threatened. As a part and consequence of this work in increasing sensory awareness, the therapist must work in many ways to reduce all forms of chronic tension or spasticity in the affected areas of the body. Initially, this increased awareness and emerging letting go may be associated with physical pain, but eventually it will reduce experienced pain and affect any psychosomatic illness which has not already produced lasting physical damage.

As with all clients, it will be useful to increase the schizoid's awareness of and identification with his own defenses. It is always useful for one to be aware of how one has and does defend himself, to respect the survival qualities of these defenses and to understand how they were appropriate choices under the circumstances of one's development. In the schizoid case, for example, it will be useful to help the person identify his tendency to "go away," to ask him to do that deliberately, and to assist him in monitoring its effects.

As one works on the emotional level with the schizoid individual, one will confront deep-seated and profound hostility and terror. As the person begins to trust his body and feelings, more and more of these feelings will emerge to be owned, expressed, and eventually integrated into the self. Although getting to the terror is essential, it is in the retaliatory rage that the individual often experiences the surest road to finding his true self. When he experiences the power and realness of that rage, he begins to have the power base for self-expression. There is at last, in that rage, a self to experience and express. The alternating of experience and insight around that emotion, as well as around the terror, will initiate the emergence of self. In the expression of the rage particularly, the schizoid person restates his right to live and to be in this world.

As with the rage, the schizoid's ability to experience the terror and to tolerate it is an empowering experience. He can discover that the terror, like the rage, is within him, that it can be expressed, and that he will not disintegrate with its expression. Additionally, he can have someone to assist him and be in contact with during and after the emotional experience. The increase in feeling through the body and contact with the ground, the environment, and others allows him to experience the intensity of these feelings without needing to "go away."

A central objective throughout this process is to increase the schizoid's tolerance for feeling and expression. He can learn that neither rage nor terror results in annihilation or disintegration. He can be asked to reach out and maintain contact with the therapist, thereby reinforcing the notion that he can be expressive, identified with his negativity, and still not lose himself or the support of others.

In simple affirmation terms, we seek for the schizoid individual to experience the following on a physical, feeling level: "I am welcome here. I belong here. I can trust life. I can trust my own feelings. I am a member of the community. I am capable of love and lovable. I can and will take care of and love myself. I can enjoy the movement in my body. I can run, jump, yell, express myself. I am safe. I am loved. I can relax."

Although it is not completely possible to separate therapeutic objectives into the organizational structure used thus far in the book — affect, behavior, cognition — such an organization is nevertheless heuristic. The therapeutic objectives of a sensory, kinesthetic, or affective nature may be summarized as follows.

1) Increase sensory contact with the environment — the sense of touch, hearing, visual, olfactory, and taste contact with the

world—and develop an appreciation and awareness of the human touch of others.

2) Increase the sense of stability or *grounding*—the sense that one's feet are planted firmly on the ground, the sense that one can stand one's ground.

3) Increase the feeling sense within the body—the feeling of all movement, breathing, the sensations of tension versus relaxation, the specific bodily sensations associated with hunger, pain, joy, laughter, etc.

4) Reduce the chronic tension or spasticity in all affected areas of the body and the associated physical pain.

5) Open the feeling of rage and direct it at the appropriate target. Integrate the rage within the self until it becomes a source of power and assertiveness; in the simple poetry of the bioenergetic therapists, "Claim it, aim it, and tame it."

6) Open the access to terror in the person and assist in the recovery of its initial causes. Integrate the terror within the self until it becomes a source of the ability to feel fear, awe, and vulnerability.

7) Access the grief associated with the loss of love and the loss of self. Integrate that grief as a part of the reality of the person—a reality of tragedy and irony. Eliminate the denial of what was, so one can experience what is.

8) Develop the physical relationship between the person and the physical world (e.g., food, nature, home, familiar objects, etc.).

9) Open the feelings of love and the experience of joy grounded in reality.

Behavioral-Social Objectives

Since, in the schizoid problem, the main failure is in attachment, it will be the therapist's objective to establish that attachment. In some cases, the therapist may be the client's only meaningful human contact and it may be necessary to establish and then resolve a symbiotic attachment. In other cases, where there are relationship or attachment difficulties, the therapist will also work to assist in the development of those attachments and commitments. In general, growth in the schizoid character will involve an increase in commitments to love, friendship, and work relationships. Establishing or increasing involvement in some nonthreatening small group experience can often be very useful. In short, the individual needs to learn that he is a member of the group and equal to all other members, that he can take what he needs and give what he is able. Assistance in discovering that perfectionism or special performance is not required for acceptability will often be needed. Decreasing the perfectionism and need for specialness will usually result in decreasing procrastination and/or performance anxiety if these are a problem.

To facilitate and expedite increased social involvement, it may be necessary to give feedback on, teach, or arrange for the teaching of simple social skills. The behavioral programs in personal effectiveness or assertiveness training may be useful in this regard, since these individuals may need to learn both verbal and nonverbal social skills.

While the aggressive impulses are almost always denied in individuals with this basic character structure, the aggression or hostility always finds an outlet in one form or another. Thus, it is an objective to help the individual discover the ways in which she unwittingly aggresses against others. Commonly, individuals with this character structure engage in passive-aggressive patterns such as withdrawal, or they provoke aggression in others to justify retaliation or provoke rescuing from others. The essential objective here is to discover the "games" that these people play, which in a very general way tend to operate by the presentation of the schizoid individual as understanding, accepting, and even weak, but which culminate in withdrawal, rejection, hatred, and the humiliation of others. As outlined earlier, the characterological pattern is expressed here with the individual offering what was not forthcoming to her but ultimately delivering to others what was earlier received. In other words, we offer what we didn't get and we ultimately give what we got.

As the aggressive impulses are integrated, the individual will begin to behave more aggressively and assertively in the social world. The therapist will serve to smooth out this transition so that aggressive and assertive expressions in the real world are relatively appropriate and effective. The direct expression of aggression and assertiveness in appropriate ways and contexts will be encouraged in therapy. Similarly, therapists can encourage and facilitate the smooth and appropriate expression of other affective experiences in the real social world — sadness, anxiety, laughter, joy, etc.

Again, in list form, here are the behavioral-social objectives of therapy with the schizoid individual:

1) Initially establish or strengthen attachment and eventually resolve the symbiosis.
2) Strengthen the conscious and deliberate use of defenses such as social withdrawal.
3) Increase small group and community involvement.
4) Decrease perfectionism and specialness in performance and thereby affect procrastination and performance anxiety.
5) Help the client to discover current outlets for the denied aggressive impulses (i.e., the "game" patterns in social relationships, passive-aggressive or withdrawal patterns, aggressive fantasies, and so on).
6) Teach or arrange for the teaching of social skills (e.g., personal effectiveness, assertiveness, eye contact, display of affect in social situations, etc.).
7) Increase appropriate aggressive and assertive behavior in the person's social world.

Cognitive Objectives

There are two basic areas of repair which need to be considered in addressing the cognitive problems. The first involves the client's attitudes, beliefs, and processes of self-identification. These structures are represented by the "script decisions," "ego ideals," "false self" identifications, etc. Here we are talking about beliefs, attitudes, points of view, etc. The second area involves cognitive abilities or, in psychoanalytic terms, ego functioning. Here we are discussing the individual's cognitive strategies in dealing with the external world, the defense mechanisms used internally, and the quality and robustness of cognitive abilities (e.g., assimilation and accommodation). In the first case, the therapeutic objectives center around the restructuring of internal beliefs, while in the second case they involve the literal repair of ego or cognitive abilities per se.

Just as it is useful to help the client identify how his compromise solutions have expressed themselves in his body and behavior, it is useful to do this in the area of cognition or belief. The first step, therefore, may be to help the individual to identify the usually simplistic and exaggerated precepts of the ego ideal. In this process, the individual may find that she is demanding absolutely, "I must be all-accepting. I must be special." Or believing dogmatically, "I am my ideas. I am my achievements." Once these notions are identified and experienced in their real intensity, it becomes relatively easy to explain their origins and assist the client through interpretation to develop further insight into their operation. Identification and understanding will initiate change in the ego ideals and false self identifications and more direct methods can then be employed to further those changes.

As the defenses at all levels are systematically relaxed, the therapeutic objective of uncovering the various "script decisions" about self, life and others in general will be facilitated. In this character structure, these tend to be of the following nature: "Something is wrong with me. The world is a threatening place. I have no right to exist." In general, the "script decisions" in this structure will reflect self-hate and paranoia.

With the identification of the ego ideals and script decisions, the very basis for the false self will begin to erode and there will begin to be greater opportunities to strengthen a real self-identification. The therapist can begin this with strategies that strengthen the identification of the self with the body and its life processes. In this structure, that would amount to replacing the identification, "I am my ideas and accomplishments" with "I am my body and the life therein."

In the second area of cognitive or ego functioning, the therapeutic task, simply stated, is to assess and repair the areas of cognitive weakness. In relation to the perception of external reality, for example, the client may need direct instruction in the processes of assimilation, accommodation, discrimination, integration, and generalization. The therapist may serve not only the role of reality tester but also that of instructor in the strategies for accurately perceiving and testing reality. Just as the schizoid individual may need to be directly taught simple social skills, he may also need to be taught strategies for simple social perception. How does one know when one is liked, disliked, or responded to with objective neutrality? How does one know whether the negative behavior of others is the result of their internal preoccupation or their specific response to us personally? Similarly, the schizoid individual may be helped to sharpen his cognitive strategies for discriminating internal affective states. How, for example, does one discriminate anxiety from excitement or sexual arousal from love?

The schizoid individual will usually also need to be taught better or more evolved defense mechanisms than the ones she already has. The schizoid defenses are primitive and few in number and most of these individuals are capable of learning far more efficient and less costly internal defense mechanisms. Particularly where used consciously and deliberately, such methods of internal defense are extraordinarily useful. A number of strategies are available from the cognitive wing of psychotherapy (e.g., rational emotive therapy, neurolinguistic programming) to teach such defenses. A part of this teaching, of course, would be the identification and strengthening of existing defenses, increasing appreciation of their survival function and rendering them conscious and under voluntary control.

The schizoid individual can benefit greatly from direct instruction in dealing with the harsh and anxiety-provoking parts of the real world. Much of this will involve behavioral instruction; however, on a cognitive level the therapist can assist with cognitive maps concerning how to approach and think about the demands of adult reality. Thus, the therapy may at times deal with strategies for managing one's time, dealing with the demands of others, or simple strategies for living life: how to clean the house, pay the bills, study for exams, etc.

Finally, a great deal needs to be done in the schizoid case on the integration of the "good parent-bad parent" and "good self-bad self" representations into a healthy, ambivalently experienced self-concept and view of others. The "good parent" is usually deficient in its representation in this structure and is particularly deficient in the nurturing functions. As a result, the schizoid individual is usually poor at self-soothing or self-nurturing. She may be directly taught to strengthen those self-soothing abilities which she does possess and to learn anew those which she does not.

In the course of the treatment, a central theme must be the identification of the unintegrated introject — the "bad parent." It is often so split off from the rest of the self that the patient feels literally possessed by an alien and destructive force which is aimed primarily at himself. The therapist's task is to assist the individual in identifying and taking responsibility for this negative force, in understanding its origins, and in beginning the process of integrating it into the ambivalently experienced self and other representations. In any person so hated, there will be hatred. To erode the denial of that hatred, to admit its existence, to aim it at its appropriate target, to accept it as part of one's reality, and to release its expression in a manner which will reduce tension without undue harm is perhaps the central therapeutic task with the schizoid character. As this is accomplished, an integrated representation of the self with all its real components will be established at a cognitive level. Such a representation may be facilitated by intervention at the cognitive level directly.

An appreciation of the need for strengthening of the cognitive ego abilities yields a solid theoretical justification for methods of direct instruction or influence. The theory presented here does so, however, without the extreme oversimplification in theory characteristic of those who espouse an exclusively cognitive understanding of the complex human condition. With this knowledge, one can engage in very simple and direct cognitive restructuring with an understanding of how that fits into a broader perspective of what the human dilemma is all about. One can help another to think differently without having to believe that thought is all there is.

Here is a listing of cognitive therapeutic objectives in the two categories.

Attitudes and beliefs

1) Identify, interpret, develop insight into, and change the ego ideal or false self (e.g., "I am all-accepting, understanding, and special. I am my ideas and accomplishments.").
2) Identify, interpret, develop insight into, and change the "script decision" (e.g., "Something is wrong with me. I don't belong. The world is frightening. Others can't be trusted.").
3) Strengthen identification of the self with the body and its natural life processes.
4) Strengthen the identification of the self with the person's history and its resulting vulnerability. Eliminate the denial of what happened and its effects.
5) Strengthen identification of the self with natural aggression, assertiveness and power.

Cognitive ego abilities

1) Identify, strengthen, and bring under voluntary control existing ego defenses.
2) Teach ego defenses not yet learned (e.g., suppression, dissociation).
3) Reinforce, repair or teach strategies for dealing with harsh or anxiety-provoking environments.
4) Promote or teach self-soothing and self-nurturing.
5) Establish the ambivalent experience of the self, others, and the world and increase the tolerance for ambivalence. Discriminate and integrate self- and object-representations with particular attention to the negative parental introject.
6) Assess and repair where appropriate: Assimilation, accommodation, discrimination, integration, and generalization.

It may be useful at this point to remember that there is no such thing as a schizoid character. This is merely an archetype in a model which identifies basic human issues. Those who have been terrified early in life by the harshness or coldness of the environment they found then will usually still be operating with the adaptations to that reality formed by a weak and frightened child. Understanding this element of any person seeking psychological assistance can guide the therapist in a useful way. Imperfect and incomplete, this map of the invisible territory is worth having.

CHAPTER III

HEALING THE
HATED CHILD:
PART I

THE PURPOSE OF this chapter is to present and integrate therapeutic strategies from many schools which are applicable to the initial
treatment of the schizoid elements of any personality. The organization of this presentation follows a sequential outline of the general
course of treatment for the generalized case. Within that sequence, the
specific therapeutic techniques will be presented and integrated to accomplish a more or less broad general case scenario. I suggest that you,
the reader, orient to this and the following descriptions as you might
to a generalized map to the home of a friend. I, for example, have had
to prepare a general map to my home for colleagues, friends, and
clients. The map and accompanying text must cover all possibilities,
including the cases in which people are coming from out of town from
any direction. Thus, the text of directions starts with the most easily
identified and generally applicable starting point and proceeds from
there. Obviously, the person following the map or text picks it up at
the point where it becomes relevant or interjects with his knowledge
of the town and the location of my home. As a person becomes more
familiar with the particular location of my home, he may find short-
cuts to it which I have not even put on the generalized instructions.

The current map on the treatment of the schizoid character is guided
by the therapeutic objectives outlined in the last chapter and organized
around a sequential course of treatment for the most general case.
There will, of course, always be a great deal of variation in the treatment of any individual who falls within this broad general category
and the dimensions of variation will include the severity of the schizoid
issue, the level of defense or compensation developed, the length and

nature of prior treatment, the other core issues present, the acceptability to the client of various strategies, etc. The map is just that—a map. In using such a guide it is essential to keep your focus on the client as he is rather than on the guide, which can never fully capture him.

PRESENCE AND COUNTERTRANSFERENCE

I would like to share first the best single piece of advice I have ever received regarding how to treat the schizoid patient. That is: *be there— be available, present, and congruent.* While this is, of course, good advice with any client, it is probably most essential with the person with a strong schizoid character structure. This presence orientation begins to repair the original experience of being unwanted, hated, and the target of the caretaker's rage. Additionally, it models the orientation of being enough in one's presence. As therapist, I model not having to do anything "special" to justify my existence. I am enough as I am and can be healing in the wholeness of my presence. I provide contactfulness and acceptance—that which the schizoid did not originally receive. In this, the therapist will need to be willing to assume a nurturing, even parental, role with clients, a stance which may lead to a symbiotic-like attachment. The attachment must be established before it can be resolved. Concomitant with this orientation is the willingness on the part of the therapist to be real herself and to share with the client aspects of her own life when it is called for.

This more humanistic orientation to the treatment process is not always easy to maintain and risks the stimulation of many of the therapist's countertransferential issues. That is, to the extent that the therapist herself requires a symbiotic attachment, needs for her own ends to be trusted and needed, or is threatened by a too-close relationship, this prescription of presence will be problematic. To the extent that the therapist is herself needy, she will be inclined to seduce the client into that symbiosis and have difficulty letting go or resolving it. To the extent that this much closeness is threatening, she will be inclined to role play the nurturing therapist while covertly distancing, thereby reinflicting the original wound. This is not to say that the therapist need be perfect. It is likely that there will be some countertransferential issue of this nature and often both polarities of the closeness issue will be represented in the therapist. All that is asked is the therapist's awareness of the issue, an openness to supervision and feedback concerning it, and a dedication to resolving it.

The position presented here, of course, runs counter to the classical analytic position or attitude, but it does not run counter to the suggestions made by several of those analysts who have extensive experience with the borderline patient (e.g., Kernberg, 1975; Horner, 1979; Masterson, 1981). What the schizoid individual needs to learn in a purely experiential way is that human bonding is safe, that it feels good, and that it produces good results. The hated child in the schizoid patient has a residual hope for that but a persistent doubt that it can be true for him. As a consequence, he may repeatedly test the therapist and in one way or another withdraw just at the point where hope is at its highest. In doing this, the client will often attempt to stimulate the therapist's rage and rejection. If he succeeds in this, the therapy not only will have failed but also will have established one more supporting situation for the primary script decision. It will be in the handling of this very issue that the treatment will succeed or fail.

Unfortunately, the healing professions have no shortage of people who nurture out of their own compensatory patterns and who deny their anger and disappointment in interpersonal situations. In response to this kind of frustration, the therapist will err by unconsciously denying it and by compensating with his or her characteristic, artificial response. To be present, available, and congruent in this situation is to be frustrated, disappointed, and even angry at the withdrawal or provocation of the patient. The job of the therapist is ideally to work through on his own time that part of this reaction which is countertransferential and to work through with the client that part which is currently involved in their ongoing relationship.

As a part of learning all that human bonding can be, the schizoid client needs to have the experience of real relationship, including the elements in which his behavior is disappointing, frustrating and anger-provoking without its eliciting destructive rage from others. He needs to learn that the expression and working-through of such frustration and anger are among the most intimate and caring things that people do with one another. Because of the schizoid's history, however, he will usually need a period of positivity and nurturance to stay present through the resolution of such conflict. In sharing my countertransferential reactions with clients, I have often found it useful to educate them a bit about this concept. I may explain, for example, that in therapy I have my human reactions and my professional judgment or observations. My human reactions include not only compassion, love, and caring but also anger, envy, frustration, etc. My job is not to cut off my human reactions but to use them. My job as a professional is always to keep a trained observer's eye on them and, at times, share and explore them with the client in an effort to work them through as a part of the therapeutic process. I may explain that whenever these human responses seem to be getting in the way of my professional judgment it is my job to know that and to use my regular peer supervision contacts to resolve the issue. It is not my job to be perfect, but it is my job to be a professional.

As is often the case, this therapeutic prescription, which is on the face of it so simple, is at base so crucial and so often the most difficult to follow. To simply be present, available, and congruent—to be a real human being—is what the schizoid client needs most in her therapist. Because of the distrust, she will test this and this testing will pull at the therapist's most profound difficulties and call upon his most important resources. Presence must be the basic orientation to the treatment of the schizoid client, to which the therapist returns again and again, irrespective of whatever other orientation or technique is used. There may be the continued temptation to retreat from the demands of a real relationship to the security of technique of whatever kind. But to come home to the reality of the human relationship, as difficult as that may be at times, will be a relief to both client and therapist and will be the real cement which holds all the rest of the treatment together. Though we leave it now in this context, we will return to it periodically throughout the text, just as the therapist must return to it consistently throughout the treatment.

EXPLANATION

In addition to establishing a therapeutic relationship, the early stages of therapy will, of course, be involved with the reporting of problems and resources, as well as the development of a historical understanding of them. As in all cases, the therapist will be involved in identifying the characterological issues, the historical antecedents, the ego or cognitive resources and deficits, the script decisions, ego ideals, etc.

Although the extent to which all this can be shared with the client will vary, the schizoid patient can often be greatly helped by building a cognitive map of his particular dilemma. This may be accomplished in many ways and, in general, the impact of such understanding is more far-reaching when the client's own insightful "aha" is spontaneously forthcoming and when there is an emotional catharsis or even abreactive release around the content of what is understood. Nevertheless, such broad spectrum insight and emotional awareness are often not possible in the early stages of treatment, and the schizoid client may be greatly benefited by simple explanation of the therapist's hypotheses regarding the client's central issues. In accomplishing this myself, I often explain that I use a knowledge of child development to help me understand people's emotional problems in adulthood. The emotions or strategies for dealing with adult problems are often childlike, and the *metaphor* of child development can promote not only understanding but also compassion for the difficulties in ourselves and others.

The strategy of explanation is also useful in the schizoid case for other reasons. The schizoid person tends to be the most comfortable in his head and the therapist joins or paces him by initially operating at this level of abstraction. The explanation can be made nonthreatening, sympathetic, and tentative, resulting in the client's beginning to have an understanding and compassionate orientation toward the child in him. This is an initial means of dealing with the introjected, judgmental, self-hating aspect of the schizoid character. Of equal importance in this process, the client may begin to be encouraged to view all problems encountered in daily living as opportunities for greater self-understanding. This adoption of the new "analytic attitude" or the "observing ego" can give the client a new and powerful cognitive ego ability, the impact of which is far-reaching. This will be particularly valuable to the more borderline or less well-defended client in giving him an extraordinarily powerful and useful defense.

This "up leveling" orientation to a problem often allows for a good deal of self-control not hitherto available. Beyond that, it suggests to the client the ways in which she needs to develop and may even prescribe modes or situations in which that development can take place. It will become most valuable when the individual is capable of not only migrating into her head but also migrating back again to the feelings and memories. This migration from understanding at a cognitive level to feeling and remembering will provide those cathartic, abreactive experiences which are a part of a deeper healing. In this connection, I wish to share a process or exercise which does enhance the possibility of a broad range of primary experience, facilitating understanding and emotional completion.

Persistent Problem Exercise

In the following exercise, a process which I have labeled "the persistent problem exercise," the client engages in exclusively internal exploration. As in every such process, it is well to assist the client in achieving an at least slightly altered state of internal focus. This may be accomplished through general relaxation or hypnotic induction. Particularly where hypnotic induction is used, it is often facilitative to foreshadow age regression, since this process ultimately calls for memories usually involving childhood or adolescence.

Prior to the initiation of the process, the therapist and client together choose a persistent problem of the client, which may be affective, behavioral, or cognitive. A persistent problem may be elicited through questioning or, more commonly, an incident occurs in the patient's day-to-day life which is obviously persistent and taps a core issue. The eliciting of a basic issue is, of course, most apparent when the response to external situations is obviously overdetermined or out of proportion to what would ordinarily be expected. Once the persistent problem or situational occurrence is elicited and the altered state is achieved, the therapist simply assists the client in reexperiencing the problem state in all sensory modalities. If the problem is initially experienced primarily in the kinesthetic channels (e.g., headache, sinking feeling in the stomach, weakness in the knees, etc.), this sensory experience is elicited first and the client is asked to notice all other primary *kinesthetic sensations* associated with the problem. The client is then asked to fill out the experience in all other sensory channels. For example, the client may then be asked to notice any *emotions* or *feelings* concurrent with the problem. She then may be asked to be aware of any *attitudes, beliefs*, or *self-statements*. In each sensory category, it is well to repeatedly ask the client to reexperience the situation in emotions and feelings, attitudes and beliefs, etc. The client may then be asked to image herself experiencing the problem and, in relation to that image, notice any *behaviors, postures*, or *facial expressions* associated with it. In an effort to elicit what the client may have been told or heard about the problem, she may be asked, again repeatedly, to be aware of anything she has *heard* or *read* about the problem. This filling out of the sensory experience of the problem is done primarily to elicit as full an experience as possible.

Frequently, it is not necessary to go through the entire list of sensory categories, since a person may obviously drop into the experience very fully and continuing of the process in a rote manner will tend to pull her out, rather than get her more deeply into it. When it is apparent that the person is in the experience, or when the process outlined has been fully completed to the satisfaction of the therapist, the key step is then made. The therapist asks the client to passively allow an *image or scene from the past* to simply pop into awareness. It may be suggested in varying ways that the remembrance can just rise to the surface in its own good time and in its own way and that the resulting memory may have little or nothing to do with the persistent problem.

Since it is usually disruptive for the client to talk during the early part of this process, I have found it useful for the client to signal by nodding the head or raising a finger when such an image presents itself. A memory or image from the past may not always be immediately forthcoming and it may be useful to seed that possibility and indicate that memories or images may come up at other times, perhaps when least expected. This reduces any performance anxiety about "coming up with something" and reinforces the very real possibility that further experience around the problem may pop up at any future time.

Once an image or scene from the past does come into awareness, as it usually does, the therapist may then ask the client to expand the image to include all the circumstances of the episode recovered from what she considers to be the very beginning to the very end. It is useful for the client to take her time and to recover as many details—visual, auditory, and kinesthetic—as possible in this recall. The therapist then asks for the client to signal again when she has completed this episodic recall. When the end signal is given the client is then asked to recall any *conclusions, decisions*, or *judgments* she made at that time regarding herself, others, or the world. This request obviously elicits script decisions—generalized statements about oneself, others, or the world.

The strategy from this point on is to simply ask the client to repeat the recall one to several more times. Sooner or later, it is useful for the client to verbalize the content of the recovered experience as she goes through it. It is the clinician's judgment which will determine the number of repetitions and the time at which the verbalizations should occur. In general, I usually ask the client to verbalize on the second or third run-through and ask for two to seven repetitions.

These decisions are based on several factors. First, if I determine that the initially recovered experience is fairly trivial, I may ask the client to reach for another. If the experience is fairly recent, I'm inclined to believe that more powerful effects can be gathered through a recovery of an earlier memory. Sometimes, the verbal report of the incident will elicit a charged phrase in an otherwise relatively uncharged experience. I may then ask the person to focus on this phrase and again look for an image or scene from the past triggered by that. Ultimately, this process can yield one to several recovered memories which are of central importance in understanding the person's basic characterological issues. The results of this process are most rewarding when it elicits powerful, suppressed emotion surrounding the earlier events. This process can result in a powerfully abreactive response and is one of a handful which I view as the most useful in my practice. When the recall does elicit powerful abreactive emotion, it is useful to repeat the sequential recall until that emotion is substantially diminished. When that is accomplished, the client may then be asked to simply take note of any *insight* or *awareness* that she has gained during any part of the process.

Finally, it is then often useful to ask the person to image herself as she will be when the problem is no longer an issue. This step suggests a positive outcome and gives the person a vicarious experience of a symptom-free existence. This process, which is very consistent with a number of schools of thought, was first introduced to me in my own *est** training in 1979. Here is an outline of this process as I have presented it here.

Persistent problem exercise

   1) Relaxation or hypnotic induction
   2) Establish experience in all sensory channels
       a) Body sensations and location

*Ehrhart Seminar Training created by Werner Ehrhart.

b) Feelings and emotions
c) Create a scene of the client experiencing the problem and
   ask for behaviors, postures, facial expressions
d) Attitudes, beliefs, points of view
e) Reasons, causes for the problem
f) Things read or told about the problem
3) Call for the memory of an image or scene from the past associated with the problem.
4) Ask for recall of the decisions, conclusions, and judgments
   made at the time of the memory.
5) Repeat steps 3 and 4.
6) Ask for realizations, insights or knowledge coming from this
   process.
7) Ask client to visualize self without the problem.

It is well to note that while this is one of the more valuable exercises I have ever encountered, it may very well be too much for the
relatively undefended or borderline schizoid patient.

Persistent Problem Case Examples

Ralph: "Is this all there is?"

Ralph was a 30-year-old investment banker who came into therapy
complaining of chronic indecision and lack of any depth of feeling or
commitment to his girl friend, his work, or anything else. There was
a chronic low level depression obvious in his way of being and a total
anhedonia in his experience of life. The persistent problem was the "Is
this all there is" feeling state surrounding his girl friend, with whom
he lived, and with whom he had a topographically satisfying relationship. The persistent problem exercise, experienced by him in a mod-
erate hypnogogic state, yielded a powerful adolescent memory which
he claims to have repressed until that time.

As a junior in high school, he had been passionately, uncontrollably
in love with a girl who attended another school. He recalled very vividly
the scene on the front steps of his high school in which she walked up
to him and told him their relationship was over. This came as a complete surprise to him. He recalled responding back with shock and ultimately with the decision, "I will never care for anyone like this again."

It then became apparent to him that he had had no real depth of feeling for any woman since that time and that his protective shell had been a result of this early experience.

It is common in this process, particularly when it is used early in therapy, that an adolescent scene will be recovered which recapitulates the parent-child situation experienced earlier. This particular recovered memory is remarkable because of the dramatic nature of its paradise lost quality and the resulting defensive detachment, which is definitional of a schizoid issue.

Jane: "Men can't be trusted."

Jane was a 38-year-old businesswoman who was divorced and plagued by a history of putting her trust in men who would betray it. In the most recent case, she had loaned $40,000 to a boyfriend who had skipped out on the debt. In the persistent problem exercise she recovered an earlier adult experience in which, while in Holland, she had extreme difficulties in delivering her first child. She had difficulty getting into the midwifery facility which she had picked at the last minute, and her husband failed to be supportive during the process. Rather than staying with her and assisting her, as did the other husbands in the facility, he left her and went out for a hamburger. She had a difficult delivery with much pain, anxiety, and hyperventilation and, during that, received no sympathy from the midwives who had barely let her into the facility. One of them slapped her and said, "Others here are having babies and not carrying on. Go ahead and have your baby and be quiet." The husband was expected around 10 o'clock the next morning to take her and the child away but did not appear until 2 p.m. She experienced this as "absolute and total rejection." This marriage lasted for 14 years and was sprinkled throughout with many occurrences of this unsupportive and unreliable behavior on the part of her husband.

In the recovery of this memory, the sentence kept coming up, "I have to do it all myself." I pursued this line with her and asked for the recovery of another memory, perhaps further back in time. She then remembered an incident which occurred when she was five. She had had her tonsils out, as did many children at that time, but she had been told by her parents that it would be a fun experience and that she would be able to eat ice cream and sherbet for days afterwards. In fact, the surgery was so badly botched that she was unable to eat anything for several days thereafter and was seriously ill for a year following the tonsillectomy. A goiter-like growth appeared on one side of her neck and she was taken from doctor to doctor all over the state to find a solution to her problem. She remembers going to at least 12 doctors. One of them lanced the growth, but it grew back. There was a good deal of pain for her during this crucial year of her life and, because the diagnosis was unknown and she was obviously ill, she had to be isolated from other children and was not allowed to go to school. She played on a farm with animals during that whole year and remembers as a consequence preferring animals to people and beginning a life of withdrawal and involvement with animals and books rather than people.

Eventually, it was determined that the initial surgery, done in a doctor's office, was incompetently performed and created some type of infection in the lymphatic system. Eventually, the lymph nodes on one side of her neck were removed and this solved the problem. The primary decision that she remembers from this was, "Men can't be trusted." In relating this back to her present-day problems, she noticed how her attraction to "men with a fatal flaw" always included the real hope that she could change them, and that the original decisions, "men can't be trusted" and "I have to do it all myself," were repeated each time.

At times, the changes which follow the recovery of these memories can be profound and wide-reaching. More often, however, they not only begin a process of analysis of the deeper origins of the problem but also lead to an awareness of the recurring nature of circumstances which lead to the same general pessimistic conclusions about oneself, life, or others. In Jane's case, some further analysis led to uncovering the ways in which she collaborated in picking unreliable men and participating in the setting up of the eventual betrayal. Here there had evolved an extraordinarily competent women who could handle things herself but who was chronically unable to find a man in whom she could really place her trust and to whom she could really open her heart.

Persistent Compensation Process

There is a reciprocal process or exercise which can yield equally dramatic and useful results. In this one, the therapist simply begins by eliciting a positive experience in which the client found satisfaction with himself and his resources. It is usually useful to ask for a time when the person felt particularly self-satisfied, on top of things, optimistic, and in charge. From that memory, a similar fully represented state is recreated, just as in the persistent problem exercise. At that point, the person is again asked to allow an image or scene from the past to pop into awareness. The client is asked to reexperience this scene as fully and completely as possible and asked to recover any decisions, conclusions, or judgments made at that time about himself, others, or the world. This process typically elicits very direct statements of the ego ideal—decisions about how to "make it" or compensate for whatever rejections one has experienced of the real self.

Bob: "I'll be special."

Bob was a 35-year-old research scientist who, in spite of a good deal of worldly success in his field, was persistently depressed and seriously psychosomatic. To initiate this process he remembered an instance in which he was very pleased after the presentation of a scientific paper at a national convention. After the presentation, he received a good deal of acclaim and was able to celebrate very heartily that evening, feeling worthwhile, accomplished, and acknowledged. The associated flashback was to childhood, when he was the only child of older, rather constricted parents. He remembered a time when, at church, he served as acting minister or priest to the other children and then sang a solo in the church choir. Again he received a good deal of acknowledgment and praise, particularly from his parents. He decided, "I'll be special, I'll get recognition," and remembered that this was one of the few places in which he could fully express himself and be safe from the parental ridicule or anxiety that was stimulated by other forms of spontaneous self-expression.

Both of these processes are of quite general applicability, but the examples given here are rather typically schizoid. What are elicited in the first exercise are examples of rejection or betrayal which result in script decisions concerning trust, worthiness, and involvement in life. In the second exercise, typically decisions are elicited concerning how one decided to cope with that reality using compensatory adaptations and construction of an ego ideal which embodies the idealization of that compensation. The initial stages of therapy can often be very profitably spent in eliciting this kind of information, particularly if there is a feeling associated with the memories. The degree to which this is advisable will depend on many factors, including how able the individual is to handle the uncovering of this much information and the extent to which such uncovering has already been done. Schizoid patients will often tend to stop at understanding even though it is ultimately unsatisfying. It is at this point that the solid, safe therapeutic relationship will provide the necessary grounding for approaching rougher territory.

BODY WORK AND AFFECT

Implicit in this book is the thesis that it is often useful to shuttle around in the treatment process from strategies which primarily affect cognitions to those that are aimed at changes in behavior to those which emphasize contact with and expression of affect. While there is more to say here about the understanding and explanation of script decisions, ego ideals, ego abilities, and awareness of one's existing defenses, I wish at this point to shuttle away from that area and begin to discuss more kinesthetic approaches to getting the schizoid client literally grounded and in touch with himself. In a sense, we have been studying the development of the false self in the preceding pages, and it is useful to begin the appreciation and development of the real self before getting too lost in the understanding of repetitive patterns.

Increasing the sense of grounding and developing the client's sense of his body and environment are the very beginnings of realizing the real self. In a bioenergetic sense, grounding means having a real experience of one's legs and contact with the ground—feeling the support of the legs, the contact of the feet with the floor, developing the sense of one's place in the world. The well-grounded person knows where he stands, or knows when he is not on solid ground and his stance needs to be changed. He is in good contact with reality and with his position in the world. He is not a pushover but can stand his ground.

The schizoid character is not well grounded. Appropriate treatment for him will address this objective. Understanding himself and his history will be a part of accomplishing grounding but, in addition, literally and concretely enhancing his contact with the ground will be useful. This will pave the way for an increased capacity to experience and tolerate feeling and to literally have a greater sense of himself from the ground up.

When one develops a greater kinesthetic sense of the body, one simply has greater sensory awareness of feelings, along with greater awareness of sensory contact with the environment. In other words, there is greater consciousness of what is felt both internally and externally, as well as of what is heard and seen. When I write, for example, I am "in my head," meaning that there is a good deal of my consciousness devoted to ideas and a good deal of my energy absorbed in this activity. I may be totally unaware of what I am seeing or feeling and impervious to sounds in the environment. When I do push-ups, on the other hand, it is difficult not to have some awareness of my body, particularly the muscles in my upper arms, and particularly toward the end of my capacity to do the exercise. In this sense, the schizoid patient spends a lot of time in his head and can be greatly benefited by increasing the awareness of his body and sensory functioning. There are many physical exercises from a variety of sources which will accomplish this purpose. Bioenergetics offers some but others are available from yoga, Tai Chi, ordinary calisthenics, exercises for skiers, etc. There is really nothing sacred or mysterious about physical exercises for the purpose of enhancing the quality of life. The exercises outlined in this book are illustrative rather than exhaustive. These physical exercises are often best demonstrated person to person rather than in print, but some good books listing exercises with illustrations include the following: Lowen, *The Betrayal of the Body*, 1967, and Lowen and Lowen, *The Way to Vibrant Health*, 1977.

Passive Awareness Processes

For a number of reasons, it may be advisable in therapy to delay any very active work with the body. Body work as a part of psychotherapy is unusual and for this reason many therapists and clients alike are resistant to it. In addition, because of the borderline nature of some schizoid patients, very little movement or affective release can be overwhelming. Consequently, it is useful to have a repertoire of processes which enhance sensory awareness without requiring that the patient become very active.

An excellent initial choice for this is a process which I label the "I am" exercise or meditation. In this process, simply ask the client to close her eyes and focus her attention inward. Then ask her to silently say to herself "I am . . . " filling in that blank with whatever body sensation comes to mind. The sensation may change or stay the same as she repeats this mantra-like statement. Tell her that this process will probably produce a state somewhat different from her ordinary one and label it "being with yourself." Ask her to notice how this state feels and determine if it is continuous or variable. After allowing the patient to engage in this process for several minutes, the therapist may either bring her back to contact with him or add the following steps: 1) When the desired state is reasonably achieved, ask her to open her eyes and look around the room slowly while attempting to maintain the state. 2) Instruct her, "If you begin to lose that contact with yourself, close your eyes and repeat the exercise until you regain the state of being with yourself." 3) Finally, ask the client to look at you while following the same procedure—"If you begin to go away or lose yourself, close your eyes, go inside, and repeat the exercise until you can come out and once again look at me." At the end of the process, the client is asked to share her experience.

This meditative process can also be a very useful self-help device for many clients. The research results for the effects of meditation and general self-administered relaxation programs are impressive (e.g., Benson, 1975; Orme-Johnson & Farrow, 1977). To my mind, the research results on the effects of transcendental meditation are more uniformly positive than are the research results on the effects of psychotherapy. I am not convinced from the research that the effects of TM are necessarily better than the results of any other similar method, though there is more research on this than on other methods. In any case, I believe the effects of meditation and relaxation training are so profound that I recommend them to practically every one of my clients. The "I am" exercise appears to be a viable method for this kind of work.

Another sensory awareness process which involves no movement is the "visual clearing exercise." In this process, simply ask the client to breathe, look around the room, and see everything that is green in color. After about 30 seconds, ask the client to see everything that is round, then everything that is made of wood, then everything that is rectangular, and so on. As a final step in this exercise, one may ask the client to totally relax his focus and not look at anything in particular but to see how broad and deep is his perspective of vision. "How far can you see to the right, the left, up and down, deep and near at the same time? Breathe and take your time." At the end of this process it is often useful to instruct the client, "Now simply close your eyes, breathe, and notice how this was for you." In addition to enhancing the visual awareness of the client, this process, particularly the latter phase, will have the effect of opening and relaxing the eyes. That opening may be experienced as somewhat fear-provoking for some clients; if that is the case, some reassurance in this regard can be useful. Additionally, when the eyes are finally closed, it is often useful to instruct the client, "Now, put the palms of your hands over your eyes so that the palms cup your eyes but do not touch them. Feel the warmth, see the darkness and breathe."

This process may be followed by auditory and/or external kinesthetic clearing. In auditory clearing, simply ask the client, "Now, with your eyes closed notice every sound around you. Some sounds are close; some are at a distance. Some are very faint while others are very obvious. Hear everything." External kinesthetic clearing simply involves the following instructions: "Now, with your eyes closed, feel some things around you: your clothing or skin, the arm of the chair, the plant nearby, etc. As you feel, notice the texture, the temperature, and the sense of touch, perhaps in a more profound way than you ever have before. Just breathe and feel and notice your reactions." At the end of this process, it may be useful to summarize its objectives, suggest its use in the future, and make some general suggestions for the possibility of deliberate manipulation of one's focus of attention. For example, "Your awareness is always moving and changing. That awareness can be focused inward or outward. You can feel sensations in your body, think thoughts in your head, or see things in your mind's eye. Or, you can focus outward and see things in the environment, hear the sounds around you, and feel the world in all its expressions. It is nice to know all of the dimensions of your awareness, to shift from inside to outside, from seeing to feeling, to do one almost exclusively or to do all at once. Your awareness can flow. You can have greater and greater control over where your awareness is placed. There may be a time in the future when you deliberately wish to change your focus of attention. If, for example, there is something you will be worrying about, you may wish to remember to breathe and to change your focus of awareness to seeing and hearing and feeling the outside world. When you want a rest from the outside world, you may close your eyes, go inside, relax, breathe, meditate and enjoy a vacation inside yourself. It may be useful now to anticipate some circumstances where you want to shift your consciousness in to out, feeling to seeing, thinking to feeling. How nice it is to know that you can control the content of your awareness."

A third method which may be used in this context is that of focusing, as introduced by Gendlin (1978). Because the purposes of this process go well beyond those being discussed here, this technique will be outlined in detail later. The general strategy is to initiate the client into the ability to feel things in his body and achieve more clarity about himself through this method. If, for example, a client indicates that he has a worry or emotion, he may be asked to simply close his eyes, focus inward, and see if that worry or emotion can be located by a physical sensation in his body. Once the worry or emotion has the beginnings of a sensory representation, the client is asked to make ever more refined or precise distinctions about it. Central to the effectiveness of this process is helping the client take his time in reading the bodily sensations. Many of us, if not most of us, can think more quickly than we can sense. We need assistance in muting the chatter of thought long enough for the wisdom for the messages given by the body to be registered and clearly understood. The focusing process is particularly useful for this and is another strategy which may be undertaken without any movement.

Active Techniques

Enhancing kinesthetic awareness and particularly strengthening grounding can always be greatly facilitated by more active techniques than those mentioned above. Nevertheless, because the exercises presented in this section are primarily aimed at enhancing grounding and sensory awareness, they are among the "softest" or least intrusive body processes to be presented. It is important to be aware that borderline individuals with a basic schizoid structure may be overwhelmed by active body techniques and may find them to be a real intrusion if they are not preceded by considerable work of a "softer" nature. Most exercises used in bioenergetics or other body therapy can be broken down into three basic categories, though there is overlap between categories. A number of exercises are used to promote the relaxation of chronic tension and increase sensory awareness. These exercises often involve some form of stretching the body together with focus on breathing and will be called *awareness-relaxation* exercises. The second group of exercises is devoted to *building an energy charge* in the body; these exercises substantially increase respiration, circulation, and movement. In simple language, these exercises "get the blood pumping." A third group of methods is devoted primarily to the *discharge* of energy or affect. The exercises presented in this section are almost exclusively in the first category of awareness-relaxation.

In initiating these exercises, it is useful to have the client wear loose-fitting, cool clothing and remove his shoes. Bioenergetic work is often done without much clothing — in underwear or a bathing suit. The lack of clothes is useful to enhance freedom of movement and to permit a greater degree of observation of the body by the therapist. These advantages are, however, far less important than the comfort of the client, and it is important to avoid the kind of personal invasion that many clients will experience if asked to take most of their clothes off. It is also important to remember that many patients may not be in touch with the invasion that this may represent, so it may be up to the therapist to protect the client in this regard. Where there are issues about personal boundaries or assertiveness on the part of the client, this therapist caretaking becomes particularly warranted.

Personally, I find it very useful to engage in most awareness-relaxation exercises with the client. I believe that that kind of joining makes the client more at ease and less prone to feeling watched as a specimen. In addition, the exercises tend to make me feel more grounded and in touch with myself and therefore more present and sensitive. What follows is a typical series of body processes which enhance grounding and sensory awareness and provide a warm-up for more charging and discharging processes. Whenever possible I have provided direction, as I would to the client directly, in quotations.

Focusing and Stance

On beginning the first trial of physical exercise of any kind, I ask the client to simply stand and direct his awareness inside and notice what sensations are present in the body—comfort and discomfort, tension and relaxation, balance and imbalance, etc. As the client does this, I observe the body for signs of its dynamics, including posture, symmetry, cohesiveness, and points of over- and underdevelopment. For further instruction on body reading, I would recommend *The Body Reveals* by Kurtz and Prestera (1976) and *The Language of the Body* by Lowen (1958). After some moments of body awareness focusing by the client, I ask him for some feedback. I notice if the client's knees are locked; if they are, I ask him to bend his knees and notice the difference. When one's knees are locked, and particularly when one's feet are fanned out, a tension in the lower back is produced and there is a loss of contact with the ground. If this is the client's characteristic, comfortable position, I ask him to go back and forth between that position and one in which his knees are bent and his feet are aimed forward at about shoulder level. This posture will feel pigeon-toed and awkward to most people initially, but it is in fact a much more grounded, solid position, easier on the lower back, and conducive to fuller, deeper breathing. When the client is in the position with knees locked and feet fanned out, I may show him how easy it is for me to push him over backward and then contrast this with how this task is more difficult when he is solidly on his feet and his knees are bent. With the client in the more stable position, I will ask him to adjust his stance so that his weight is evenly distributed heel to toe and perhaps to bounce slightly so that he can feel the ground and the solidity of his stance. In many ways, this stance mirrors that of a skier and those who ski may more easily appreciate the sensation and advantages of being solidly over their feet and firmly grounded in this way. From that solid position, I will ask the client to rock forward and then backward onto his heels. Then I will request, "Relax your belly and breathe. Put your hands on your lower back and allow the muscles there to relax as much as possible. Feel the warmth and the letting go. Now let your arms hang loose and allow your jaw to relax, opening your mouth just a little and feeling the jaw letting go. Allow your eyes to go out of focus as much as you can. Shift your weight to the left, now to the right, and then come back to center."

Forward position

Now, demonstrating as I give the instructions, I lead the client into one of the most basic bioenergetic positions. "Let your head drop down to your chest and slowly allow the upper part of your body to bend forward till your fingertips touch the floor. Bend your knees and breathe. Now begin to add a little movement. As you breathe in, bend your knees a little more. As you breathe out, straighten them a bit, but not to the point of stiffness. Let yourself have nice and easy breathing and move up and down to the rhythm of your breathing. Shift your weight slightly forward so that you are sure to *push* your body up as you breathe out. Let your feet and legs do the work. Feel your feet and legs and let your upper body just hang. Be sure to leave your fingertips on the floor so that just your lower body is moving while your upper body simply breathes and hangs out." The length of time of this process will vary depending on the tolerance and needs of the client. After it is finished, it is always useful to ask for some feedback or debriefing about it. This process enhances grounding in the literal, physical sense, as will the two that follow.

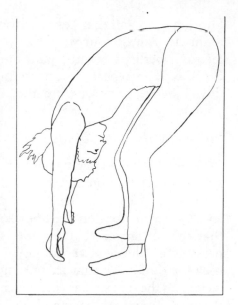

Figure 1. Forward position

Footwork with the dowel

For this exercise, a three-fourth to one and one-fourth inch dowel approximately two and one-half feet long is required. I usually place the dowel in front of the client and say, "Begin by rolling your foot over the dowel which I've placed in front of you. First one foot and then the other. Allow the muscles in the bottom of your feet to relax and notice those points which hurt. When both feet seem sufficiently relaxed, walk across the dowel, starting just below the toes and proceeding slowly back to the beginning of the heel. This will probably hurt in places and that's okay as long as you don't force it and bruise a muscle. Adjust your weight as you walk so that you can feel your feet and perhaps feel the pain but don't be too hard on yourself. Breathe. Now repeat this one to four more times. Now come off the dowel, bend your knees, breathe, and feel the increased sensation in your feet."

Loosening the joints of the toes

"Now, from the standing position, bring your left foot out, forward about half a step, and slightly to the left. Curl your toes on the floor so that the toenail of your big toe is pressing on the floor. Now slowly rock forward and backward putting weight on the toes so that you stretch the toes. Now rock back and forth slowly, breathing fully and stretching the toes. When you have had enough of this, bring your toes out flat very slowly and rock forward on them. Now repeat this with your right leg." This exercise comes from Tai Chi. It is best accomplished when the center of rocking is that Chi center of gravity located just below the belly button. What is desired here is slow, rhythmic rocking from the center in stretching the toes with full and easy breathing. (See Figure 2.)

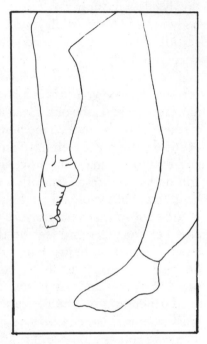

Figure 2. Loosening the toes

Stretching the ankles

"Using the same position as in the former exercise, now bring your weight on the outside ridge of your foot. As you rock forward on your left leg, feel the pressure of the floor on the side of your foot and the pull in the muscles on the outside of your left leg. Rock back and forth in the same way, breathing slowly and fully, stretching the muscles in this area. After two repetitions on both legs, come back to the regular stance and feel your feet, your toes, and your ankles. To enhance the feeling in your ankles, shift your weight on both legs as you stand there to the outside of each foot. Then rotate your knees in together so that the weight is on the inside of your foot. Now back to the outside with your knees out, and back inside again." This rotation can be accomplished rather quickly and further enhances feeling and the flow through the ankles.

Return to forward position

Throughout these and many other exercise sequences in body therapy, one cannot make a mistake by returning to the forward position too often. It enhances grounding, deepens breathing, and can be used to build a charge. In the current case, the purpose is primarily to further enhance grounding and help the client to get the full advantage of the stretching and loosening and enhanced awareness of the feet and ankles which come out of the former exercises. If there is lower back tension in the client, one may help alleviate that by a light hitting of the lower back as it is stretched in the forward position. In such hitting, I prefer to use an open hand and make contact with the side of my hand opposite the thumb. Thus, I lightly pummel the lower back with light karate chops using both hands simultaneously for a massage effect.

Lightly pummel the upper back, shoulders, and neck

To accomplish a pummeling massage of the upper back, shoulders, and neck, ask the client to come up from the forward position about half way. Stand just in front of him and with both hands lightly to firmly strike the upper back on either side of the spine, being careful to stay away from the spine and high enough so as not to inadvertently strike the kidneys. Ask the client for feedback on the desired lightness or firmness of this hitting massage. Although this may sound abusive in writing, most clients welcome this massage and contact. Go up through the shoulders and into the neck, considerably lightening the blow as you reach the neck, and continue up to the very base of the skull. The hollow area at the base of the skull on either side of the spine is often very constricted in the schizoid patient and may be very sensitive. This area is involved in the "ocular block" noted in this character structure and will be the focus of considerable other work on these patients. As the client experiences this exercise, it is often useful to ask her to make a low level "ah" sound and to let the sound reverberate as you strike the body. When this is finished, ask the client to come up to the full standing position, always remaining sensitive to the client's experience of the process.

Neck stretch and roll

Simply ask the client to perform the popular neck roll exercise which most people already know. To do this, one simply drops one's head all the way forward, slowly rotating it all the way to the right side, all the way to the back, all the way to the left, all the way forward, and so on, for two to three repetitions in one direction, followed by two or three repetitions in the other.

Summary

This sequence may be quite sufficient for initial sessions and with some patients may be all one would want to do for quite some time in therapy. This sequence may, of course, be reduced or supplemented with exercises from elsewhere, particularly when one deals with specific areas of bodily tension. It is just a basic, easy sequence, derived from several sources, which is relatively nonthreatening and which most people will experience positively. It is often important to permit people to have an initially positive experience of body work, which, in its more advanced and hard stages, can hurt.

This particular sequence is for the most part easy to self-administer. The only exception to this is the light upper back, shoulder, and neck pummeling, which can be accomplished alternatively. One alternative for the longitudinal muscles along the spine involves the client's simply leaning up against a corner where two walls meet. In this position, one can rock such that the pressure of the wall goes from the middle to upper back. A more powerful self-help alternative involves the use of a tennis ball. To accomplish this technique, you simply lie on the floor and place a tennis ball in the midback region on one side of the spine just above the kidneys. You then roll your body in a downward direction so that the tennis ball comes up. Wherever it hurts just "breathe into" the pain and allow the muscle to relax. When one side of the spine is completed, simply repeat the process on the other side. The loosening up that was accomplished by pummeling the neck may be accomplished by using the dowel. The dowel needs to be at least two and one-half to three feet long for this application. Lying on your back on the floor, simply bring the dowel behind your head and onto the neck, locking your elbows around the dowel such that it is resting on the inside of your elbows lifting your neck above the floor. Then simply roll your head slowly from one side to the other. Stop and breathe into the pain wherever it hurts. This self-help sequence, like regular yoga or meditation, can bring one back to contact with one's body, to breathing, grounding, and an enhanced kinesthetic sense of the self.

Exercises for the Ocular Segment — Opening the Eyes

The former sequence may be used simply by itself as an awareness-relaxation device or as the precursor to a number of other more active, intense techniques. Work on the ocular segment can also be mild and directed primarily to enhancing relaxation and visual awareness. Exercises which do this are described below.

Breathing and seeing

After some initial grounding and sensory awareness work with the client standing in the usual position, simply ask her to bend the knees and straighten them as in the forward position. While doing this, ask that she simply move the focus of her eyes far away in breathing out and closer in as she breathes in. Be sure that she blinks and ask her to keep scanning even as she moves her focus from distant to close objects. It is useful to remind her to feel her feet and legs on the ground as she breathes and sees.

Neck stretch

In the same position, ask the client, "Now, simply let your head fall all the way to the right side as in the neck roll. When it is stretched as far to the right as possible, tilt your chin up and out until you feel a pull at the very base of your skull on the left side. This feeling of pull is in that ocular hollow at the very base of the skull just to the left of the spinal cord. When you feel that pull, extend your head even further to the right, extending the pull down into your shoulder up through the spot at the base of your skull. Breathe and continue this until you've had enough. Then slowly roll your head over to the other side and repeat the process on that side. Remember to tilt your chin up and out a little until you feel that pull at the very base of your skull." Two repetitions on each side are usually enough for this exercise. After that, a brief return to the forward position is often useful to further relax the muscles stretched by the preceding exercise. Then, a brief period of bending and straightening the knees while standing and shifting focus near to far as outlined initially may also be useful.

The gate

"Now, pick a vertical object in the distance—a pole, a tree, a corner—and focus on it. Then bring the index finger of your right hand up in front of that vertical object. As you focus on the object in the distance, you will be aware of seeing a double image of your finger in front of you with the distant object in the middle of that 'gate' or double image. Breathe and allow yourself to see both images at once. Now, switch to focusing on your finger and see the double image of the vertical object in the distance." After a lapse of several seconds (10-20), ask the client to shift back. Continue this shifting for several repetitions. After this exercise, it is also useful to return to simple seeing and breathing. Some clients may experience some anxiety at this and other exercises which play with or alter systematically one's focus or way of seeing things. Whenever that occurs, or where there is visual fatigue, it can be useful to do a few moments of "palming," in which one cups the palms of each hand over the corresponding eye and breathes deeply, appreciating the darkness and warmth this procedure produces.

The swing

This is a gentle exercise which first involves the whole body and then incorporates a change in vision. To accomplish the exercise, simply instruct the client, "With your arms relaxed at your sides, just begin to swing your arms and body as far as you can to the right and then slowly back as far as you can to the left. See if you can enjoy this rhythmic swinging movement, breathing easily and being sure to do it slowly. As you swing to the right, lift your left heel up so that you are balancing on your left toe and thereby able to swing as far to the right as possible. It may be nice to visualize that you are massaging your own spine in this exercise. Now as you continue this swinging, allow your focus to relax so that the room goes by in a blur. Try not to hold on to anything. Allow your focus to go and just see the room blurring by first one way and then the other." This easy exercise can be engaged in for some length of time without testing the limits of most patients, though the loss of focus may sometimes be experienced as a loss of control and therefore be fear-provoking. If this is true, a period of palming and perhaps some mild reassuring contact with the therapist can often be useful.

The gate and swing

This exercise simply puts together the gate and the swing. "First, establish the gate by putting your finger out in front of you and focusing on a distant perpendicular object. Now, slowly begin to move your whole body to the left or right and maintain your focus on the distance so the gate is maintained." As with most of the other exercises in this series, this one helps the patient to let go of a fixed perspective and a holding on to things with the eyes. Eventually, this will be experienced as enlivening, but initially it may be anxiety-provoking.

The infinity swing

"Standing in the usual grounded position, see all of the room in front of you or outside to the horizon. Look to the left and right as all of this scene will be involved in the exercise you are about to do. Now, imagine that you have a weightless paintbrush coming out the end of your nose and you are going to just paint an infinity sign or a figure eight on its side over this scene in front of you. Now do that, swinging your head perhaps down and to the left, and then up to center, and down to the right, and then up and back to center, and so on. Keep doing this for some time as you allow your focus to be relaxed and aware of how you are massaging the muscles in your neck with this movement. Remember to breathe and see."

The neck press

This maneuver involves the therapist's applying considerable direct pressure to those hollow sensitive areas on either side of the back of the neck at the base of the skull. This should not be done in the very initial stages of therapy, but should wait until there is a good therapeutic relationship established when the therapist can be reasonably sure this will not be experienced as intrusive. The object is to produce relaxation and increase the flow of energy through these blocked areas at the base of the skull. This can be done by putting one hand on the patient's forehead and the other on the back of the neck and pressing the thumb and index finger hard into those areas. The amount of pressure can be increased substantially in an alternate position which imitates the "full nelson" in wrestling. Get behind the client and ask him to raise his arms and allow you to put your hands underneath his arms and up to his neck. Put your thumbs in the hollow areas on either side of the neck. By pulling his arms forward the client may put considerable pressure on this area.

This pressure point maneuver can have rather profound effects, letting in more light and releasing more energy through this whole ocular segment. Here again, the client may experience the anxiety associated with loss of control of fixed focus in the release of the ocular block. In this case particularly, the palming technique is particularly useful, with full and easy breathing. When sufficient client stability has been achieved, this exercise may occasion the accessing of terror and may elicit repressed visual memories which evoke fear.

EVOKING THE ENERGETIC DEFENSES

The kind of body work outlined above can lead the therapy right back to the process of evoking, acknowledging, and eventually melting the defensive structure. The demand for greater movement and life in the body elicits feeling and that feeling triggers the defenses against it. As one begins to breathe, for example, one begins to feel more, and it is not at all uncommon for schizoid individuals, as they tune into their bodies, to feel pain, fear, or anger. As a client said to me once, "I see why I think so much. If I feel my body all I feel is pain."

Not infrequently, the client will feel that she wants to breathe but her body will not cooperate. Or, as a person begins to relax in the lower body, and to breathe more fully, he will experience increased tension in his upper back, shoulders and neck. At these times, it is often useful to ask the person to exaggerate the tension and be aware of what that tension does for him—how it defends or serves him. Then, the client can begin to identify with the resistance or defense. He may say, for example, "I don't want to feel fear. I don't want to feel this sadness. Holding back the feeling allows me to do my work and get on with my life."

Giving the resistance a voice in this way and acknowledging its value has a number of beneficial effects. It renders the defense conscious, thereby encouraging its use voluntarily when necessary, relaxing its hold on the person at other times. When that part of a person knows that it is acknowledged for its positive intent and appreciated for what it has done to serve, it is more likely to let go of control and be more amenable to discrimination concerning when its functions are less necessary. When unconscious, the defense tends to be operative much if not all of the time and the person typically has little or no awareness of it or what it is responding to. As it becomes conscious and its intent clarified, it can begin to "listen to reason." It can begin to discriminate that the environment is not always threatening and that negative feelings are not always bad.

The defensive parts of any of us are very much like frightened little children. They need lots of love, attention, and reassurance. They need to tell what they are afraid of and have those fears dealt with in an adult way. They can, over time, be relaxed by this kind of attention and reassurance, as well as by an intelligent explanation of their origins. In short, there is nothing more likely to relax the defenses than their acknowledgment and support.

By the same token, it is often necessary to bring to full conscious light the price that is usually paid for the rigidity of the defense. This is particularly true when it results in egocentric behavior or thinking. The early stages of therapy described here will typically enhance the awareness of and conflict between the real and false self. Thus, the schizoid person may begin to realize that he is holding himself together and damaging his body in order to live up to his illusion of being special or accepting. At these times, it is often useful to make this painfully explicit. That can be accomplished, for example, by having him look at the therapist or the image of a significant other and simply state the compromise decision that negates the real self in service of the illusion. In the schizoid case, these compromise decisions are often stated as follows: "I'd rather not feel anything than feel this pain. I'd rather be special than feel good. I'd rather hurt me than you."

Though it may seem cruel, bringing these decisions into consciousness and eroding the denial of their reality may be one of the best things you can do for another human being, if it is not done before he can handle the reality. In my experience, it is often useful to make this realization as dramatic as possible and then leave it—either change the subject or finish the session. This prevents the therapist and the client from wrapping up the problem in a pretty package before it is really resolved. It promotes the very real working-through of a very real and serious dilemma. Ultimately, however, it will be very useful to assist the client in seeing how this decision, too, was reasonable, justified, and sensible under the original circumstances and to appreciate how it allowed him to move on with his life and survive. As in the case of physical defenses, this increased understanding and conscious acknowledgment will allow the eventual relaxation and change to occur.

Also, it is useful to help the client understand that even though his assets were developed in a defensive, compensatory way, they are still developed and will not fail him if he begins to indulge the body and the real self. This simplistic, either-or way of perceiving the world is infantile and can be changed with the generous administration of self-love. The actor who denied all in order to become a star will still know how to act when he begins to breathe and feel himself, though his fear that he will not want to act anymore because the original motivation will be eroded is not entirely ill-founded. He can be reassured, however, that usually the loss of motivation to exercise one's skills is more or less transitory and that one can be taught to enjoy the expression of one's abilities for other, healthier reasons.

Reframing

Bandler and Grinder (1979, 1982), in their application of neurolinguistic programming to the clinical situation, have institutionalized some of these basic insights into a general set for therapeutic work, as well as in a specific process called reframing. The reframing process outlined here can be very useful in helping a client orient to appreciating the function of his resistance or symptoms, as well as in coming up with new ways of accomplishing that function. The reframing process per se is predicated on the useful fiction of separating one's ego states or ways of being into "parts," as has been done in much of Gestalt therapy and transactional analysis. The process itself involves

communication with and between these parts, with a focus on understanding the underlying *intention* or purpose of the troublesome "part"
and then finding new, less troublesome behaviors or attitudes which
accomplish that intention. A brief overview of the reframing process
is given below, followed by detailed instruction for its use.

The reframing exercise may be aimed at any problematic behavior,
attitude, or feeling. After identifying the target of the process, it is often
useful to produce in the client a state anywhere from mild relaxation
to deep hypnotic trance before proceeding with the following steps.
In this altered state of consciousness, the client is asked to establish
communication with the part of him that generates the problematic
pattern. Having established communication, he is then asked to discover the positive intentions of that part. Following this, he is asked
to contact that part of him which is creative and ingenious. Using all
the resources of his creative part, he is asked to generate new ways of
accomplishing the intentions just discovered. Next, the part in charge
of generating the problematic pattern is asked to examine, correct, or
assist the creative part in perfecting those new solutions until they are
acceptable all around. When all new solutions are acceptable, the part
in charge of generating the former problematic pattern is asked to take
responsibility for generating these new solutions in the appropriate contexts. Finally, the client is asked to check and see whether there are
any remaining considerations which would prevent him from adopting the new solutions.

The process does not, of course, always go as smoothly as outlined,
nor does it always produce immediate or profound change. Yet, I have
found the outline of this reframing exercise to be extraordinarily valuable in changing my own and my clients' orientation to the problems
brought up in psychotherapy, particularly the problems of resistance.
All resistance is essentially self-protective and much can be achieved
when this is fully appreciated by both client and therapist. Once this
is known, many measures can be taken to accommodate resistance's
self-protective intent. Following is an outline and suggested text for
Bandler and Grindler's reframing process. The process itself can vary
considerably and often certain steps may be deleted or expanded for
a given case. The outline is deceptively simple in that the exercise does
not always go as smoothly as presented and much additional work will
often be needed just to complete one step. Yet, this process, like many

coming from Bandler and Grinder, represents a masterful integration of a number of therapeutic principles and offers a useful guideline for an entire course of therapy, particularly around resistance issues.

Reframing outline

1) Identify the pattern or problematic situation to be addressed.
2) Establish an altered state.
> Through relaxation or hypnotic induction, establish an altered state of consciousness in which the person is more inwardly focused and more capable of suspending disbelief than in his usual conscious state.
3) Establish communication with the part that generates the problematic pattern or problematic situation.
> "Now as you are focused deeply inside and aware of yourself, I would like you to remember a time when this problematic pattern occurred. I'd like you to be highly aware of the situation and more and more in contact with that part of you which generated it. As you do this, I want to prepare you for the question that I will soon ask you. When I ask this question, I want you to become exquisitely aware of any changes that occur inside you. It may be a feeling or an image, or you may hear a word or sound. Just be exquisitely aware of the change. The question is, 'Will the part of you that creates this situation communicate with us in consciousness?'" Wait and ask the client to signal nonverbally when some change or changes have occurred. When you see the signal, continue, "Good. If those changes represented a yes, a willingness to communicate, I would like that part to intensify the changes to further signal that yes. If it is a no, I'd like it to diminish the intensity of the changes to signal no." Assuming the answer was yes and the signal intensifies, continue, "Good, now diminish the signal so that you know what a 'no' will look and feel and sound like. Now, I have another question for this part of you. It is this: 'Are you aware of your positive, beneficial intention in creating this situation?'" Assuming a yes, move on to the next step.

4) Elicit the intention of the pattern or situation, "Will the part of you that creates this situation be willing to communicate it to us?" Assuming a yes, "Do that now."

5) Generate new solutions to satisfy the intention.

"There is a part of you which is creative and ingenious. It is the part which you have used on other occasions when a problem needed a novel solution. When the old ways did not fit, or when you came up against a new situation which required a different approach, the part emerged. Perhaps in your personal life or your work or in fixing something. Let this part emerge now—allow it to begin to generate new solutions to satisfy the intention we have just uncovered. Allow it to present at least three new alternatives and signal me when this is done. You may not be aware of all the solutions that you create now and those discoveries may continue for some time to come." When the new solutions have been generated and shared, move to the next step.

6) Integrate the new solutions.

"Now I want to ask that part of you which creates the pattern or situation to pay attention and answer another question. 'Will you accept the new solutions and accept the responsibility for generating them when your intentions need to be fulfilled?' " This step will provide very useful opportunities for editing out and adding new solutions if there are objections to the solutions already generated. There can be a dialogue created here between the part which creates the pattern and the creative part which suggests the solutions. When this is accomplished the client is ready for the final step.

7) Check for ecological balance.

"Now go deeply inside yourself and see if there is any other part of you which is holding back or concerned about the solutions and agreements that have been made here." This, too, is a very useful step for editing and additional solutions. The basic idea here is that whatever solutions are generated should not violate any other part of the person

or any of his other intentions. Once this editing is performed, the process is complete.

An exercise of this kind can take from a half hour to many sessions
of intensive work. Indeed, as indicated before, this overall outline can
encompass a good deal of the therapeutic process itself. In cases in
which the person is unaware of the intention or the part responsible
is unwilling to communicate or share that intention, the whole process can be done at a level outside conscious awareness. This is not
at all difficult for therapists who are comfortable with hypnotic procedures, though it probably will be uncomfortable for anyone who is
not. Those therapists uncomfortable with the useful fiction of parts
communicating through internal sensory experience may not wish to
use this process at all. But they will be assisted, I think, in acknowledging and following the basic underlying intention of this process—
appreciation and respect for the intended function of any persistent
pattern and assistance in generating more evolved methods for fulfilling that purpose.

For additional assistance in working with processes that require communication with "parts," feeling senses, or the unconscious, the reader
is referred to Eugene Gendlin's (1978) focusing process, reviewed in
chapter IV, pages 153–158.

In addition to these and other processes aimed at the defenses and
resistance, simple discussion of the advantages of the defenses, such
as social withdrawal and the denial of unpleasant feelings, will often
prove useful. Giving permission for withdrawal and encouraging the
client to withdraw deliberately and enjoy it will assist her in utilizing
and appreciating this sometimes adaptive strategy. Similarly, the process of making someone aware of how she suppresses anxiety in a performance situation and then instructing her to do that deliberately
allows conscious use of an automatic and perhaps overused defense.
It assists the client in discriminating the settings in which this or some
similar defense may be useful from those in which it is neither necessary
nor useful. If this is coupled with a sensitive and compassionate discussion regarding how these defenses were necessary in the client's childhood, these defensive maneuvers can be integrated and provide the basis
for a healthy appreciation of self.

Typically the schizoid person is an expert at self-hatred and, as he becomes aware of his defenses, he may add them to his storehouse of ammunition for attacks on himself. "Reframing" the defensive structures, incorporating them into a broader range of defensive maneuvers, and appreciating the circumstances of their origin can do a great deal to eliminate this largely iatrogenic complication of psychotherapy for the schizoid patient. I often use the phrase "You came by this honestly" to help the client see the legitimacy of his attitudes, behaviors, or feelings as they emerge in the therapeutic process. Whatever can be done to cut short the tendency for negative self-judgment about the defenses and resistance will facilitate therapy.

TEACHING NEW DEFENSES

One constructive way of looking at the schizoid problem is to see the hated child as one who has a great deal to defend against but with only limited and primitive defenses. The feelings in the schizoid's body are overwhelming and the demands of the environment are much more than can be handled given the arrested functioning in the early symbiotic period of development. Before this person will ever be able to relax and confront the terrible feelings within him, he must feel safe not only with the therapist, but also with himself. That is, he must feel that he can put himself back together if he allows himself to come apart and that he can stop the release of feeling short of disintegration or destruction. The simple defenses of denial and projection are generally not sufficient to provide that kind of safety and it is therefore useful to teach him other ways of defending against the internal emotions and coping with the external environment before more internal, affective objectives can be realized.

In general, many of those practicing cognitive-behavioral treatment programs, such as rational emotive therapy, neurolinguistic programming, and behavior modification often seem to do little more than this, and in that I feel their work is seriously incomplete. At minimum, however, these techniques represent some powerful strategies for ego building which those in the analytic school talk a great deal about, but which they offer little of in writing or direct instruction. It seems to me that this is one of the most fruitful bridges between these two schools of thought. I believe that behavioral-cognitive therapeutic approaches can do far more than provide people with better defenses than the ones they already have. Yet, this is one valuable contribution which they do make. Without this valuable step, a purely affectively oriented treatment, which aims only at releasing the underlying feelings in the schizoid structure, may well lead not to mental health but to the mental hospital. The possibilities for creative therapeutic intervention in this area are numerous if one is fluent in the cognitive-behavioral therapies. All that is required is some specificity regarding the cognitive or behavioral component of the problem and then the application of selected procedures to the difficulty.

One problem area which is almost always of concern in schizoid patients is anxiety, particularly in performance and social situations. I have found two therapeutic strategies from neurolinguistic programming to be particularly valuable with this issue.

Resource Accessing

The initial strategy of the process labeled *resource accessing* is to help the client discover those personal resources which he will require in the situation which brings him difficulty. Then, one simply assists him in remembering times when these particular resources were present. In the course of this remembering, the therapist assists the client in collapsing all of these useful memories or ego states into one representation. Finally, the client is asked to imagine future situations in which these resources will be necessary and, in imagination, to bring them forth in those situations. It is usually useful for the individual to have a triggering stimulus or "anchor" (a word, scene, or even a special self-touch or movement) to facilitate the eliciting of the latent ego state. When this "anchor" or discriminative stimulus is a physical one, the individual may, for example, touch his left wrist or alter his posture to elicit the state. I have found this remarkably simple process to be most effective, though not uniformly so, for a wide variety of situational problems, particularly those involving social relationships or performance anxiety. A brief example from my own practice may help in understanding the specific ingredients of this process.

Matt was a 34-year-old trial attorney who would frequently experience debilitating anxiety, sleeplessness, and unnecessary compulsive work surrounding his appearance in a trial. The more important the trial, the more disturbing the symptoms, to the extent that the issue of his performance in the trial often took on the quality of a life and death matter. The dynamic significance of all this was becoming clearer in analysis, but I felt it would be useful for many reasons to provide him with a tool for dealing with his anxiety, thereby making his day-to-day life more comfortable and reassuring him that the anxiety could be handled.

In every case of schizoid personality there is, or will be in the course of treatment, the emergence of underlying terror. The client is more likely to allow that to emerge and be worked through if he knows that it will not severely disrupt his normal day-to-day life. Processes such as the present one can have that effect and thereby hasten and smooth out the course of affective release therapy.

In discussing the necessary resources in this situation, Matt and I decided that two powerful ego states would be sufficient. The first was "confidence in my abilities," and the second was "acceptance of whatever happens." I asked Matt if he could remember a time when he was confident in his abilities. He remembered an incident of trial work in which he was particularly brilliant and effective and during which he felt solid, grounded, and alert. The representation of this incident was enhanced by the fact that he remembered wearing a particularly pleasing dark blue suit during that trial. The suit was important because he was particularly comfortable in it and liked the feel of the texture of the garment. In addition, he had a very solid, positive memory of how well he looked in that particular suit. Finally, he could remember what he sounded like on that particular occasion, including his voice tone and pace of his speech. Thus, he had a solid visual, kinesthetic, and auditory remembrance of this particular *confident* incident. In response to inquiry about a former experience in which he felt acceptance, he came up with a time during which he was waiting for a jury to return a verdict. The case was important and the outcome uncertain, but his pretrial and trial work had been to his satisfaction and he was able, after trying the case, to simply release its outcome to the jury and to fate. He remembered this experience as an almost transcendent one and could recall particularly the kinesthetic feelings of relaxation which went along with it.

After the recovery of those memories, I asked Matt to relax and took a few moments to reinstate relaxation and internal focus, a state which had been repeatedly established in earlier work. I then asked him to remember the *confidence* scene as vividly as possible, requesting remembrance in all sensory channels. As he remembered this, I asked him to put his left hand on his left knee and kept repeating the word "confidence." I then called up the acceptance memory in all sensory channels. As this memory was relived in the altered state condition, I repeated the word "acceptance" and again instructed him to place his left hand on his left knee. The neurolinguistic programmers refer to this classical conditioning process as "anchoring." It appears to me that the more powerful and numerous the anchors are, the more powerful the results can be in the real world. In the final step of the process, I simply instructed Matt to visualize himself in future circumstances where these resources would be necessary, to use the anchors that had been established, and to go through and meet the challenges in question.

The process worked particularly well in this case and two years later Matt was still using it on occasion to enhance his effectiveness in the courtroom. By that time, most of the debilitating anxiety symptoms had been relieved as a function of the emotional work done in the context of bioenergetic, Gestalt, and interpretive psychotherapy. I believe the resource accessing had a very instrumental role in this and that it continued to be used as an enhancer of effectiveness even when it was unnecessary as a stopgap for debilitating anxiety.

Occasionally, one or more of the desired resources will not be present in the client's history or she will be unable to remember an incident involving them. In such cases, the therapist may suggest that the client literally borrow a resource from another who has it. The client may know someone who had the desired resource or she may have seen a portrayal of the resource in a public figure, movie actor, etc. In that case, she is simply asked to recall that instance and, in the altered state part of the process (step 5 below), "step inside" the other and exercise the resource just as the other person did originally. This action is then anchored just as it is when the resource comes from the client's own personal history.

Here, in outline form, is the sequence for resource accessing:

1) Choose the problem to be addressed.
2) Assess the personal resources needed to deal with the problem.

3) a) Elicit recall of times when the desired resources were present in the person, or b) elicit memories of others exhibiting the
desired resources.

4) Establish a relaxed or altered state.

5) a) Repeat the recollection of the exercise of each resource in
all sensory channels and anchor each resource, or b) repeat the
recollection of another exercising the desired resource and then
request the client to "step inside" the other and exercise the
resource himself. Anchor each resource.

6) Ask the client to imagine himself in the relevant situation(s),
use the established anchor, and employ the relevant resources.
This step is called "future pacing" in NLP.

Visual-Kinesthetic Dissociation

The second procedure, which has wide application to circumstances
of anxiety, particularly phobic response to certain stimuli, involves the
direct teaching of dissociation. In neurolinguistic programming the process is called visual-kinesthetic dissociation (V-K dissociation). It is a
process developed initially for phobias and involves the dissociation
of the visual memory of an early traumatic event which presumably
created the phobia from the feelings involved during the trauma. The
result is that the memory of the earlier event or events can be elicited
without the traumatic feelings which have accompanied them.

The most dramatic use of this process in my own work was with
Bill, a Vietnam veteran with post-traumatic stress disorder. He had
a number of horrifying memories which could be triggered in many
situations, including any discussion or allusion to the war, instances
of hypocrisy or unfairness, or any event which was disappointing or
involved personal loss. In any of these circumstances, he would have
one or more flashbacks to the horrifying events in Vietnam and break
down in uncontrollable crying or rage. It was essential to gain some
control over this pattern before anything else could be done.

The first step in the dissociation process is to establish in the client
an ego state of comfort, security, and safety. Before this could be done
in any instrumental way in this case, several sessions were devoted to
establishing a trusting therapeutic relationship, which included an open
and frank discussion of his suspicions of me, disappointments with pre-

vious counselors and other establishment figures, and some minor disappointments that he encountered with me in these early sessions. Throughout this process, it was more important for me to "be there" genuinely than for me to do anything specific.

It was only after this process had established some camaraderie between us that the process of dissociation could even be initiated. To further establish the comfort ego state, I performed an induction which achieved deep muscle relaxation and then asked Bill to remember a time when he felt particularly safe. I anchored this state with the word "safe," while suggesting that in that state of mind he place one hand over his heart and feel the reassuring warmth that produced.

I then asked Bill to visualize a photograph of himself in Vietnam just before the first horrifying event occurred. I had him project this image or "photograph" onto a "screen" in front of him. When that scene was established, I asked him to actively dissociate. That is, I asked him to imagine himself floating out of his body, viewing himself sitting in my office. To achieve this, I said, "Imagine that you are watching a TV program with your twin brother and you look over at him and see him watching TV. You are not him. You are watching him watch." I anchored this dissociation with the words "outside yourself." I then instructed Bill, "Stay outside yourself in viewing the scenes that are now to come."

Being assured that the state of safety and the perspective of "outside" were maintained, I asked Bill to *watch himself watch* his younger self going through the horrifying event in Vietnam as in a movie from the very beginning to the very end of the incident. I tried to maintain the safety state and the dissociation by repeating the words "safe" and "stay outside."

On the first trial of this process, Bill collapsed into the former scene as he had always done before and broke into terror and sobbing. While this is exactly what I do want in a number of bioenergetic, affective psychotherapy sessions, it is exactly what I did not want in this session. Unable to regain the ego state of safety and the dissociative perspective, I stopped the process and then was able to bring Bill down and regain the safety ego state.

It took an additional session to completely regain the feelings of trust and safety that had been established prior to the initiation of this process, and in the following session Bill asked me, in a very firm and adult-like manner, to try the process with him again, as he felt that it could be of real assistance. We did this and this time he was able to maintain the ego state of safety and the dissociated perspective through three horrifying events in his Vietnam experience. At the end of each recall, I terminated the dissociative stance and asked Bill to come back into his own body. I then instructed him to imagine his present-day self going to his younger self in Vietnam and giving reassurance, comfort, and appreciation to that boy who had to deal with the horrors of war. I said to him, "Reassure that young man that you are from the future. Tell him that he survived and give him the kind of reassurance that only you know he needed then. Do whatever you need to do to assist him. Be sure to tell him that he did the best he could with his knowledge and the circumstances present at that time. Stay with your present self but continue to be with him until you see that he is comforted and reassured." When all three earlier traumatic situations had been dealt with in this way, I instructed that he reintegrate the younger self into his current self, come back to the room, and reorient to the here and now.

The dissociation process is not always effective in my experience, and often other things must be done to deal effectively with these kinds of problems. In this particular case, however, the process was extraordinarily effective and in the weeks and months to come there were very few repetitions of the earlier common pattern of emotional breakdown. Where this pattern did occur it was considerably milder than it had been before and Bill attributed this to the dissociation process. His ability to deal with the world more effectively affected problems of drug use and permitted him to begin vocational training, which he had postponed because of his serious emotional state.

While this has been my most dramatic use of this particular process, I use it frequently in other contexts. Where individuals have difficulty with performance anxiety or in situations where they have difficulty with interpersonal conflict, it can be most helpful. One can rehearse the actual dissociation so that one can see oneself in the problematic situation and observe oneself as if observing another. Taking on this position as observer and, in effect, dissociating from the debilitating feelings brought up by the situation can have the effect of allowing one to perform more effectively in the situation.

In outline form, here is the V-K dissociation process:

1) Establish and anchor an ego state involving comfort, security and safety.
2) Have the client visualize an image of his younger self just prior to the traumatic event.
3) Establish the dissociation such that the person is able to watch himself watch his younger self.
4) With dissociation and comfort solidly established, have the client *watch himself watch himself* during the earlier traumatic event.
5) Discontinue the dissociation when the recall of the earlier event is completed and request that the client's present-day self return to the traumatic event involving the younger self and reassure that person as outlined above.
6) Integrate the younger self with the present-day self.

Where dissociation is used for social or performance anxiety, the therapist may have the client rehearse in imagination the dissociation in the relevant situation. An anchor may then be established for the dissociated state so that the person may elicit that state when it would be useful.

Self-Soothing

The hated child also usually needs to be taught self-soothing or self-nurturing, but because this is an even more central requirement for the oral character, the presentation of these techniques is presented in the treatment of that structure. For an outline of self-soothing treatment, the reader is referred to chapter VI, pages 202–206.

SUMMARY

The objectives and techniques outlined in this chapter have wide application for both the well-defended schizoid character and the more borderline or less well-defended individual. At this point, however, there exists a crossroads at which the well-defended schizoid character goes in one direction whereas the borderline character must stay behind, strengthening the gains outlined in this chapter and further developing ego abilities. Because the borderline issues and ego-building techniques will be essentially the same in both the schizoid and oral characters, I have devoted a chapter to ego-building techniques at the end of this volume. When the ego abilities are sufficient either initially or through treatment, we can then move on to those objectives which require more insight and more affective release. These techniques, which presuppose a relatively high level of ego development and an effective defensive structure, are presented in the following chapter.

HEALING THE
HATED CHILD:
PART II

MOST OF THE CONTENT of chapter III, as well as that of chapter VIII on ego-building techniques, provides the groundwork for the more dramatic components of the transformation of the schizoid character. While the work described is invaluable, it is not what will ultimately be valued most on the other side of the transformation. The early work is essential to transformation but does not represent the transformation itself. That will be achieved as the person begins to get into himself and progresses through the experience and expression of the deep feelings within toward an integration of the real self within his real world. To do this, the person must come into concrete conscious contact with the terror and rage which have, usually for decades, been repressed. He must take responsibility for what is within and ultimately stop projecting his own distress outward. While the elicitation and understanding of the core affects are necessary, that alone cannot really heal until the schizoid takes responsibility for being the host of these feelings. A good solid step in the direction of responsibility is taken when the individual is ready to appreciate how he plays the games of the schizoid: denying feeling, projecting feeling, and foisting responsibility onto others.

CASE STUDY

David was a 35-year-old man who presented with symptoms of chronic depression and repeated relationship failures resulting in extreme loneliness and exacerbated depressive symptoms. After a number of the initial psychotherapeutic steps had been completed, he began to explore the pattern of his relationship failures. David characterized himself as particularly good at initiating relationships and participating in and enjoying them during their early stages. He was a good-looking, bright, professional man who could, in his own words, "present a good front as the open, feeling, and liberated male." But, as a relationship developed, as he began to spend most evenings with his lover or they moved in together, he would begin to lose interest. There would be a gradual diminution in his excitement about the relationship and he would stop his special and romantic efforts to communicate his loving attention. His sexual interest would wane and this would often be associated with his discovering things about his partner that he did not appreciate. This "blemishing" could involve his dissatisfaction with his woman friend's body, sexual performance, intellectual abilities, or almost any aspect of her appearance or behavior. David would then begin to find ways to avoid sleeping with his girl friend such as finding work he needed to do, staying up late or developing some minor physical symptom which would be used as an excuse. The excitement associated with the relationship would wane, though typically there would be little argument or overt difficulty between the partners. After several attempts to understand and remedy this problem the couple would split. Sometimes this would be initiated by the woman and sometimes it would be initiated by David himself. Whoever initiated the separation, David would respond to it with a great deal of pain. Though he was largely unable to cry or become angry during these periods, he was seriously depressed, inactive, and unable to work.

Fortunately, the relationship process outlined here occurred during a phase of his therapy and it was possible for him to begin to come to an understanding of the pattern. Because it was fresh, the current relationship difficulties were the easiest to see firsthand, while the distance he could take in viewing his prior relationships was also useful.

In every case, David became disillusioned and angry during the course of the relationship. In certain relationships these difficulties seemed to be more projected than real, while in others there appeared to be more legitimate sources of dissatisfaction. In either case, however, David was unable to appreciate the extent of his anger or disappointment or to express it directly. His withdrawal from the woman was always an automatic and unconscious process, yet it was his most aggressive weapon against the woman at whom he was unconsciously furious. He was afraid and unable to get angry, but was powerfully vengeful in withdrawal. When the woman would become angry at the withdrawal, he was very adept at explaining away his behavior and seeing the woman as overreacting, "hostile," or "crazy" in her emotional response. Particularly in two cases, in which the woman had tired of this pattern and left him before he was willing to let go, David felt particularly victimized and wronged.

A number of techniques, including simple discussion and direct analysis of each relationship, were used to uncover this pattern. Central among the useful procedures in this case was a process which is called the *responsibility exercise*. Using this process, I asked David to reexperience fully one of those times when he was left by a woman. I asked him to remember all the feelings of loss and victimization and to tell me of the ways in which he felt betrayed and injured. Wherever I could, I assisted him in accessing that time and particularly in experiencing the feelings of victimization. When the story and its accompanying feelings had been played out about as far as I thought possible, I asked David to stop and prepare himself to shift gears in his perspective on this story. I asked that he suspend judgment for a while and assume that he was the architect rather than the victim of this historical chain of events. I suggested that he assume for the sake of further insight that he set out to create the situation, that he wanted the scenario to go exactly as it did, and that there were many advantages for him in its eventual outcome.

In helping David orient to the story in this new way, I offered some tools to assist him in achieving this perceptual shift. First, I asked him to remember back and see if he could come up with any *inklings* that the woman in question would ultimately leave him. At this question, he perked up and remembered a number of times when she had left him in small ways. He recalled his sudden feeling at these times that he did not really know her, could not communicate with her about deep concerns, and could not count on her as an emotional partner. I then explicitly asked that he remember his *denial of the inkling*—a decision to ignore the discomfort or haunting feeling that the inkling had brought. He then recovered his unwillingness to look at the possibility of their incompatibility and the fear he felt associated with going through another wrenching separation. Finally, I asked him to determine any payoffs or rewards that he got for having the relationship end and for having it end as it did.

With the enhanced perspective afforded by hindsight and the healing effect given by time, David was able to appreciate how dissatisfied
he had been in that particular relationship. The woman had been even
more reluctant than he to openly acknowledge conflict or engage in
discussion about it. She had, he said, been unreal and he had been unable to gain any sustained rapport with her. But characteristically,
rather than confront her about that issue or give up on the relationship and deal with the loss, he had merely withdrawn and punished
her for her inability to communicate. In many ways, he had lost faith
in that relationship but did not have the courage to do anything about
it other than withdrawing and leaving the active steps to her. In completing the process, I asked David to consider the following questions
in the accompanying table. "How did the situation allow you to:

be right	make others wrong
self-justify	invalidate others
dominate	avoid domination
win	make others lose?"

Finally, I asked David, "What did this outcome allow you to do,
say, or feel that you could not otherwise have done, said, or felt?" All
these question are used to elicit the payoffs in the situation and in its
outcome.

In this particular case, David could see that he had ended a relationship which did not work for him, and that he had essentially expressed his anger and disappointment by "freezing her out." She was
forced into the position of "being the bad one" in their social circle and
was perceived by all as the one deserting their love. He was, at that
point, able to feel wronged and to move on to a new relationship with
a clear conscience, his ego-ideal intact.

Through this process and others, David became acutely aware of
the power and cruelty of his withdrawal. In his current relationship,
he was able to begin to touch the real depth and intensity of the rage
which came at the disappointment, and he began to touch, too, the
fear set off by closeness and the possibility that he would be dominated
by a woman. David began to appreciate the power of his pattern of
withdrawal and to begin to experience the real depth of the feelings
which lurked beneath it. In his further analysis, it became clear that
the origins of this pattern existed in a family wherein he had been re-

jected and controlled. No one, however, could control the feelings he experienced for his parents, particularly his mother. He withdrew his love from her and in subtle ways allowed her to know it. This was his most powerful weapon and one which he retained with all its vengeance in his other relationships with women. It was the one way in which he could win in his family and in a perverse sense he could continue to win with it, though, of course, in depriving his lovers he deprived himself. Getting onto himself in this way paved the way for the emergence of the vengeful feeling and its eventual complete conscious experience and expression.

Whenever dealing with a schizoid issue, one is dealing with vengeance and a demonic force in which the vengeance is disguised beneath softness, acceptance, and rationality. The subtlety and meanness in the schizoid games can be brought to consciousness as the individual is urged not only to be aware of that meanness, but also to begin to identify with and even enjoy it. Most people will balk at this initially, but if we can get them past that disapproving hesitance, we can move them a long, long way. The devil operates best in darkness underground in the invisible heat of deception. Out in the open, in the sunlight, he dissolves. Accordingly, David was helped to acknowledge and enjoy the power in his demon during this process, as well as in others which will be outlined here. Being aware of and taking responsibility for one's demonic games are only the first steps in claiming, aiming, and taming these forces. The schizoid is a wolf in sheep's clothing. The wolf bites him and other people while denying he is doing so. A relationship with him is always frustrating in that it is always dishonest. When the wolf is owned and the costume put aside, there is hope.

The games that schizoids play may be detected in many other ways. Games tend to be repetitive and typically there appears to be an obvious winner and an obvious loser. The decisions or conclusions which one makes at the conclusion of the game are typically some version of the script decisions which run life below the surface. There are usually numerous payoffs at various levels for the eventual outcome of the game. As outlined by Berne (1964) in *Games People Play*, the advantages can be both internal and external and involve variables of a psychological, social, or even biological nature. In David's repetitive game outlined above, his withdrawal 1) permitted the expression of aggression while denying it, 2) provided the avoidance of real closeness which provoked his fear of intimacy, 3) made legitimate the conclusion that a close relationship with a woman was not possible for him, and 4) allowed him, when left by the woman, to redecide that women could not be trusted and to receive the external social support for this decision from his friends and family. Additionally, the pattern served to maintain his own ego ideal as a soft, nonaggressive person while preserving the ideal of the all-loving mother who might someday be found.

The repeated relationship failures also gave David opportunities for truly healing abreactive experiences in which he could have opened to the original, deep feelings associated with the traumatic failure of the relationship with his own mother. Without a good deal of guidance and support, however, most of us are unable to do that and merely use each repetition of the game pattern to reinforce the initial script decisions. In David's case, psychotherapy opened the door to this and thus to the transformation.

ANALYSIS OF GAMES

In my own work, I suspect the presence of the demon and a game when I notice a smile or subtle sign of demonic delight in the report of a circumstance which is otherwise unhappy. In the analysis of games, I look primarily for repetition, script decisions, and evidence of demonic delight. Whenever I deal with a problem which has been fairly persistent in spite of treatment, I am relatively sure that the demonic forces are at work and that the way out for both myself and my client is to assist him in identifying the demonic glee associated with the unfolding of the repetitious pattern.

Games typical of the schizoid character are, in Berne's entertaining language, "See What You Made Me Do," "If It Weren't for You," and "Wooden Leg." Each of these games emphasizes the denial of responsibility and projection of that responsibility onto others or external circumstances. The games of "Blemish," "Why Don't You . . . Yes, But," and "Let's You and Him Fight" are also games to which this character structure may be attracted. In each case, there is the opportunity to express aggression while at the same time denying it or making it appear harmless.

The foregoing discussion of responsibility and games is an example of the kind of synthesis of various schools or practices which I aim for in my practice and in this book. The responsibility exercise, per se, was a part of the consciousness training, "Awareness Responsibility, Communication" (ARC), designed by John Enright. The table for recognizing payoffs of a game was derived from Werner Erhardt's *est* training, and the inquiry of what the game allows one to do, say, or feel is derived from Eric Berne's game analysis. The concept of the demon as the designer of games comes from the writing of Alexander Lowen in *Betrayal of the Body* (1967), and the prescription for what to do with the demon—bringing him out of the darkness and exposing him to the sunlight through appreciation and enjoyment—comes to me most directly from my teacher Edward Muller.

The analysis of games as a way into the conscious experience and beginning expression of the underlying emotions is bolstered if one understands that games are typically learned in the family by the developing child in a more or less conscious way (see Berne, 1964, pp. 58–60). The origins of the learning are lost through time, and the awareness of the game must be suppressed in order for one to keep playing it without feeling entirely foolish or evil. The awareness, however, can be regained; the nasty enjoyment of winning can be experienced and better strategies can then be initiated.

There is another process which I frequently use with those who have learned so well to withdraw and hide out as a retaliatory method. This technique comes from psychodrama. I say to the client, "There is a little exercise I'd like to do with you which I hope will help you discover some important things. I want you to stand up and get behind me. I am going to look for you in the room very thoroughly and very slowly, and I want you to remain exactly behind me so that I cannot find you. Are you willing to do it? See if you can enjoy the game."

I then proceed through the room very slowly and meticulously and, if so inspired, may say things like, "I wonder where Janet is? I know I saw her a moment ago." I know that this has succeeded to some degree when the client experiences the demonic glee in being so well hidden though so close. It also succeeds somewhat when the client experiences the poignancy and tragedy of that position in life and realizes how she is stuck there withholding from herself what she withholds from others.

Provided that the game will not be terribly disruptive to others, I will also sometimes instruct the client to deliberately play it out in day-to-day life. In couples work, I am often able to outline both sides of

a repetitive game for clients and then prescribe to both of them the initiation and each subsequent step of the game. When the game is finished, I instruct one or the other to say, "Are we doing this because
we really mean it or because Steve told us to do it?" I call this game
"Who's Conscious?" and the winner of the game is whoever is conscious
—whoever engages in the game consciously under instruction rather
than automatically. If both parties are conscious, they both win, but
if one tricks the other into playing the game without remembering the
instruction, he or she wins. I have found this strategy extraordinarily
effective in working with couples' repetitive patterns, though by itself
it often produces a transient "cure" which dissolves in a few weeks.

There are certain attitudes on the part of the therapist which will
facilitate insight about the games a client plays. A healthy sense of hu-
mor will help, as will a benevolent, appreciative attitude toward the
cleverness and power exhibited in the game. Modeling the compassion afforded by reframing and understanding the original purpose of
the game will help avoid negative judgment and encourage the client
to own her own demon. The therapist who is in touch with his own
demonic force will help much more than the therapist who is still ego-
invested in the denial of any such thing. If your demon can laugh with
your client's demon about his cleverness and the satisfaction of his aggressive urges, you will be on the road to real change. If you have any
vestiges of phony sainthood, work on it. Your client's more creative
demon will bring you crashing down, and his demon's hidden nature
will be fortified. Your owning of your own nastiness will be your best
credential for handling the nastiness in others.

Particularly with a client who is bright, insightful, and motivated,
some pointed questioning can often best elicit the demon initially.
James, a professional man of 39, came to see me for work anxieties,
a pattern of overwork, and chronic noninvolvement in relationships
with women. In the first six months of treatment there was a good deal
of progress in the first areas of concern involving work; however, in
spite of repeated attention to the social problems, there was little progress. In one session, James said, "No matter what I do, no matter what
I have done, I just can't solve this problem." I suggested to James that
there were possibly some very real advantages to not solving this problem and asked him to look at me and restate what he had just said in
the following way, "I won't solve this problem." I asked that he iden-

tify with that part of him that was refusing to solve the problem and to appreciate that part. In doing this, I tried as much as possible not to be confrontive, accusatory, or blaming, but rather to side with that part of him myself. In this kind of discussion, I often find it useful to ask, "Who else has tried to help you with this problem? Did they succeed? Were they confounded, frustrated, or stumped in trying to help you? Whom else have you confounded by refusing to solve this problem?"

In making this internal exploration, James discovered that his refusal to solve the problem had several payoffs. Because of his history, he tended to pick women who were demanding and to further project demandingness onto them. By refusing to solve the problem, he was free of "demanding women." He was also free of worrying about his attractiveness or whether he was sufficiently charming. Whenever he would begin dating, he would be consumed with this concern but otherwise he could just be himself.

The most pay dirt was found in answer to the question, "Who else have you confounded by refusing to solve this problem?" In exploring this, he discovered his delight in frustrating all of the older members of his family (parents, aunts, uncles, etc.) who pressed for his settling down. He was also somewhat gleefully aware of confounding the women who were his closest friends—women whom he dated and occasionally slept with but who were not really romantic lovers. He characterized these women as nurses and, in the laughter of recognition, also looked at me and said, "And, of course, I also confound the doctor." With some animation, he concluded this part of the therapy session by saying, "I don't want to be tamed. I don't want to be housebroken. I don't want to be a good boy and do what is expected of me."

This enthusiastic outburst allowed me to reframe this stubborn and aggressive part. I told James I felt that this was his best part, a part of him that was alive, aggressive, independent, and a part that would be the most attractive to women. I indicated that the kind of woman he would really want would not want to tame him anyway, and prescribed that he let his bad boy chase the girls. I indicated that I wanted no part of the role in which I had been cast—tamer, parent, demanding authority figure. The session ended with a suggestion from me that he continue to explore the benefits and advantages of this side of him. Integration would come later. It is often important to simply acknowledge and strengthen the resistive part before jumping to any rapprochement.

It is difficult to convey in writing the fun, camaraderie, and quality of laughter that best accompanies a session of this kind. I enjoy these sessions thoroughly, not only because I feel that we are really getting somewhere but also because my own demon thoroughly enjoys hooking up with that of another and participating in the appreciation of the cleverness and essentially positive intention of that demonic force. To the extent that I still need to justify this degree of demonic glee, I can by the knowledge that the open expression and appreciation of it will provide the surest route to its resolution and the healing of its destructive effects.

This same method of inquiry and sharing has been effective for me on numerous occasions with the problem of procrastination. Among other things, this problem is almost always a passive-aggressive maneuver which repeatedly confounds and challenges authority, often internalized authority. Questions about how long the problem has maintained, who else has tried to assist with its solution, who has been confounded in those tries, etc., will all serve to elicit the demonic component in the problem. As indicated, whenever there is a particularly resistant problem in the face of many attempts to solve it, you can almost be assured that the demon is at work. In cases where the resistance is too great to employ these "conscious mind" maneuvers, I tend to borrow from my hypnotic training and tell the client stories about other clients or friends of mine who have discovered the gleefully demonic aspects of their own resistant behavior. I will make these stories less transparent in their intent as I find the client more rigidly resistant to this aspect of himself. Some clients will require quite a bit of time and gradual work before they will be willing to relax their rigidly held self-concepts and embrace their demonic elements.

The analysis of the client's games can probably be most powerfully accomplished in the context of the therapeutic relationship itself. The client will do in therapy what he does outside. Perhaps the most common consulting room game of the schizoid character could be labeled, "Do me something." In this game, the client is superficially cooperative in every respect except the most important one. He will come on time for therapy, religiously pay his bill, and cooperatively engage in any dialogue, activity, or exercise suggested by the therapist. He is present in the room but not really involved in the therapeutic process, and this lack of involvement is a secret to him and will often be, for a while at least, a secret to the therapist as well. To the extent that the therapist is fooled, she will tend to come up with more and more avenues of treatment with which the client will superficially cooperate. She will take increasingly more responsibility for the progress of therapy while accumulating more and more unexpressed resentment. If she is relatively unconscious of this process and is not obtaining the appropriate supervision, at least one round of this game will end either with her angry confrontation of the patient "for his own good" or in the drifting away of the client, who will typically redecide the classic schizoid script decision, "I'm not OK, you're not OK." The therapist, unconsciously delighted to be rid of one who makes her feel inept, will "forget" to follow up on the case and generally repress the unpleasant experience.

My own most common strategy for dealing with this situation is to begin to elicit the demon in the client with the kinds of dialogue outlined above. As the client and I are both celebrating the clever aggression of the demonic force, I will begin to lead the client to see the expression of that force in our relationship. Then, I will share with him my own countertransferential reactions in hopes of getting him to enjoy the ways in which he makes me inept, wrong, and foolish. In this way, I attempt to increase the therapeutic alliance and establish a precedent for the nonthreatening labeling of this consulting room game in the future. The therapeutic alliance is between the adult ego state of the patient and the professional, adult ego state of the therapist, taking joint and cooperative responsibility for the therapeutic process.

Most therapists tend to give themselves a very hard time when they find themselves caught up in the game maneuvers of their clients. Hopefully, an antidote to that will be the realization that the client is far more expert at this particular game than the therapist will ever be. The function of getting caught in the game is to learn how it works in the very human world in which the client lives. One may need to be caught in the game more than once before it can be fairly understood and appreciated. The greatest deterrent to that outcome will be the therapist's perfectionistic arrogance, which will prevent him from seeing when he has been caught. The professional obligation of the therapist is not to be so perfect that he never gets caught. Rather, it is merely to have the strategies and resources available to catch having been caught and reverse the pattern.

The demon work is particularly effective because it begins to elicit the aggressive part of the real self and to increase the client's identification with this denied part. Because the demonic solutions were originally arrived at consciously, they are more easily brought back to consciousness. In this respect, the demon represents an unlocked window in what may otherwise be a well-locked fortress. Once the therapist is able to elicit any real affect, this will open the way for the triggering of other affects. In the schizoid character, the anger is, at core, about being punished and frightened out of his natural self. That anger will elicit the fear of punishment and the emotion of fear itself will eventually elicit the core fear of people, leading back to the initial fear of the parent or guardian of childhood. The rage and terror will also eventually elicit the grief surrounding the loss of self and the loss of the nurturing relationship that should have been. Thus, because all of the affects are interlocked, any unlocked window may provide an opportunity to elicit, and ultimately resolve, all interconnecting feelings.

The exception to this rule exists whenever there is an "affect defense" or "racket feeling." Any experienced clinician will have the experience of treating a client who appears to be quite capable of feeling one of the basic emotions. She is easily and repeatedly incensed with anger, capable of tears at the drop of a hat, or easily overwhelmed with fear or anxiety. In these cases, however, the affect never seems to complete itself or lead anywhere. While there may be some relief after an angry outburst or crying episode, there is a repetitive "racket" quality about the affective release and although there may appear to be some movement or insight on the first few occasions, after a while the clinician will see that nothing of any substance is really going on. In these cases, the available affect is not an open window at all, but really represents a bolted iron door to the internal affective structure. The racket is a clear signal to the clinician to keep looking for another way in to the internal affective structure. In these cases, one possible response is to interpret or analyze the affect defense and to make an agreement with the client to move around it looking for another way in.

The transactional analysis school has been particularly helpful in elucidating the characteristics of the affect defense or racket feeling. The essential payoff is to cover the experience and expression of one or more real feelings. Another salient quality of racket feelings is that they require an excuse for expression. In other words, we tend to set up situations in which we can express the racket feelings and re-express the script decisions which accompany them. An important payoff of a game, therefore, is the opportunity to experience the racket feeling. In the analysis of the demon and her games, the client may be introduced to this very useful insight and begin to appreciate that indeed her games are in part an excuse for the experience and expression of the racket feeling. Thus, in Berne's (1964) entertaining language, one may be vigilant for another to make a mistake so that she can play the final move in the game, "Now I've Got You, You Son of a Bitch," experiencing the racket anger which accompanies this final move. Alternatively, a person may set up a rejection so that he can play "Poor Me" and experience the racket grief which elicits sympathy from others. In each case, the racket feeling will be associated with the repetition of some core script decision about oneself, the world, or others. Another possible response to the affect defense is the orientation suggested by the reframing process described in the last chapter, so that the client may discover the underlying intention of this repetitive process.

Whether there is an affect defense or not, the analysis of the demon and of games will almost always provide some opening to the real self. The very existence of the demon is dependent on its deceptive or hidden quality, but the underlying feelings are real enough. As they emerge, more active techniques may be used to further this experience and expression. To facilitate aggressive release, it may be necessary to do further processes which reduce chronic tension and build a charge in the body.

BODY WORK

By way of review, the four stages of a typical bioenergetic affect release session are as follows: 1) reduction of chronic tension, 2) production of a charge in the body, 3) affect release or discharge, and 4) rest. The following is a presentation of a sequence of exercises which realize these objectives, particularly around the affect of aggression.

Relaxing and Charge-building Exercises

A number of the general warm-up exercises presented in chapter III will be useful for the objective of reducing chronic tension and producing fuller respiration, firmer grounding, and better contact with the environment. In addition, it may be necessary to free up even more chronic tension that tends to exist in the upper trunk, shoulders, neck, and jaw before engaging in processes which pull for aggression. The exercises which follow are among those which speak to these objectives.

The bow

The bow is a classic bioenergetic posture which expands the chest and affects the entire upper body. Instruct the client, "To do the bow, stand with your knees bent, feet at shoulder level aimed perfectly forward. Now clench your fists and bring them into your lower back and slowly move your hips forward and your shoulders and elbows back, so that your body comes into a bow, like that of a bow and arrow. Breathe and stretch your shoulders and elbows back. It is usually more comfortable to keep your head erect as you do this." In addition to stretching the entire trunk of the body, this exercise will also build a charge in the body if it is maintained for any length of time. It is useful to ask the client to return to the forward position after the bow in order to stretch out the back, particularly the lower back, which can be very strained in this exercise. Clients having any significant lower back problem may do well to avoid this particular exercise.

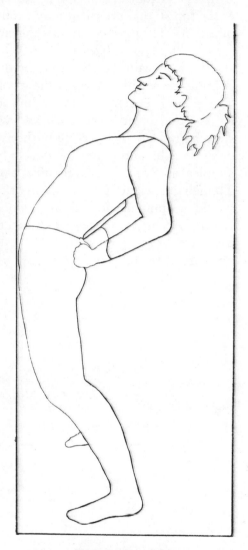

Figure 3. The bow

The stool

The bioenergetic stool is a custom made tool for this work which may be purchased from Realto Furniture, 214 Sullivan Street, New York, NY 10012. It is a stool approximately three feet high and resembles a sawhorse, though it is narrower in width. The stool is padded at the top so that the client may extend himself over it in various applications. The most common application of the stool involves another form of the bowed back stretch. When I first introduce the stool to clients, I typically demonstrate the desired posture. I lie on my back over the stool with the top of the stool just below my shoulder blades. This point is exactly corresponding to a woman's bra line across the back. I extend my arms back and with each exhalation attempt to stretch my back by lowering both my hips and shoulders as much as possible. The same stretch may also be accomplished over the arm of a typical sofa or over a large towel placed on top of an ordinary stool. Though the height of the sofa arm or ordinary stool may be lower than would be optimally desired, these more common structures can be used for any self-help stretches prescribed for the client. This stretch opens the chest, bringing movement to chest breathing and expansion in the abdominal region, lower back, shoulders, etc.

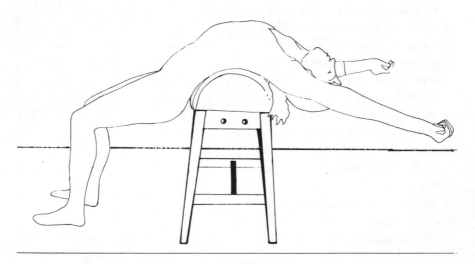

Figure 4. The stool

The stool is also very valuable in the diagnosis of body blocks in that one can typically see and feel the areas of blockage in this posture. There may, for instance, be whiteness, coldness, or immobility in the upper chest of the schizoid client and a similar blockage in the neck. The stool will almost immediately show the rigidity in the body and will persistently demand that that rigidity be relaxed. I suggest to my clients that they make friends with the stool as quickly as possible as it will always be more rigid and less yielding than they. Though the stool is initially often met with a good deal of resistance, after a time most clients find this stretch to be particularly relaxing and relieving. After each stretch on the stool, at least a brief return to the forward position is useful to stretch out the back in the other direction.

The stool is also useful to assist in releasing tension in the neck area, particularly in the front and on the sides of the neck. To assist with that release, the therapist may massage lightly the front of the neck between the Adam's apple and the sternocleidomastoid muscles located on the sides of the neck. Relaxing this area will help with freedom in vocalization. In addition, the therapist may massage or apply pressure to the sternocleidomastoid muscles more vigorously to force release in these muscles.

Jaw exercises

The clenched jaw is a classic and widely recognized expression of inhibited aggression. Loosening the muscles which control the jaw will always be involved in enhancing aggressive expression. It is easiest to work on the jaw when the client is either over the stool or lying on his back. A number of alternatives are possible. A beginning, simple procedure involves simply asking the client to stick out his chin as far as possible, bringing the lower teeth forward of the upper teeth. The effect of this may be enhanced if the therapist places his hand on the client's chin and applies some resistance or pressure. If the therapist is prepared to pull for a little aggression at this point, she may ask the client to growl a little on each exhalation. After 15 to 60 seconds of this posture, the therapist may remove the pressure and ask the client to move his jaw around from side to side, opening his mouth widely and otherwise exercising the muscles that have been held tightly in the exercise.

Further work on the jaw may be accomplished by the therapist's applying direct pressure on the muscles directly around the joint of the jaw. Since this maneuver can be intrusive and sometimes quite painful, it is important to approach it with caution. On occasion, I have solved this problem by asking the client himself to accomplish this maneuver or I have waited until there was a very solid therapeutic relationship before attempting it. After the jaw exercises, it is often useful to ask the client to relax the jaw, opening the mouth and breathing. A slight opening of the jaw on exhalation is particularly important and indicative of a natural pulsatory movement congruent with letting go in the body.

Pulsatory and counterpulsatory movement

In these processes, particularly where the therapist is leading up to affective release, it is important to look for pulsatory versus counterpulsatory movement in the body. By pulsatory movement I mean the natural flowing movement which the body expresses when it is in a state of relaxation or uninhibited energy flow. The most easily observed natural flow occurs with respiration. In lying over the stool or lying down on the floor or on a mat, pulsatory movement includes, with exhalation, slight opening of the jaw and extending or dropping the hips and shoulders. The opposite occurs in inhalation—the jaw closes slightly, and the body raises slightly. When movement is pulsatory, there is respiration in both the abdominal and chest regions with visible expansion apparent first in the abdominal region and then in the chest region.

Counterpulsatory movement—the opposite of that outlined above— is generally a signal that the defenses are being mobilized. Counterpulsatory movements signal the therapist to respond to the resistance by calling the client's attention to it, enhancing the client's identification with it, exaggerating it or otherwise working it through. It is important not to further escalate the body or affective work before responding to the resistance. In the schizoid personality, the counterpulsatory movements will often be accompanied by a general "going away" on the part of the client. This can be seen by a vacant look in the eyes and can be repeatedly checked out with the client by asking him, "What are you experiencing now?" or "Are you here?"

Charging and Releasing Exercises

All of the foregoing exercises can be used not only to reduce tension but also to build charge in the body. If they are engaged in long enough and with deep breathing, a charging effect will be realized. The exercises presented here can be used to continue the building of charge or to begin the release of aggressive energy. A number of these exercises involve hitting; when this hitting is done in a standing position, a bed or other cushioned, elevated structure is required.

Hitting the bed or couch

To accomplish this simple hitting exercise, I instruct the client, "Stand with your knees bent, solidly grounded, in front of the bed. Clench both fists, bring them over your head and repeatedly hit the bed as hard as you can. With each blow, make some sound." During the hitting, I watch the client carefully to see if she is simply flailing with her arms only or if she is hitting using the power in her legs, back, and shoulders. Where the force of hitting is less than it could be, I intervene. I will ask her to cock her body back in preparation for the hit, to stop and feel the cocked power in her body, and then to come forward with full force using legs, back, and shoulders to fully connect in the blow. Typically, I will demonstrate this action. Unless it is too threatening or there is a problem of containment, I will ask the client to hit to the point of exhaustion. Frequently, I will add aggressive content to the vocalization, asking the client to yell something with each blow, such as "No," or "I won't" or "I hate you."

In this, as in all similar exercises, the client will experience either the release or the resistance. If she experiences the release, it will be obvious, and relaxation, insight, and further release will follow. If she experiences the resistance, a therapeutic opportunity is at hand. This is a win-win situation. Resistance is not failure; rather, it is the emergence of that part of the patient which requires expression, appreciation, and integration. The nature and purpose of the resistance will be the focus of early affective therapy. Thus, in response to the resistance you may ask for its exaggeration, communicate with its positive intent, ask how it is being of service, or use any other method to bring it into the open. This may well lead to asserting the resistance out loud (e.g., "I won't get angry, I won't give you the satisfaction").

The client may achieve both the experience and the resistance serially. He may release for a while and then, as the intensity of the emotion grows, become threatened and lock up to the experience. This very typical reaction is a triple win. There is the release with its accompanying changes, the enhanced awareness of the defensive structure, and the opportunity to observe the change from release to defense.

Defensive tension is also a signal to re-engage in whatever processes have in the past reassured or relaxed it. This may include therapist-client contact, literal physical support of the client, or other similar maneuvers. I, for example, have found it useful at these moments to move behind the client and put my hands on his shoulder blades. I then ask him to lean back slowly and take whatever support he can from me. This literal, physical reassurance often results in the relaxation of the defense and the continuance of flow in experience or insight released by letting go. This effect may be enhanced by suggesting relaxation in those areas observed to be tense in prior work or by direct, hands-on work in these areas. I may ask the client to close his eyes, drop his jaw, breathe into his chest, or stretch his neck. Or I may go directly into the muscles of the neck or upper back with light or firm massage. Additionally, dropping back into the forward position will ground and reassure the client and further facilitate a letting go of tension and feeling. Even no response to any or all of this is a response and represents important feedback. This no-lose attitude will be critical in the use of all similar active techniques.

Hitting exercise 2

This exercise can build a considerable charge. The first two sequences require a release, but with containment. The third repetition, however, encourages the client to discharge freely. The exercise pulls for anger but, as in other hitting exercises, can pull for other affects as well. This process may be particularly useful when it is difficult to establish a sufficient charge by other methods.

Ask the client to hold one end of a rolled-up bath towel in both hands, to get on his knees, and to assume a "Muslim prayer position" with his arms extended in front of him. He should push his buttocks down as far as possible toward his heels and put his face close to the floor. Ask him to do deep breathing in this position. During the first such sequence, ask him to 1) take 10 deep breaths, 2) rise up on his knees swinging the towel up over his head, 3) then hit the floor with the towel — just once. Tell him to look at you, as you sit in front of him, and to repeat the exercise.

The second time, the client should breathe deeply 10 times, hit the floor with the towel three times, and again, look at the therapist. For the final repetition of the sequence, ask him to take 10 deep breaths, then slam the towel against the floor until he is exhausted.

Building the charge, containing its release, and then encouraging a total release is a combination that often breaks through rigid defenses when other techniques have failed. As in the previous exercise, vocalizing while hitting may enhance the release.

Figure 5. Hitting with the towel

Kicking or hitting while in the supine position

Ask the client to lie on her back for this exercise, on a bed or mat if one is available. Tell her to begin to kick or hit, or to do both simultaneously. To enhance the charge-building effects, tell the client to keep her legs relatively straight — and to kick hard, slamming her heels deeply into the bed. Clients with relatively poor defenses may have trouble with containment of the energy charge. For them it is useful to prescribe a limited number of kicks to contain the release of energy. A more well-defended client may tolerate extended kicking, to the point of exhaustion, and this may be necessary to break through the defense. Asking the client to accompany her kicking and hitting with an appropriate word or phrase will enhance the effect. Therapist and client can collaborate to come up with an appropriate individualized statement or use the most universally applicable word, "No!"

Hitting and kicking may be more effective when combined in synchronized movement analogous to a tantruming child's. In this alternating method, the client first hits the bed or mat with her left arm, the impact just left of her thigh, and her right arm is extended above her head. She strikes the next blow with her right arm down and left arm extended upward. The furious left-right, up-down movements are similar to those of an out-of-control child's temper tantrum, so the exercise tends to pull for anger or rage. For even greater release, ask her to fling her head from side to side as she simultaneously kicks and hits. This exercise requires moving the whole body, substantially increases the breathing, and pulls for aggressive affect. Vocal expression of anger or resistance further enhances the probability that the aggressive affect will "connect," so the person will really feel the expression. The therapist can intensify this connection by, for example, countering with "Yes" every time the client yells "No!"

These techniques require a well-established therapeutic relationship with a client who has reliable ego strength. Use them to aid connecting and expressing affect. The processes are ordinarily designed simply to build a charge or to pull for aggression, but they frequently elicit inhibition, fear, or terror. When inhibition is elicited, another opportunity arises to exaggerate, explore, and interpret such resistance. When fear or terror are elicited, the therapist can quickly shift to enhancing that expression if he determines that the client can handle it. It is particularly crucial that the therapist keep his eyes on the client at these times. If he expects the client to stay with a difficult emotion, the therapist must stay with the client.

It helps for the therapist to remember that the clear experience and expression of these emotions is the safest avenue both for him and the client. There is no real danger as long as the client experiences the affect with clarity and expresses it directly. Furthermore, the therapist knows that it is impossible for the client to stay in peak rage or terror forever. The affective expressions will naturally decline after the peak. At that point, the opportunity arrives to relax, report memories, and acquire more precise insight. Throughout the sequence of building and releasing the charge, the therapist may need to intervene with hands-on methods to reduce any spasmodic muscular defense elicited by this sudden increase in energy flow through the body. It is always better to learn these techniques, which will be presented in part throughout this text, through direct person-to-person instruction. This book is meant to be an adjunct to direct therapeutic training, particularly with these deepest level and hands-on interventions.

The final movement

After the affect peaks and gradually calms, there is a period of rest conducive to integration. During this time, it is essential that the therapist stay out of the way of the natural healing process. It may be useful for the therapist to gently ask, "What are you experiencing now?" in order to keep tabs on the process. It is not, however, a bad sign if the client is unable to report on this, as it may be necessary for the internal reverie to be largely at an unconscious level. Insights, memories, or a developing sense of what the affect is all about are possible at this time. The client is in an altered state of consciousness at this point in the process and material of incredible value may come spontaneously. I tend to believe in erring in the direction of saying too little rather than too much at this very crucial time.

In addition to whatever content may be extracted at this point, there is a very important lesson about the life process itself here. This is the final step of a natural sequence — charge, discharge, and rest. There are clients who will almost automatically try to skip this last, valuable part of the natural sequence. They may easily develop a charge and achieve discharge, but fail to come down and relax. They will ask, "Well, what's next?" One may bring this disruption in the sequence to the client's attention and discuss it in regard to his history and current life. I often use my hypnotic skills at this point, however, to elicit the desired relaxation response. I may, for example, make very generalized statements about the naturalness of relaxation and rest following exertion. I may say, for example, "It is nice to rest when one is tired — to know when it is time to *do nothing*. After one has worked hard, it is such a release to just *stop, rest* and let the mind wander where it will. *Nothing to do, nowhere to go.* You can drop into the middle of nowhere, thinking nothing, doing nothing, letting the mind go on vacation as the body relaxes and melts. Perhaps there has been a time when you just allowed your body to completely relax, perhaps in the warmth of the sun, or before a warm fire, you just allowed your body to *be* completely and totally *at peace*. Whenever there is exertion there can be relaxation, just as the night follows the day and the sun follows the moon. Rest is such a natural part of life, a part of the natural cycle. It is the down in up and down, and as there is no up without a down, there is no activity without rest. Rest, enjoy, be easy, relax."

While tending to err on the side of doing too little rather than too much in this crucial phase, I like to remember that it is an altered state having great potential for hypnotic processes. It is a period in which one can profitably use a number of hypnotic or neurolinguistic programming strategies to further growth and integration. If, for example, the client comes forth with a traumatic childhood memory in which she was horrified or brutalized, I may use the final step of the NLP dissociation process. I will ask that her current, older self return to the traumatic scene and comfort her younger self, reassuring the child that she survived and reminding her that she did the best she could at that time with the resources she had. I will say, "Do or say whatever that younger person needs from you now." Alternatively, should the person have some insight, or reach some ego state which she wishes to carry forth into some real-life situation, I will be inclined to *future pace* this—that is, to suggest that this insight or ego state occur in the imagined situation. The material shared in this important time may spontaneously suggest to me a metaphor or story which I feel will consolidate or further the gains already achieved.

AGGRESSION, ASSERTIVENESS AND THERAPEUTIC TECHNIQUE

The release of pent-up anger and aggression can be a very useful precursor to the expression of appropriate assertion in the world. Part of the inhibition of assertion and aggression in the schizoid personality is his realization, at some level, that there is a well of rage within him which could burst forth if accessed. The release of the tension will facilitate the more appropriate expression of assertion and aggression. In those cases where a real-life situation currently calls for assertion, I often first encourage the expression of rage using the methods outlined above. After the final movement of this rage work, I will call for the behavioral or imaginal rehearsal of the desired assertive behavior. At this point, the client typically does not have to struggle to hold back the inappropriate rage but can more calmly state her position and demand appropriate attention and action. After using role playing or behavioral rehearsal, I will also future pace the assertive behavior in the target situation. The preceding represents a combination of bioenergetic, affect release techniques with the strategies of cognitive and behavior modification.

In addition to these more active techniques for eliciting and releasing aggressive impulses, there are many interview-oriented methods which can be used for the same purpose. The ordinary events of the client's life, as well as his relationship with the therapist, provide a number of opportunities for expression and analysis of aggressive impulses. With the schizoid client, one will find repeated examples of the denial of aggression together with its "leaking out" in unconscious ways. Particularly where this is true in the therapeutic relationship, it is useful to bring it out, thereby giving the client the experience of acknowledging aggression, expressing it directly, while staying and being accepted in the relationship. To further this end in a systematic way, I often ask clients periodically during the therapy to list reluctances or resentments towards the therapeutic process or toward me. In this process, I simply ask the client to list, without censorship, all reluctance, resistance, considerations, or resentments which he may have toward me, the therapeutic process, or any circumstances surrounding our relationship. I indicate to the client that the most revealing reluctances or resentments may come up after the first, fully conscious ones are brought forward. So, I use the Gestalt therapy frustration principle and simply request the client to list all conscious resentments and then wait quietly for more.

Similarly, I may look for the appropriate opportunity to ask the male client, for example, to list all the resentments he has against his wife, mother, or women in general. As with most exercises of this kind, the client's reactions to doing it are often far more important than the content revealed. As a result of the listing of resentments, for example, the client may discover the powerful prohibitions within him against the awareness or expression of such negativity. The therapeutic session may then be devoted to further exploration of these prohibitions, their survival value, historical origins, and so forth. This may lead quite naturally to focusing more deeply on the client's resentful part and reframing it, or to engaging in dialogue involving explanation, interpretation, or integration of the negativity polarity and its inhibition.

What is being offered in this presentation of psychotherapy, then, is the integration of techniques such that, with practice, one procedure naturally flows into another and, over time, the discreteness of techniques begins to dissolve in the natural flow of their collaborative function. The techniques are presented in a discrete, stepwise fashion to facilitate their learning; however, the eventual therapeutic product will, it is hoped, look much more natural and free form than the step-by-step presentation of technique would suggest. In the present discussion, for example, the release of aggressive and rageful impulses may naturally elicit a change in one's cognitive self-representation and that may lead to new behaviors in the person's day-to-day life. The discovery that one harbors a pool of primitive rage challenges the false self concept of the all-accepting, unaggressive self and permits insight into one's destructive social games. This, in turn, paves the way for more direct assertive behavior in one's social context. Those therapeutic techniques which pull for affective release may be indispensable during certain parts of this process but totally off target during others. Similarly, therapeutic procedures which are aimed at affecting appropriate social behavior may be very superficial if they do not involve the affective and cognitive components, yet absolutely indispensable in cases where these other elements are considered and treated.

Many of us have seen those sad cases in which an individual can provide a very lucid analysis of all the familial circumstances which led him to be socially shy and inept, yet, after five years of some form of analytic treatment, is still unable to ask a woman for a date or be comfortable at a party. Similarly, we may know of others who, while they have been taught to put on a good show behaviorally, still feel anxious, depressed and socially alienated. The quality of their behavior is acceptable but the quality of their experience is unchanged. Finally, we may also be acquainted with those individuals who have learned to "blow off" affective steam when under pressure and who always feel better after dumping a load of negative affect. They may go for a primal scream or a bioenergetic session instead of taking a Valium, but they are still as immature, irresponsible and unclear about themselves as ever.

In bringing this back to the current concerns of the schizoid dilemma of repressed aggression and rage, it is important to tie these affective experiences to the cognitive and the behavioral objectives outlined earlier. Strategies for generalizing the appropriate behavioral expression of assertiveness and aggressiveness have been presented. Rage release offers opportunity for historical memories and the associated interpretations. Such opportunities force the client to further develop the representation of self in a more realistic and ambivalent way. Thus, he can see where he is a natural product of his environmental history and can begin to accept his personality with all its strengths and weaknesses. He can identify himself with the feelings in his body and the affects, both positive and negative, which are there. The feelings, in turn, will strengthen the experience of his real self and ultimately the real contactful experience of others. Such interactive changes will enable him to act in a more adult fashion in the world, with more realistic expectations of himself and others and more appropriate handling of feelings. Some of this generalization of effect will occur naturally without the therapist's attention or intervention. Yet, an awareness of the nature of these interactions will enable the clinician to enhance, foreshadow, predict, and program such changes in many ways.

Personally, I rely on my skills as a communicator influenced by hypnotic training to help the client in choreographing these changes. Just as in the prior paragraph, I generously use *presuppositions* to suggest that *as changes occur in one area of life, they will, by natural extension, occur in others*. I may, even in ordinary conversation, elicit in the client realistic pictures of how these interacting effects will accumulate. In good hypnotic tradition, I am careful to use maximally general terms and descriptions for suggesting how the release of rage in therapy can most naturally yield creative and effective uses of assertiveness on the outside, how an awareness of the historical antecedents of the rage will naturally assist in the discrimination concerning when assertiveness or anger should be exhibited, or how the erosion of the idealized self will naturally result in the reduction of perfectionism, performance anxiety, and procrastination. This "hypnotic talk" can have many positive effects, including giving the client an internal rehearsal and representation of these outcomes. Additionally, stories about other clients, friends, family, and myself assist in this essentially verbal intervention.

In the discussion of affective release techniques it is probably important to highlight two considerations. First, it is impossible to provide, even in a general way, a typical course of affective treatment or to accurately predict the extent to which it will be repetitive and cyclical. Because the aggressive responses are slightly more likely to be accessible initially, at least at a superficial level, I have dealt with them first. But it may well be that grief, fear, or perhaps even some initial euphoria will come out initially. It is, however, typical that each affect needs to be worked through again and again and it is generally the case that affective treatment in one area will springboard to another both within the same session and across sessions. In particular, the affects of rage and terror will tend to "ping pong" one to the other and back again even from moment to moment within a session. It is also probably necessary to highlight the fact that within this often protracted course of affective treatment a broad range of therapeutic techniques will be used. Thus, there may be a session, in the midst of serious affect-related treatment, devoted exclusively to interview, explanation, interpretation, or problem-solving. Indeed, after a particularly intense affective session, it has been my experience that the client often needs one or more subsequent sessions of quiet interaction, integrative hypnotic work, or other internal focusing to come down from and incorporate the emotional work.

ANXIETY, FEAR, TERROR

With these clarifications in mind, let us now consider the issues and techniques surrounding the problem of accessing and eliciting anxiety, fear, or terror. There will typically be a strong automatic resistance in the body to the experience of deep terror. There can, however, be an easier entry into that emotion, the release of which will be necessary for the eventual transformation. Very often, the schizoid individual is aware of anxiety surrounding any number of situations, or he may experience generalized anxiety much of the time. An easy entry into the exploration of this emotion is to require the client to focus on this emotion and free associate about it. As in former exercises outlined in this book, an initial step to such focusing could involve the client's closing his eyes, attending inwardly, and being aware of all the body sensations involved in anxiety or fear. This could then be expanded to include emotions and feelings, behaviors, postures, facial expressions, attitudes, beliefs, and points of view associated with anxiety. The client may then simply free associate about anxiety or fear using a repetitive phrase such as, "I am afraid of . . . " filling in the blank with whatever comes to mind.

After this initial anxiety-directed warm-up, the client can then be encouraged to free associate in the classic way, that is, to say whatever comes to mind about anything. At the end of some period of this, the therapist may then ask the client to review any insight, realization, memory or feeling coming out of this process.

Active Techniques

At a more active level, the affects in the range of anxiety, fear, and terror may be elicited with varying degrees of intensity or intrusion. For example, as a client sits in a chair, he may be asked simply to breathe more deeply, open his jaw somewhat, and open his eyes more widely, allowing some of the fear or anxiety to be there without trying to change it.

The basic strategy for eliciting the emotions of anxiety, fear, or terror is to require the client to assume the postures and expressions associated with these emotions. Thus, expanding on the former example, one may get more fear by asking the client to open her eyes more widely and put her hands up in front of her face as if warding off something threatening. Deep breathing with eyes wide open, mouth open, and hands up in front of the face will tend to elicit more fear.

Still more active elicitation of the fear or terror should be preceded by establishing solid grounding and developing a charge in the body. The following process may be done with the person erect but I've had the best experiences with it with the client in the recumbent position, lying down on the mat or floor with knees up and the bottoms of the feet pressing downward. I ask the client to breathe deeply, in this position, for some period of time. If there appears to be a good deal of resistance in the breathing process itself, I typically ask the client to engage in *paradoxical breathing*. In this form of breathing, you fill up the chest with air first, followed by filling the abdomen. You then release the air all at once and repeat this for a minute or so. If this works to enhance breathing, I ask the client to breathe more normally, while keeping it full and deep. I then request that the client bring his hands up in front of his face as if shielding it, open his eyes widely, and scream as loudly as possible while looking at me as I stand over him. The client may require encouragement to stay with this, to scream louder, or to scream at a higher pitch, intensifying the pull for terror.

Additional physical maneuvers may be used to stop the typical defensive contractions associated with the inhibition of this emotion. Mild pressure applied on the client's cheekbones just on either side of the nose will inhibit those facial muscles usually used to smile in defense of this and other unpleasant affects. Additionally, you may put some pressure on the sternocleidomastoid muscles on either side of the neck. This pressure will inhibit the spasmodic contractions of these muscles, while additionally metaphorically replicating the strangling of the patient, thereby pulling for the terror response. Obviously, good therapeutic rapport is necessary before one can engage in this very intrusive maneuver.

Hypnotic Technique

As with rage, terror will need to be experienced repeatedly and worked through. Particularly with this affect, one is engaging the client in a desensitization process so that she can experience more and more of this emotion without cutting off the body. Most of us are very much afraid of being afraid. Continual suggestions for the removal of the fear of fear can be useful. Perhaps my most successful experience with hypnotic work was in one session with a 12-year-old boy who had witnessed the remains of a horribly violent suicide committed by his uncle while he was staying in the boy's home. After this traumatic event, the boy was unable to sleep well at night, suffered recurrent nightmares, was unable to go to the bathroom at night, and experienced panic attacks associated with sirens or anything which triggered memories of the incident.

While the boy was in a conscious state, I made the interpretation that fear was not his problem, but that his fear of being afraid was his problem. I then created a hypnotic state by telling him story after story about all the things people do to deliberately experience fear—roller coasters, ghost stories, circus fun houses, horror movies, sky diving, etc., etc., etc. I suggested to this young man that if he could conquer the fear of fear, he would be ahead of most grownups in the world and that he would learn a valuable lesson never to be forgotten. After 45 minutes of storytelling, I suggested to him that this session would probably alleviate the problem but that he could always return to see me for any reason. At three- and six-month follow-ups, I learned that his symptoms had literally disappeared after that session and that he was in every respect a normal child as he had been before the incident.

Similar suggestions can, of course, be made to any client, particularly after the experience of terrifying feelings. Frequently, too, after such experiences, physical contact with the therapist, as well as eye contact, can be reassuring and bring the client back to better current reality relatedness. Personally, I find it is often helpful to hold the client's neck and head in my hands in a kind of reassuring support which is intimate yet nonintrusive. The essential thing in this entire process is staying in contact with the client and remaining sensitive to him.

ELICITING SADNESS OR GRIEF

Sadness or grief may also be easily elicited during the processes described above. Indeed, often all that is necessary is to slightly reduce chronic tension and build a mild charge for this affect to come forth. The deeper accessing of terror and rage will be even more likely to trigger this response, though in many schizoid clients there is a severe constriction around the experience of deep sadness and its expression in crying or sobbing. Here it may be important to clarify that depression is usually not sadness or grief. I view depression as more commonly a holding back of all feeling. Wherever there is real feeling, there is usually a change in respiration and vocalization, such that there is an increase, a peaking, and an eventual decrease in the expression of the feeling. In other words, there is some movement or change in real feelings, whereas in depression there tends to be a frozen immobility.

Focusing

It is not uncommon for the schizoid client to experience some vaguely unhappy sensations or feelings of sadness without knowing exactly what they mean or understanding their cause. The process of focusing (Gendlin, 1978) is directly suggested to me whenever I am faced with a person reporting some vague or incompletely understood feeling. Gendlin's focusing process is similar to a number of others outlined in this book but it has some unique and valuable features. It is another example of a relatively less intrusive body-oriented approach which does not require movement on the part of therapist or client. Although it is useful for a wide range of therapeutic applications, I present it here as a nonactive technique for getting at sadness or grief.

The following is a brief description of Gendlin's focusing process in six steps.

Step 1: Clearing a space

As with many other processes involving attention to internal processes, this one begins with a procedure aimed at facilitating uninterrupted internal attention. Gendlin prescribes an initial clearing process in which you list all of the things which are troubling you at the moment. Don't get hung up or stuck on any particular problem but simply allow the list to emerge, temporarily putting each item on the shelf. This meditative attitude of letting things come up and go by is represented in many such techniques. When you seem to have the list completed, Gendlin suggests that you use the sentence, "Except for all of this, I am fine." Often, this sentence will lead to other items for the list until it seems completed. At this point, you may experience a settling down or settling in such that you can say with some confidence, "Except for all of this I am fine."

As is true of the listing of reluctances or resentments outlined earlier, a common result is a kind of detachment from the list itself. While it is all so, there is a release in the listing and a disengagement which can come from separating the list from yourself. As with other Gestalt processes, this one demands awareness which goes beyond what is already consciously realized. In this, there is both clearing for the process of focusing and the beginning of the process itself.

Step 2: Feeling for the problem

In this step, you begin the process of *feeling for* the essence, heart, or core of the trouble. Essentially, you ask your body to send you the message in a kinesthetic, sensory way. You avoid labeling, understanding or analyzing, but give yourself time to feel the message in the language of the body rather than in the language of the mind. All of us, but particularly the schizoid part of us, will almost automatically tend to analyze and jabber during this second step. What is required is patience and time for the feelings to present themselves. The body generally speaks more slowly and, particularly where unpleasant emotions are concerned, there are often well-established habits of mental exercise which close off feelings.

This is the primary reason why the focusing process is so valuable to the schizoid individual. Though this process is presented in the context of dealing with sadness and grief, you must be open to letting it flow and allowing the content to emerge. Gendlin suggests that in this second phase, you ignore the details of any concern and just feel for the totality of the problem. He suggests such questions as, "What does this whole problem feel like?" "What whole problem feels worst on this particular day?" "What does this whole thing feel like?" In this second step, you are trying to arrive at the single whole *feeling* that includes all that is central in the sadness. Just as it is important not to intellectualize or analyze the feeling, it is also important not to try to change it — simply hold and deepen it. It is like calling up the central feeling you have when thinking of a certain other person. The details, the visual experience, the understanding of that person may be there, but they are not essential to the feelings called forth as you think of that person.

This part of the process is in some ways the most difficult, especially for a schizoid client, because it is teaching him a new language — a sensorily based form of communication with himself which will be relatively foreign. There will be some real difficulty in describing in words the language and messages of sensation.

Step 3: Finding the crux

The process of focusing is essentially a training for communicating with the feelings, the body, or the unconscious. The secret of this kind of work involves asking open-ended questions and waiting for answers, avoiding any rational, conscious mind responses arrived at rationally. This third step may be the most difficult to explain and differentiate from the ones preceding and following it. It, too, involves the asking of verbal questions and remaining open to answers which are often nonverbal, kinesthetic or visual. The key questions in this third step are, "What is the crux of this problem? What is the worst of it? What is the main thing in it that makes me feel bad?" You then wait for the answer to come, just as you would wait in the reframing process outlined earlier for the signal from the part generating a problem.

Gendlin indicates that in this phase of the process you may find the problem changing. That change will be at a feeling level, so that you know that you are making progress in this third step if there is a definite shift in bodily feeling. You know that you are on the right track in answering the crucial question of the third step when the bodily shift suggests, "This is right, this is it." The shift resembles that feeling you have had when you suddenly remembered something you knew you had forgotten but couldn't place what it was, or when you have recalled where you left something you had lost.

In this third step you may begin to come up with a verbal label or discover an image which gives some understanding of the crux of the problem. While this is all right, it is not necessary and it is more important to slow this process down than to rush to complete it. We learn to use a new language correctly much more slowly than we can use the old one and it is always a temptation to return to the ease of the old language. If you slow down the process of focusing, you are more likely to be learning the new language of feelings. The secret of focusing is to ask open-ended questions and then wait for the body, "the part," the unconscious, or whatever you want to call it to slowly give you the answer.

Step 4: Labeling

In this step, at last you begin to ask for pictures or words which come from the feeling and, in effect, label it. Once again, however, the process is not from the top down but from the bottom up. The label must flow out of the feeling rather than be imposed upon it. Essentially, you are looking for something you don't know already and the old labeling and understandings will not give you the kind of body shift that is the measure of a successful focusing process. In this fourth step, you may ask of yourself, "What is this feeling?" and then wait for the words or images to emerge or pop up out of the felt sense. Frequently, this labeling may quickly and naturally fall out of the third step and that is fine as long as the label comes from the feeling and there is that concomitant shift in the body which signals a completion, resolution, or change. The bodily shift in this fourth step will often involve an "aha" or a "that's it" which signals that more has been accomplished than the repetition of some old insight or way of looking at things.

Step 5: Checking back with the feeling

In this step, you simply check the image or label received in step 4 with the felt sense of the problem to see that there is a fit. You ask in this step, "Is this right?" Once again, wait for the response to this question to be felt rather than thought. If the sensation which answers the question is a confirming, settling one, you can move on to the next step. If the felt response is less settling, wait and see if a more precisely fitting label or image emerges from the feeling. Whatever the answer is in this step, it is important to hold on to the feeling rather than to stop feeling it once you have a label for it. You must have the feeling and the label together before you can check one against the other. In this step, too, the feelings may change. It is advised that you allow all of this to flow—to let both the words and the feelings shift until there is a match. When that occurs, let yourself feel the feeling and experience the words for a minute or two.

It is important to let the feeling be, and not try to change it. It is during these minutes that there can be a continued changing, releasing, moving, and resolving. Often the tendency, especially in the schizoid, is to rush on and escape or change the feeling. It is important to counter this tendency and stay with the feeling and its matching label for a while.

Step 6: Recycling at deeper levels

In succeeding rounds of this exercise you look for successive feeling experiences and their accompanying labels at deeper and deeper levels. You assume, for example, that what you have arrived at so far may be only the first layer of this feeling state. By returning to Step 2 you ask again, "What is the whole felt sense about that problem?" Again the body, the feeling, or the unconscious is allowed to begin to present that answer slowly. In repeating the third step, you again ask for the crux, and in the fourth for the label. In the fifth step you again ask for the match between words or images and the felt sense. This process can seemingly go on indefinitely, as ever deeper experiences of settling and shift occur around the feeling or the derivatives of that feeling which emerge as the process evolves. The stopping point may be dictated by the end of the therapeutic hour or, more fortunately, by coming to a place at which the shifts and settling in the body signal that one has arrived at an appropriate place to stop.

The focusing process involves learning a new language. It takes time and practice and an increasing faith in one's ability to communicate with one's own body and unconscious. For the schizoid client particularly, this may be very much a *foreign* language and much repetition and patience may be required. Very often, I have found that hypnotic trance induction is particularly useful for the initial stages of the process to encourage the client to suspend his ordinary conscious judgments while he learns this new, often threatening language.

The preceding is only a brief outline of Gendlin's focusing process, and while this description may enable you to understand it, it may not be enough to allow you to practice it effectively. Gendlin's book covers many of the difficulties which people typically have in learning the process and, though repetitive, gives the reader a deeper understanding of the process, so that it becomes possible to guide others through focusing after one has been through it again and again in the process of reading the book. Because this is a new language for most therapists, as well as clients, the repetitive and even drilling nature of Gendlin's book is, I think, often necessary and beneficial.

Active Techniques

It is often necessary to involve the schizoid client in more active bodily processes to access the deepest sorrow. For many such clients, this emotion has been so locked up that crying is impossible. A program which literally retrains the crying response may be necessary. Such a program, of course, will begin with the loosening of chronic tension, particularly that which blocks respiration, or disrupts flow, in the neck, jaw, and ocular segment. All of the warm-up and eye exercises presented earlier will be useful for this, as well as the following exercise.

Following the light

This process is best done in a darkened room and requires a penlight. Do the basic warm-ups first, building a mild charge in the body. Ask the client to lie on his back with the bottoms of his feet touching the floor or mat. Stand behind the client and move the light in an irregular pattern above his eyes. Ask the client to follow the light by moving his head from side to side. Suggest that he relax his vision and take in the light as he breathes and moves his head. Continue this for several minutes until you see the client breathing deeply, relaxing, and opening to the light. At this point, ask the client to repeatedly say the word, "Why?"

Particularly where grief is just beneath the surface, this energetic process will bring forth tears or even sobbing. In cases where the disinhibition is particularly successful, the client may require some encouragement to stay with the feeling and may benefit from some physical contact. After the affect release has peaked and settled there is once again the opportunity for insight, historical recall, or productive visualization. As with other affect release sequences, this point offers the opportunity for creative hypnotic process. The schizoid client may need a good deal of permission to cry, as well as a good deal of reassurance that his vulnerability will not be used against him. In this structure, there is often resistance to crying with the attitude, "I won't give them the satisfaction." The schizoid client needs to be encouraged to give himself the satisfaction and know that he no longer needs this defense around most others with whom he is or could be close.

I often use my hypnotic skills, especially metaphorical communication, to encourage crying. Particularly when this emotion seems just below the surface, I may elicit or utilize an altered state and begin to offer suggestions to disinhibit crying. Because I live in the Northwest where natural beauties abound, I enjoy using many natural metaphors. For crying, I often use the metaphor of a waterfall and describe in repetitive detail the "collapse" of water as it "relaxes" and falls to the ground. I allude to the "release" that water could feel as it allows itself to just fall down and down surrounded by other water to the pool which awaits it. "As the water flows and falls it is not alone and it is not hurt in the falling. It collapses, releases itself, allows the fall, and lets go." Thus, in these and other ways one can hypnotically suggest a letting go and a collapse into crying. While I am aware that this metaphor may sound strange to the conscious mind, the suspension of usual judgment which occurs in trance can result in the first escape of tears from a formerly armored individual.

During the period in which a person is liberating her ability to experience and express grief, I often prescribe homework to facilitate that expression. Those exercises which reduce chronic tension and build a little charge in the body, followed by exercises on the eyes and then the expression of a key word or phrase, will often have this effect. Similarly, the prescription to read specific poetry or prose or to watch certain films will often stimulate this affect. The availability of large film collections in readily accessible videotape form now makes it possible to prescribe movies to cry by and thereby expands our ability to help people experience and express this emotion.

PSYCHOTHERAPY'S "CRAZY" PHASE

As the schizoid individual begins to open to powerful emotions of all kinds, he may go through periods during which he experiences himself as somewhat out of control or "crazy." There may be times when he cannot stop crying, when he experiences outbursts of frightening anger, or when he is overcome by anxiety. The ordinary defenses have begun to be eroded and the underlying feelings are beginning to emerge, but there is less solidity in the real self than there ultimately will be. Among other things, the therapist will need to respond to such periods with understanding, explanation, and reassurance. Typically, I assure my clients that these periods are a sign of movement and, uncomfortable as they are, "the only way out is through." I have a number of stories, about myself and others, concerning how we went through similar periods in our own lives and therapeutic work. These stories are reassuring in that they come from the other side of this relatively out of control crisis and document the benefits of these necessary periods. It is useful to remind the client during these times of the resources, strengths, and ego control which he does have. Additionally, it is helpful to remind him of the defense structure which he still has and which can be employed voluntarily. This can be a particularly useful time to teach the client new defenses or review the ones that have already been taught. There usually are repeated episodes during which one will work through a layer of anger, fear, or grief followed by a period of consolidation and then a period of deeper working-through of one or more of these emotions. This ongoing working-through with accompanying consolidation and rest represents much of the hard work in this hard work miracle of characterological transformation.

The most obvious gains in the client's day-to-day life may well come during the periods of consolidation and rest. At these times, there may be a systematic increase in social involvement, more occasions of self-assertion and healthy aggression, and a progressive desensitization in opening to feelings of love. The periods of calm between the storms will typically be the most valued by the client and seen as evidence that the therapy is working. As these calming periods are progressively longer and more productive, the termination of therapy is being foreshadowed. Breaks in the therapeutic contact may also occur at these times and I feel it is important for the therapist to assent to these breaks whenever possible and to support the client's independence and individuation from the therapeutic process. A decrease in the frequency of sessions may be useful during these times and the therapy may be construed as a resource for the client to use as he needs it. In this way, it is made clear that the therapist and the therapy are for the client rather than the other way around. The difficulty in terminating therapy is, I feel, often as much a function of the therapist's theoretical biases, his need to be needed, and even his tendency to reject anything less than perfection as it is an expression of the client's legitimate difficulties with the separation itself.

THE SCHIZOID HEALING

Though there are some universals in the healing process and the evolution toward maturity, each basic characterological issue will lead to a unique set of discoveries and pleasures as real health is approached. The theme of these discoveries and pleasures for the schizoid is the discovery of life itself. There is a joy every spring when the trees which have seemed to be dead suddenly blossom. This is analogous to that special joy which the schizoid feels as he begins to discover he is really alive. It is often difficult for him to express this verbally because it is so kinesthetic and so profound. It is most clearly and simply felt in a slow, relaxed, full and deep breathing which occurs not deliberately, but spontaneously. Naturally, the body breathes itself. The lungs take in air through the principle of vacuum, and when that process is unencumbered yet consciously experienced after a lifetime of restriction, it can be awesome. It is at once profound and nothing special. As the schizoid experiences the life within and around him, so extraordinary yet so simple, he begins to lose the need to be something special. His consciousness migrates downward from the head and from ideas and comes to reside more and more in the sensations, particularly the kinesthetic sensations of movement. The schizoid discovers that his body is alive and physical movement becomes a great joy. Concomitantly, physical relaxation becomes profound realization. As the chronic muscular bracing against the terror and horror of life is relaxed, the pleasant sensations of a body at rest are realized. This represents an altered state of consciousness leading to deeper rest, both in wakefulness and sleep.

All of the repetitive and intense work on the darker affective experiences begins to have its payoff in the experience of an aliveness without the terror, grief, and rage which it would otherwise bring up. What has inhibited the schizoid's experience of aliveness is the intensity of these debilitating emotional states.

Particularly in the schizoid, the experience of life itself brings up a rage of particularly demonic proportions. Mass murderers are essentially schizoid and, to a greater or lesser extent, every schizoid character carries with him a truly murderous rage which is elicited by the experience of life itself. As this is relieved and worked through, he can more simply and clearly experience his own life force. The same, of course, is true for the chronic terror locked in the stiffly frozen body and for the grief similarly suppressed.

With these factors eroded, the schizoid can simply be alive and feel his life, thereby achieving incredible pleasure. From that grounded life force, then, can come all forms of self-expression. There can be a good deal of joy for the healed schizoid in learning dance, drama, music, etc. Similarly, forms of self-expression which have been learned and well-developed, but not connected to a grounded life force, can be pleasure-giving in a new way. The body is now not treated like a machine—manipulated or forced to perform. Rather the body is the vehicle for self-expression and that expression is integrated with the natural demands and flow of the body's energy.

As the schizoid improves, she will increasingly trust herself—her impulses, her needs, her intuition, her judgment, etc. Through reconnecting with herself and her body, she will know what is right for her and what is wrong, not on the basis of an adopted philosophy or unassimilated introject, but on the basis of her feelings and her grounded judgment. She will know how she feels about things, not because science or religion prescribes those feelings, but because, with a sense of herself intact, she developes her own *common sense*.

As this realistic and concrete sense of self is developed, she will be more and more free of the introjected self-hatred. The mysterious sense that "something is wrong with me" will diminish and she will experience a right to life even though she may have been damaged by life. As social relationships improve, she will gradually be able to introject the loving care of others and to replace the hatred or coldness which she originally received with the real love of others around her. Thus, as the schizoid improves, there will be an increase in core self-respect and self-love.

The schizoid person will begin to see other people as a source of comfort and joy, rather than a source of threat. As a result, he will seek out rather than avoid social contact and take pleasure in that contact even when it is somewhat superficial. Interaction with others can be pleasurable even if it is not highly meaningful or intellectual in its content. The schizoid may then be a member of a group without having to be special to justify his presence and get attention. Again, he gives himself permission to be nobody special and to have simple pleasure from human contact.

Sondra Ray has said, "Love brings up everything unlike itself for release and healing."* As the schizoid is more and more able to love, all of the other darker emotions will be brought up for release and healing. This may well be a life process for the schizoid person, perhaps even more than it is for the other character structures. As this is worked through, the schizoid will less and less avoid love and experience it more and more clearly.

As love becomes *unencumbered*, it too will become a grounded yet altered state of consciousness. As with the newly acquired contact with the self, this newly experienced love of another person will be awesome. With respect to these two basic healed experiences, the person may well say to you, "I never knew it could be like this."

*This statement is part of LRT—Loving Relationships Training.

CHAPTER V

THE ABANDONED CHILD:
THE SYMBIOTIC WITHDRAWAL

> There is no experience to which a young child can be subjected that is more prone to elicit intense and violent hatred for the mother than that of separation.
>
> —John Bowlby (1960, p. 24)

> Sometimes I feel like a motherless child . . . a long way from home.
>
> —Odetta, *A Motherless Child*

ETIOLOGY

JUST BEYOND THE right to existence emerges the human infant's need for nurturance, sustenance, and touch. Where these needs are incompletely met, another set of core issues will be established, yielding a characterological adjustment traditionally labeled "oral."

Not all children consciously wanted are adequately cared for and even those who are given what they appear to need are not always provided the consistency of a single, emotionally available caregiver capable of eliciting and maintaining a firm, healthy attachment. Orality will develop where the infant is essentially wanted and an attachment is initially or weakly formed but where nurturing becomes erratic, producing repeated emotional abandonment, or where the primary attachment figure is literally lost and never adequately replaced. The symbiosis is begun but never fulfilled and therefore never really resolved. The mothering anchor is not reliably available and thus secure "confident expectation" is never established. While the schizoid character structure revolves around the central issue of existence, the oral character's life will revolve around the core issue of need. There will be, in his behavior, attitudes, and perceived feelings, a polarity around this issue—tendencies toward desperate clinging, fear of being alone or abandoned, and poor self-care juxtaposed with a reluctance to express his need or ask for help, an overnurturing of others, and an independent grandiosity in elated or manic periods.

The case histories of individuals with severe orality are often characterized by maternal abandonment or serious illness in the mothering person. While the effect of the actual loss of a good mother figure has been documented to be most profound after seven months when differentiation has begun, the more common case appears to involve a weak or erratic symbiosis extending to chronic insufficiency in the need-gratifying ability of the mothering person. As opposed to the schizoid character, there is a "paradise lost" quality about the oral. She has experienced some adequate contact and at least begun an attachment when the caretaker is either lost or experienced as repeatedly unable to hold up her end of the attachment. Chronically ill, depressed, or alcoholic caretakers, who have relatively little outside support, are among the prime creators of the oral character. To understand this, imagine yourself the primary or sole parent of one or more very young children while you are dealing with the worst illness you have ever had outside a hospital. You might love your children and wish to give them every possible advantage, but you have barely enough energy to handle the illness and certainly you could not meet the demands of an active brood. Short of chronic depression, alcoholism, or illness, the parents of the oral character are often simply oral themselves. As chronically low energy individuals, they repeatedly fail to adequately meet the dependency needs of their children.

As in the etiology of the schizoid issue, the external circumstances under which the parent must live can contribute to or detract from the adequacy of early nurturance. A mother who may have the energy to be "good enough" for one child with the support of husband and/or extended family may be totally inadequate with two or three children, as a single parent, or when isolated from an extended family. Indeed, I believe that the vulnerability of the nuclear family in our highly mobile industrialized culture is largely responsible for the preponderance of both schizoid and oral issues in psychotherapy clients.

The young infant is, of course, oblivious to these sociological insights. He knows only that he hurts, physically or emotionally, and that the hurt is not being relieved. Bowlby (1973, p. 23) writes, "whether a child or adult is in a state of insecurity, anxiety, or distress is determined in large part by the accessibility and responsiveness of his principal attachment figure." In studying children separated from their mothers, Bowlby has observed a three-stage reaction process in which the infant first protests acutely, second, falls into deep despair, and third, finally gives up and becomes superficially adjusted but detached. In the third phase of the process, the child will respond to the mother's return by either not recognizing her or retreating from her. This will be followed by a period of marked ambivalence toward the mother for some period of time after the reunion.

We may extrapolate from these observations to hypothesize that the infant, repeatedly left or disappointed, will eventually do whatever he can to adapt to the disappointment or abandonment. Chronic upset, protest, and despair are too painful to live with. The infant (or his ego if you prefer) will try to find a compromise solution to deal with the pain and heartbreak of abandonment or chronically unmet needs. As with every character structure, the self-negation begins when the natural response to chronic frustration becomes too much to bear. At this point, the child looks for ways to cut off his own natural organismic self-expressions to stop the pain. In the oral case this step very logically becomes, "If I don't *need* anything, I can't be frustrated." This stoic position, while somewhat satisfactory in lessening immediate pain, is not very realistic for a totally dependent being. Other maneuvers must be sought to complete the compromise.

The anthropologists of infancy have given us clues concerning the types of ego defense available at various developmental stages. In summarizing this work, Blanck and Blanck (1974) have outlined the defensive concerns and functions available to children at six to nine months of age—the period when maternal separation seems to produce the full loss reaction just outlined. According to this summary, the child's primary anxiety response at this time shifts from the fear of annihilation to the fear of the loss of the caregiving object. Additionally, to the earlier available defense mechanisms of projection, introjection, and denial are added the defensive functions of identification, displacement, reversal, and turning against the self. With all of these abilities available at a primitive level, the oral child begins to develop his defense against the pain of needs unmet.

The first step, to repeat, is the denial of need. That is the central element in the self-negation process of oral character development. The person literally *contracts against* his own need. "If my need makes me hurt, I will stop needing." By limiting breathing, activity, and output of energy, the oral child will, in fact, need less input. This solution, which chooses depression over expression, will result in the low level chronic depression which is often definitional of the oral character. However, still more must be done because the needs still exist. The more evolved defense mechanisms provide ways for either bootlegging the gratification of the need while denying it or controlling the natural rage which the chronic frustration has created.

Let us briefly define these defensive functions.

Identification: The process by which one either blurs or eliminates the distinction between self and others by extending his identity into another, borrowing his identity from another, or fusing identity with another.

Displacement: The process by which the direction of feeling is transferred from one object to another — the substitution of one object for another as the target of feeling.

Reversal: In classical analytic theory this is an instinctual vicissitude by which an energetic expression is reversed to its opposite. Through this mechanism, hate may change to love, sadism to masochism, longing for an object to rejection of that object, and so on. Reaction formation is a defense mechanism which is based on this process.

Turning Against the Self: Another instinctual vicissitude described by Freud (1915) which is used to explain the phenomenon often observed in obsessional neuroses in which a person directs his hatred inward against himself. The desire to retaliate becomes the propensity to self-torture.

You will notice that all four of these defensive functions rely on the individual's ability to substitute one object with another (identification, displacement, and turning against the self) or to substitute or replace one feeling for another (reversal). This ability to change the object or reverse the drive can explain many of the oral's ego defense maneuvers which have been observed by the characterological theorists (e.g., Lowen, 1958). An understanding of these defensive maneuvers will do much in assisting your comprehension of the oral adult to be described presently.

Irrespective of the cognitive defenses chosen to resolve the conflicts, the child, unable to be satisfied in symbiotic attachment, moves prematurely to individuation. Typically, the oral child walks and talks early, embracing activities which will gain him attention and provide independence from one who cannot give what is really needed. The second subphase of individuation, practicing, includes some pretty high times during which many wonderful discoveries are made. The infant can do many new things and explore the wide world with a beginner's mind. This is a manic time and a time of natural grandiosity and narcissism. "So what if mama isn't here, look what I can do. I don't need her. Let the good times roll." The despair is escaped in the elation of individuating and moving out into the world. Such is the beginning of the manic defense, grandiosity, and narcissism that characterize many an oral character.

In a heretofore unpublished paper, Dr. Alan Levy has presented a most lucid description of oral character development. With the use of musical lyrics, he has delineated and illustrated the sequential development of this character structure by amplifying on the classic character analytic outline presented in chapter I: self-affirmation process, negative environmental response, self-negation process, and adjustment process in the oral case. With his permission I reproduce it for you here to enhance both your understanding and feel for the oral dilemma. To assist your understanding of the dynamics of the oral character, you might find it useful to see how many of the defensive functions you can find in the adjustment processes as outlined by Dr. Levy.

THE LOVE SONG OF THE ORAL*

> Where do I begin . . . to tell the story that is older than
> the sea? . . . the simple truth about the love she
> brings to me . . .   — *Love Story*

Self-Affirmation Process

The story starts immediately at birth. Contact with mother's warm, giving body is all that the newborn organism has to replace their confluence, the previous totally dependent, symbiotic connection. From its very core, the

---

*A musically illustrated story of oral character development, presented to the Southern California Bioenergetics Society Basic Training Group by Alan W. Levy, Ph.D., September 15, 1975. More musical illustrations were contained in the original paper.

neonate says "I need you" by virtually sucking in all of the emotional and physical nourishment that it possibly can absorb. Research findings amply demonstrate that bodily intimacy is essential to the neonate's survival.

> I'll get by, as long as I have you . . .
> Tho there be rain and darkness too,
> I'll see it thru
>
> — *I'll Get By*

Without that vital maternal closeness, the newborn would die. Such contact is more than vital to life; it is also pleasurable and is the prototype for the development of the capacity for affection and sexuality. There are many ways to express the relationship between pleasure at the breast and the experience of being loved. Here is but one:

> Warm . . . touching warm, reaching out, touching me, touching you . . .
>
> — *Sweet Caroline*

To the neonate, mother is the world. When she really is there, the experience of the contact merges on the miraculous, perhaps the closest event to paradise on earth!

> I have seen so many wonders. . .
> But I haven't seen anything to match
> the wonder of a mother's love.
>
> — *A Mother's Love*

Negative Environmental Response

But all too often, the paradise is lost. The environment deprives the baby of the vital contact. Mother is not there enough when needed, is there but ignores or can't respond, or leaves precipitously, and the infant is abandoned and helpless.

> Close to my heart she came, only to fly away . . .
> Now, I'm alone, still dreaming of paradise,
> Still saying that paradise once nearly was mine.
>
> — *This Nearly Was Mine*

Organismic Reaction

Remembering the pleasure and experiencing the pain of the loss, the baby naturally cries out for mother's return.

> When I remember every little thing you used to do,
>   I'm so lonely . . .
> . . . and while I'm waiting here, this heart of mine is singing;
>   Lover, come back to me.
>
> — *Lover Come Back to Me*

When mother does return, the infant has some difficulty settling down and trusting that she is there as long as she is needed. Separation anxiety is heightened; the baby clings tightly, mistrusting and fearful of the next possible abandonment.

> If you go away, as I know you must,
>   There'll be nothing left in the world to trust,
> Just an empty room, full of empty space . . .
>   . . . and I tell you now as you turn to go,
>   I'll be dying slowly 'til your next hello . . .
>
> — *If You Go Away*

The next time mother leaves, the frightened, hungry organism reacts with rage.

> Blast your hide, hear me call!
> Must I fight City Hall?
> Here and now, damn it all, come back to me!
>
> — from *A Clear Day*, "Come Back to Me"

Repeated Negative Environmental Response

If the organismic reaction of hungry rage is met with acceptance and nurturance, the desperation of the loss is only temporary and growth can continue. But if, as is often the case, the deprivation of the contact is maintained to the point of exhaustion of the crying-out energy, a chronic form of despair develops. It is as if the organism lives in a perpetual state of mourning.

Self-Negation Process

The baby now is in a dilemma. The pain of the despair is too much to live with, and each time the need for contact is felt, the discomfort returns. Yet there is no replacement for mothering. Since the neonate cannot discriminate between the experience inside its body and its experience of the external environment, the hunger sensations are perceived as the enemy. To survive, the infant must negate its own needy feelings, taking the retroflective position: "I don't need."

> What a fool I was . . . to think you were the earth and sky . . . No, you are not the beginning and the end . . . I shall not feel alone without you. I can stand on my own without you . . . I can do bloody well without you.
>
> — *Without You*

And the developing person learns to *contract against* the need rather than *reach out* with it. This leaves him with limited capacity to take in nourishment from the world, a state of chronic hunger and loneliness, yet caught between the despair of the unfilled emptiness and the fear of exposing it and being abandoned again for "being too needy." Limited intake and output of energy is part of the attempted solution; depression is a frequent consequence.

> Broken windows and empty hallways, a pale dead moon in a sky streaked with gray. Human kindness overflowing, and I think it's going to rain today . . .
>
> — *I Think It's Going to Rain Today*

Adjustment Process

The collapse into depression must be coped with in order to somehow adjust to the demands of the external world. It is as if the ego says to the collapsed, undercharged body, "We can't live this way." And, one popular form of compensatory maneuver is to act out the fantasies of oral fulfillment — the good life of overconsumption of food, drink, drugs, etc., an infantile attempt to recapture the sweetness of the nursing experience.

> Who can take tomorrow, dip it in a dream,
>   separate the sorrow and collect up all the cream?
> The candy man can . . . 'cuz he mixes it with
>   love and makes the world taste good . . .
>
> — *Candy Man*

Another ego illusion is the promise of fulfillment through material security, the ever-present "good life" fantasy.

> All I want is a room somewhere . . . with one
>   enormous chair . . . lots of chocolates for
>   me to eat, lots of coal making lots of
>   heat . . . oh, wouldn't it be loverly!
>
> — *Wouldn't It Be Loverly,* from *My Fair Lady*

The light of reality dawns, and it turns out that dreams of oral goodies or material security provide no real adult satisfaction.

> I have almost everything a human could desire,
> Cars and houses, bearskin rugs to lie before my fire,
> But there's something missing,
> It seems I'm never kissing the one whom I could care for.
>
> — *Something to Live For*

The fundamental attitude is one of dependency. The oral character knows how to wait, to long for someone to bring love to him/her, and to cling to the supplier when they find one, so as not to feel the loneliness. The result of the clinging is advertised as happiness, but the passive dependency wears through in the highly variable mood swings which are sometimes characteristic.

> Sometimes I'm happy, sometimes I'm blue.
> My disposition depends on you.
> I never mind the rain from the skies
> if I can find the sun in your eyes . . .
>
> — *Sometimes I'm Happy*

Another way to cope with the desperate longing for that "special someone" and the despair of his ever coming is to bravely resolve to "go it alone," to make an ego virtue of the self-denial.

> Easy to be a man alone,
> Just make the whole wide world your only home.
> Don't talk to strangers, someone might be kind
> And muddle up your mind.
>
> — *A Man Alone*

If someone happens to be kind and offers contact which confounds that brave resolve, the ego has to work out a creative compromise to deny the need to be loved and meet it at the same time. How? By taking an interpersonal stance of "giving and caring," a way to get vicarious mothering by ministering to others. And the target person had better respond well, or else the original loss and depression will return.

> Come to me, my melancholy baby.
> Cuddle up and don't be blue.
> Every cloud must have a silver lining,
> wait until the sun shines through.

> Smile, my honey dear, while I kiss away each tear
> Or else I shall be melancholy too.
>
> — *Melancholy Baby*

In this "mothering" personality, happiness is perceived as the assurance of never being along again — the avoidance of another abandonment. A preferred means of both guaranteeing the needed contact and avoiding being left alone is finding someone who truly needs them. But that illusion, as powerful as it is, eventually breaks down when the "melancholy baby" grows out of the dependency or is less than grateful and the vicarious feeding process no longer seems to promise fulfillment. The disillusionment is real; the sadness and longing of the inner child cry out:

> Sometimes I feel like a motherless child . . .
> A long way from home.
>
> — Odetta, *A Motherless Child*

And, for the love story of the oral character to have a satisfying ending, it must come full circle — a return to the mourning process, reexperiencing the loss of the contact with mother and the resulting fear, longing, rage, and hard work to increase the body's capacity to reach, take in, and discharge the energy needed for the person's own adult loving to emerge.

BEHAVIOR, ATTITUDE, AND FEELING

Essentially, the oral character develops when the longing for the mother is denied before the oral needs are satisfied. The unconscious conflict, then, is between need on the one hand and the fear of repeating that awful disappointment on the other. The characteristic behaviors, attitudes, and feelings you will see in the person will depend on the severity of the oral issue and on the current effectiveness of the defensive structure. Because most people seek out a therapist when their defenses are overwhelmed, you may first be made aware of the symptomatic behavior and history of the abandoned child.

Though depression occurs in other character structures and is not definitional of orality, episodes of depression always occur where there is a significant oral component. A history of major depressive disorder or dysthymic disorder is common as is cyclothymic disorder and even manic-depressive disorder. The depressions of oral characters can be distinguished somewhat from those of other character types in that they usually hit harder and are often accompanied by more exhaustion, despair, and longing. While some will present a chronic unipolar depression, these people usually show greater fluctuation than the other character types. They can often sustain a normal or even supernormal level of activity, which may extend to manic proportions. Sooner or later, however, they run out of the synthetic fuel which moves them and they crash deeply, sometimes for an extended period. The oral character is essentially an undernourished organism with a depleted life force. The mania is an attempt to deny this and to avoid confronting the underlying despair and longing. As one might suspect, abandoned children tend to get sick a lot for several reasons. First, they have not internalized self-caring functions very well, second, the ungrounded periods of elation or mania deplete their resources, and third, sickness is a socially acceptable and ego-syntonic bid for attention and nurturance.

The oral character also has real difficulty in sustaining an adult adjustment to work, family, and personal management. The oral person simply grew up too soon, and in every such personality there is an underlying *resentment* about having to grow up and assume adult responsibilities. Unconsciously, the abandoned child wishes to be taken care of and feels the world still owes him a living. Though he may jam his system into overdrive to accomplish an adult adjustment, he secretly wishes he could just stay in bed and be fed. The demands of a job, spouse, children, home, personal and financial matters are just *too much*. In part because he is working overtime to do what he can to meet these demands, he is often reluctant to accept responsibility for his failures. He often sees himself as misunderstood, persecuted, and unappreciated.

Because the oral person has essentially given up, both assertiveness and aggression are weak. He does not adequately arrange his life or aggressively set out to make it work. He does not reach out for what he needs and cannot easily ask for things. Nor can he refuse to give what is asked of him. He can wait and long for life to come to him, but he cannot reach out for it or seize it. He can resent that it does not come to him, but he cannot express the rage which he feels. Consequently, the oral person often shows a hyperirritability. Lowen (1958) has likened this to the condition of an unripened fruit. Separated from the tree too early, it is sour, hard, and bitter, missing the juicy sweetness that maturity would have provided.

I have most consistently seen all of these characteristics represented in people referred to me for psychological evaluation after an injury, often job-related, which fails to heal or ameliorate as expected. In these cases, the attending physician suspects a "psychological overlay" to the original problem. Very often I find a history of abandonment, repeated loss of the original attachment figure, or chronic lack of nurturance in childhood. Coupled with this is often a history of overwork and excessive responsibility, dating back to adolescence or before. There is often a not entirely unjustified seething resentment of the people for whom the person has worked, as well as for the doctors who cannot heal the injury. There is usually a passive or unassertive stance with regard to the injury, such that the responsibility for it is given over entirely to the doctors and there is little or no pursuit of self-healing.

These people typically really do hurt a great deal, but because they are hard to help and because they are passive-aggressive and complaining, they are usually disliked by their doctors and are not given the sympathetic ear they require. Their referral to me is often a "dump" by a frustrated physician which the patient in pain resents. Being able to really hear of the patient's pain and frustration and to acknowledge its reality has been the single most valuable response in negotiating this initially difficult contact.

All oral characters hurt and they need to be heard in their pain and despair. In this particular symptomatic expression of orality, it often appears that the person has overworked himself until he breaks at his weakest point, most often the lower back. The break or injury gives him an honorable discharge from the resented demands of adult life, which were always really too much. Because he is sick or in pain, he can get caring and nurturance without asking. Through workers' compensation and other programs, he may finally be provided the living which he unconsciously believes is owed to him. He has found a compromise solution which satisfies many conflicting demands. All he must do to sustain that solution is to stall his recovery. But to maintain his self-respect he must really hurt, and he does.

The oral character has many problems in love relationships. When she is not well-defended, or when her defenses are not working, the oral will lose herself in love. When the hope of finding the paradise lost is rekindled, the person will dissolve into the symbiosis. Her mate will complain that he feels suffocated and annoyed by this clinging behavior. The person may complain of loss of identity in relationships and will discontinue those activities which cannot be shared with the mate. Even though the oral may superficially offer a great deal of nurturance, her mate will often feel drained or sucked by the implicit demands for attention.

Sexual problems are common. The sex drive, like the essential life force, is weak in the oral character. There is a much greater need for touching, snuggling, and contact than for genital sexuality. The symbiotic nature of the relationship, which the oral craves and produces, dampens sexual passion. When the differences between man and woman are dissolved in the symbiotic relationship and when aggression and assertion are muted, passion of all kinds is suppressed and sex virtually disappears. A symbiotic relationship is a relationship without difference. Sexuality implies a set of differences too threatening to the symbiotic attachment. Oral women are frequently preorgasmic, and oral men often show a diminished sexual urge or a sexual urge which disappears once the early seductive phases of a relationship are passed. In the oral, commitment equals symbiosis and symbiosis kills sex.*

The abandoned child brings with her the fear of future abandonment in love relationships. She usually has terrible problems with loneliness and out of loneliness may prematurely rush into inappropriate relationships. Her fear of abandonment may fuel problems of jealousy or frequent panic attacks at any sign of possible abandonment. A mate's harmless roving eye or his failure to appear on time or to phone frequently or as expected may precipitate panic for which the mate is often held entirely responsible. The oral may project her propensity to leave the relationship when it is troubled onto her mate and thereby see imminent desertion when this has not occurred to the mate. As in every other character structure, we are inclined to do to others what was originally done to us. Congruent with this formula, the oral character is prone to abandoning those to whom she gets close. Because she suppresses assertion and aggression, loses herself in the relationship, gives more than she really wants to, and finds the demands of an adult relationship "too much," she builds resentment and becomes

---

*I would like to again credit Ed Muller for this most helpful insight.

irritable. She then either gives up and withdraws or arranges for her own desertion. In the words of Jackson Browne:

> When you see through love's illusion there lies the danger
> And your perfect lover just looks like a perfect fool
> So you go running off in search of a perfect stranger
> While the loneliness seems to spring from your heart like a
>   fountain from a pool
> Fountain of sorrow, fountain of light
> You've known the hollow sound of your own steps in flight.
>
> — Jackson Browne, *Fountain of Sorrow*

Particularly when not well-compensated, the oral has great difficulty with aloneness and may panic when alone or separated from his primary attachment figure. He may be prone to problematic behavior — particularly drug abuse or dependent behavior — at these times. The vicissitudes of early childhood development give some useful insights for understanding and dealing with these problems. By the fifth or sixth month of infant development, the child has formed a person-specific attachment and definitely realizes the difference between his primary attachment figure and others. "Eighth-month anxiety" refers to this discrimination such that the infant, at about eight months of age, displays anxiety or curiosity and wonderment when he is shifted from the mother or even the father to another adult for holding. At this point, he becomes more prone to separation anxiety than before.

At about this time, the infant begins to become attached to "transitional objects" (Winnicott, 1953). These objects, commonly teddy bears and blankets in this culture, tend to partially allay separation anxiety and to take the place of the mothering figure during her absences. Children tend to give up these objects as they become more secure in their representation of the constancy of the primary attachment figures in their lives. Thus, when "object constancy" is more or less achieved, they give up the transitional object.

Such object constancy is never really achieved for the oral character; thus, the nature and role of transitional objects in his life can help in understanding and treating him. Often, those with orality issues are prone to develop very strong attachments to transitional objects, particularly those which make them feel better. Thus, I believe that great attachment to drugs of any kind can often be usefully understood as transitional object attachment. The fact that many drugs produce a physiologic dependence, as well as a psychological one, will enhance this effect. This kind of attachment exists not only for obvious recreational drugs like alcohol, tobacco, marijuana, and cocaine, but also for less obvious and culturally approved drugs such as caffeine and sugar. Characteristically, the oral character is prone to addictions of dependency and helping him to establish and then forego more benign transitional objects can be of great therapeutic utility.

When the oral character is well-compensated or defended, you will see a superficially effective person whose basic needs are not being met. His own need will be *denied* and *projected* onto others. He will tend to *identify* with the other melancholy babies of this world, and take care of them. He will probably be perceived as nurturing, generous, and soft. Alternatively, he may *displace* and compensate by the over-consumption of food, drink, or drugs in an attempt to easily alter the internal experience of loss, emptiness, and despair. This solution is closely associated with the *displacement* of the need for love from other people to the need to be surrounded by those material objects which, particularly in this culture, are believed to offer fulfillment.

Alternatively, the oral may *displace* his need for love and nurturance to a need for attention. Many clinicians have observed that oral people are often verbally bright and talkative, using this facility to gain attention and recognition. But, as any star will tell you, the satisfaction to be had from this source is nonsustaining.

> A legend's only a lonely boy when he goes home alone.
>
> — Carly Simon, *Legend in Your Own Time*

Attention, in the liberal doses which the celebrities of our culture get, becomes an annoying burden. Prior to realizing fame, however, it is tempting to sustain the illusion that it will eventually fill the emptiness.

Through *reversal*, the oral person transmutes his essentially infantile, selfishly narcissistic, irresponsible, and bitter real self into a much easier-to-sell package. He often gets support for his exaggerated nurturing, which is unconsciously demanding, or for his exaggerated responsibility, which is unconsciously resented. Where this false self is well-established and highly supported, it may take serious illness or injury to uncover the real self which has been rejected and suppressed. By contracting against his own need, the oral has turned against himself. He despises the natural neediness which is his real self. The anger, which really belongs to the abandoning or withholding parent, has been *denied* and *turned against the self*, maintaining the compromise that is the false self. Thus, the oral character's ability to reverse, displace or substitute one object for another or one drive for another is a key to understanding his defensive structure. In treatment, it will be an essential key to unlocking his real self and his real feelings. The oral's problems tend to be cyclical and he usually will shuttle back and forth between compensation and collapse in the course of treatment. For his therapist, it will be important to understand the nature of the cycles and to keep him in treatment when it appears that the compensation is once again working or when he is in the manic phase of new or rekindled love when he is inclined to think that the promise of symbiosis will conquer all.

The accompanying table, though oversimplified, describes what you will see with the oral character in his collapsed versus his compensated condition. Though you may see a few clients whose collapse is chronic or some people whose oral issues are so minor that they can maintain fairly reliable compensations, the more typical pattern is one of fluctuation between the compensated and collapsed conditions. This is, of course, most obvious in manic-depressive patients or in those clearly demonstrating a cyclothymic disorder. Like all the rest of us, the oral character is attached to his ego defenses and is particularly enamored with himself in the elated phase of his mood swing. He is not easy to help in that phase, but analysis of his grandiosity and the pattern of his mood swings can assist in this part of the ongoing treatment. He is also not easy to help when he has shut off all feeling, become depressed, withdrawn, self-absorbed, helpless, and victimized, as summarized in the top section of the table labeled "Oral Collapsed." He can most reliably be helped when the real despairing and longing emerges, motivating him at last to reach for help and take responsibility for change. Helping him to reach this uncomfortable yet hopeful place is a central goal of treatment.

It is in the course of treatment that the oral's secrets will begin to emerge. As his own neediness, weakness, and self-centeredness are uncovered, he will experience the depth of his self-hatred. Unlike the schizoid, the oral experiences self-hate less as an alien force which overcomes him and more as a conscious loathing of the weak and depend-

Table
EXPRESSIONS OF ORALITY

	Oral Collapsed	Oral Compensated
Affect (feeling)	Depressed or *Lonely, despairing, and longing	Conscious: Good to elated to manic euphoria. Unconscious: Resentful, enraged, despairing, and fearful of loss.
Behavior	Withdrawn, self-absorbed, irresponsible, dependent, complaining, lacking energy or *Reaching for help	Overly nurturing of others. Takes on more responsibility and independent action than can be sustained. Makes plans which are optimis- tic to grandiose or unrealistic. Charged with ungrounded energy. Cares for self poorly—poor diet and sleep habits, overworks, plays too hard, excessive drug use.
Cognition (attitude)	Helpless and victimized or *Motivated to change	Conscious: Optimistic to grandiose Preconscious: "I am sweet, soft, and entirely giving. I am needed." Unconscious: Self-deprecating; "If I need, I will be despised or abandoned."

*Position from which most dramatic change can be initiated.

ent person he feels himself to be. The hatred is not so much an unassimilated introject, as in the schizoid case, but more a redirection of
his own hatred for the mother to himself. He may admit to long-
standing fear of "needing too much" and to the script decision, "If I
need too much I will be despised and abandoned." Frozen in his response to the symbiotic withdrawal, he is still enraged, despairing, and
fearful of further loss. That "intense and violent hatred for the mother"
of which Bowlby (1960, p. 24) speaks has been denied and turned
against the self. The oral character is in the classic depressive position
in which feelings of love and hate have been directed at the same object (the mother). The hatred has blocked the love and the love has

been instrumental in blocking the hatred. With the affect depressed, there is a consequent depression. Typically, the oral person, whose ego ideal is invested in his loving, caring, and soft nature, is alarmed by the seething rage which he finds within. As with the schizoid character, uncovering these unconscious beliefs and feelings and releasing the physical and cognitive blocks to expression constitute the road home.

There is a good deal of similarity between the issues of the oral and schizoid character, as well as a tendency for those with oral issues to have schizoid issues and vice versa. Indeed, clinicians who use the character analytic approach will often refer to their "oral-schiz" cases in conference with their peers. It is obvious that a child who is un-wanted or despised will often be poorly nurtured. Similarly, when a child is too much for the parent, as in the oral case, the child's very existence confronts the parent with his limitations. That child may then well be the target of the parent's rage as that unwanted limitation is experienced by the parent. Both oral and schizoid characters have their primary difficulty in the attachment process and experience consequent difficulties in later attachments. Both tend to be weaker, more vulner-able, and less well-nourished than the character types which are created later in the developmental process.

Because of these similarities and overlaps, it may be useful, for educa-tional purposes, to summarize the differences in etiology, behavior, attitude, and feeling. Where the schizoid's issue involves existence and survival, the oral's involves need. In other words, the oral character has relatively little concern about his right to exist and less worry over survival issues, but is more concerned with his right to need and with finding or losing his major attachment figure. As stated earlier in reviewing object relations theory, the primary anxiety shifts from the fear of annihilation in the initial developmental period to the fear of the loss of the love object. Because the oral has experienced greater attachment, he is more contactable and open, less distanced or de-tached. While the denial of aggression is central in both characters, the oral has more access to feelings. Even with the aggressive impulse, there is generally more accessibility to it in the oral through conscious bitterness and resentment.

Having evolved to a higher level of ego development before the character-shaping trauma occurred, the oral is more sophisticated in his defenses, employing more reversal, displacement, and identification. There is more poignancy and drama in his life and, except in collapsed depression, less deadness. Along with this, the oral is more prone to affective mood swings than is the schizoid. At a core cognition level, the difference is highlighted in the core script decisions: In the schizoid, "There is something wrong with me. I have no right to exist." In the oral, "I mustn't need too much. I must do it alone." In addition, of course, there are also the similarities and differences in energetic expression, which are dealt with in the next section.

ENERGETIC EXPRESSION

Here I will present the observations of a number of bioenergetic therapists on the bodily consequences of the oral etiology. The proposition is that, in the process of self-negation, the person will constrict those muscles which will restrain the natural, spontaneous, original self-expression, as well as the innate emotional reaction to the environmental negativity. For the most part, the bodily consequences of character development are a consequence of the self-negation process. To a much lesser extent, they may also be reflective of the adjustment process, such that the individual changes himself, particularly in the more developed character structures, to present the image of his ego ideal to the world in the form of an adjustment mask.

As you will recall, the oral, as a part of the self-negation process, must inhibit his awareness and expression of need. In addition, he must suppress all of his natural and spontaneous reactions to having his needs unmet. Thus, in order to get on with life, he must suppress his rage at being abandoned or unfulfilled, his eventual and profound despair at that reality, and his fear of being abandoned again, either literally or emotionally. One of the simplest ways to achieve the suppression of all feeling, as has been outlined for the schizoid, is to simply restrict breathing. Many bioenergetic therapists have noticed that those with oral histories tend to do this by pulling the shoulders forward, thereby effecting a constricted and sunken chest, with frequent actual depression in the region of the sternum. As a consequence, as depicted in Figure 6, the oral appears to have a collapsed chest and rounded shoulders.

Beyond this generalized restriction in breathing, the oral character demonstrates his inability to reach out on a concrete body level. Characteristically, there is a great deal of chronic tension in the entire shoulder girdle region and accompanying tension in the upper back between the shoulder blades. If you assume this posture, collapsing the chest and rolling the shoulders forward, you will find that your head naturally goes forward so that, as in Figure 6, you are "leading with your head."

Next, to inhibit the crying and despair even further, the oral person will tense the lower abdominal muscles to restrain the sobbing and tighten the muscles at the base of the neck and up to the jaw. These energetic changes also serve to suppress aggressive impulses and fear. The tension in the shoulder girdle, upper back, and pectorals inhibit striking out, as well as reaching out, as the constriction around the base of the neck and in the jaw inhibit the direct expression of aggression. The inhibition of breathing inhibits the experience of fear itself, as does the clamping of the jaw.

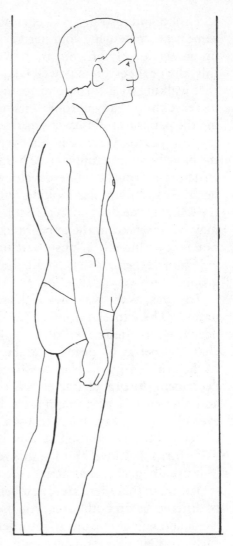

Figure 6. The oral posture

If you experiment by taking the position described and portrayed in Figure 6, you will experience that the oral character is in a difficult and uncomfortable position. Intake of the most basic environmental supply has been limited and expression constrained and held in. Chronic tension and restraint take energy, yet little is being supplied. At the same time, in denying your need and dependence you must now stand up independently on your own two feet and get on with life. To do this, the oral person may well walk prematurely and brace himself in that walking by a chronic stiffening in the knees. Such stiffening will increase the already chronic tension in the lower back, thereby causing the pelvis to roll forward as depicted in Figure 6. Typically, then, the oral person is weak in his overall muscular development. While the basic bone structure may be normal or even elongated, the muscular structure is typically underdeveloped. His legs are typically not solid, healthy, and muscular-looking but rather weak and even thin. Like the schizoid, he does not feel in solid contact with the ground and that may be observed in the appearance of his legs. Given all of this, the oral is quite literally a "pushover" in the world. In the posture pictured in Figure 6, the person can quite literally be pushed backwards off his ground with very little effort.

The eyes, as the windows of the soul, betray the oral character's true nature. The expression in the eyes has variously been described as needy, sympathetic, soulful, even begging. As the eyes of the schizoid character betray his deadness and withdrawal from the world, the eyes of the oral betray his true neediness. However giving or strongly independent the oral character may strive to be, this dependent posture and obvious lack of strength in the body and longing expression in the eyes give him away. He is really a pushover, weak, needy, and self-centered. He hates himself for this, but is still looking for someone who will affirm and love him for this real self—a very tall order.

It usually proves instructive to compare the schizoid and oral body structure, in that there are a number of similarities as well as a number of differences. In both cases, you are dealing with individuals who are weak and vulnerable due to insufficient acceptance and nurturing very early in their development. Both harbor fearful expectations of the world and are dealing with very strong negative feelings about what was done to them. In both, there is an inhibition of the life force and in breathing which sustains that force. There is a corresponding lack of firm grounding, concretely represented in weakness and stiffness in the feet and legs. Both character types tend to be prone to illness, psychosomatic or otherwise.

The classic oral energetic expression does, however, differ in several ways from that of the schizoid. The oral's musculature tends to be more flaccid and less defined than the schizoid's, which can appear contracted, compact, stiff, and dead. While the eyes of the schizoid betray the withdrawal and even shock of the hated child or the frozen terror with which he must deal, the eyes of the oral tend to betray his need, longing, and despair. The oral's eyes signal that he is more contactable—more able to establish and maintain attachment. The oral is, in short, more "there" than the schizoid. The distortion in the oral's posture, marked most obviously by the forward thrust of the head and pelvis, is more obvious than the schizoid's typical distortion. As mentioned earlier, however, these distinctions are often more academic than real, in that the oral and schizoid issues often coexist in the same person.

As mentioned in the last section, the oral character is, like the schizoid, prone to illness. Because of the general weakness of the person, deficiencies in self-nurturing, and the tendency to mania which overwhelms the already fragile body defenses, the oral person tends to get sick a lot. She is susceptible to infection and illness generally, yet there are areas of particular vulnerability. Because of the tension in the base of the neck and jaw, there is a susceptibility to headache. The constriction of breathing, as well as the general weakness of the person, makes the oral character particularly susceptible to upper respiratory difficulties and infection. Because there is chronic tension in the lower back and lower abdominal region, there is a propensity toward low back pain or injury and lower abdominal illness such as irritable bowel syndrome, spastic colitis, etc. Because of the chronic spasticity in the shoulder girdle and upper back region, there is a susceptibility to pain, injury, or spinal subluxation in this region. Finally, because of the weakness in the legs and tendency to lock the knees, there is an increased susceptibility to knee injuries. Because of all of this, and the additional secondary gain features of illness, the oral character is often perceived as sickly, hypochondriacal, and psychosomatic.

THERAPEUTIC OBJECTIVES

Affect and Sensation

In this section, I will discuss the therapeutic objectives for the oral character involving emotions and the body. It will be critical, in the case of the oral, to release for experience and expression both the denied needs and those suppressed emotions which resulted from a chronic frustration of those needs. To effect and support that, it will also be necessary to change the person's experience of his body such that, for example, he experiences his feet and legs as solidly supportive and his body as able to fully breathe, relax, and let go of the chronic tension.

The oral person will be threatened by the emergence of his own neediness. When experiencing it he will often say, "God, I hate that feeling. It is degrading and humiliating. No one wants a baby." The emergence of the real need threatens the entire compensatory adjustment with its associated self-concepts, philosophies, and coping behaviors. Working through the resistance at all levels to the real underlying need will be a crucial part of the therapy of the oral character.

Though the liberation of the neediness will be central, it is often not the place to begin because of the understandably massive resistance to its experience. Indeed, it is often in the process of liberating other feelings for experience and expression that the underlying theme of pervasive neediness will be realized. The abandoned child may most easily be reached affectively by hearing his complaints and sympathizing with his pain and sorrow, which will eventually grow in therapy to deep despair at the chronic disappointment of unmet needs. Very often he will suppress his complaining in other contexts, either because he has himself turned against such overt display of weakness or because others are simply sick and tired of hearing his whining. An accepting and sympathetic ear will be greatly appreciated and begin the process of affective expression, which will lead to reclaiming the self.

Although there is a great deal of resistance to accessing the deep rage in the oral character, its not-so-distant cousins, resentment and irritability, are usually readily available. These sparks can be judiciously fanned and the resulting flames of anger can be nurtured until a raging fire of hostility is eventually uncovered. Along this path, major resistance will also be elicited because of the deep denial of this affect and the person's great investment in seeing himself as benevolent, loving, and all-nurturing.

Throughout the release of all of these feelings, the person with an oral issue will encounter fear. The experience and release of the neediness, rage and despair will all elicit the fear of rejection and abandonment. Not without reason, the oral fears, "No one will want anybody who is this needy, hostile and desperately unhappy."

The oral person is correct in concluding that he must "grow up." Yet to do that fully, she must not skip maturational steps, as she has before. She must not try to sprint before she can walk. She must be nurtured, learn to bring the nurturing of others to her directly and, of course, learn to nurture herself.

The oral, like the schizoid, must develop *understanding*—both literally and figuratively. On a sensory level, this translates into reducing the chronic holding in the legs and arms and working a good deal on simple grounding and strengthening exercises like those described for the schizoid case. Additional work to strengthen the general musculature and accompanying sense of solidity, strength, and reliability in the functioning of the body will assist in this growing-up process. This grounding and general strengthening will serve to enhance experience and expression of the natural hostility, as well as strengthening the individual's healthy aggression and assertiveness. As this strengthening is accomplished, a therapist working on a body level will endeavor to release the spasticity in the lower back and abdomen, shoulder girdle, base of the neck, and jaw. Further, there will be repeated work on opening the chest, the breathing, and the energy flow through the neck and throat.

This general loosening and opening will usually begin to elicit the suppressed emotion without any other work on content. It is as if the suppressed emotions are locked in the chronic holding and tightness and are released through simple relaxation and breathing. When the body is nurtured, strengthened, and grounded in reality, when the breathing and natural flow of energy are opened through the body, and when the suppressed affects are released, the real loving of the oral person may begin to emerge and take on a more adult form. The oral person did make an attachment and, once the abandonment is worked through, he may begin to really trust again, grow up, individuate, and direct his love from a *differentiated self* to a *differentiated other*. Then, and only then, his legitimate adult needs can be met. He can be cared for and genuinely caring, dependent yet genuinely independent, relaxed and genuinely enthused about life.

Here in list form are the affective and body therapy objectives with the oral character:

1) Open the feelings of need and longing and assist the client in identifying with these feelings.

2) Work through the experienced sadness to the pain and deep despair at abandonment or chronic frustration.
3) Work through the rage at abandonment.
4) Work through the fear engendered by the release of all other feelings: the fear of rejection, abandonment, and continued frustration.
5) Develop a greater sense of grounding, strength, and clear energy flow in the feet, ankles, knees, and legs.
6) Strengthen the entire body and its overall musculature.
7) Strengthen assertive and aggressive expression.
8) Open the chest, the breathing, and the energy flow through the neck and throat.
9) Release the spasticity in the lower back and abdomen, shoulder girdle, base of the neck, and jaw.
10) Open the real love feelings, particularly for the central attachment figure, and develop the expression of this loving feeling.

Cognitive: Attitudes and Beliefs

It is perhaps most evident in the oral character case that the conscious attitudes and beliefs are polar opposites of the unconscious attitudes and beliefs. At a cognitive level, the therapist's job is to assist the client in identifying this polarity and developing mental understanding, insight, and knowledge about the self. Thus, the oral character must eventually realize that she prematurely contracted against her own infantile nature and developed a compensatory false self, offering to others what she did not receive. Though highly developed, and often quite effective externally, her nurturing nature is psychically an attempt to obtain nurturing either directly or vicariously. Her nurturing in very close relationships is often experienced as a demand.

The oral person may be helped to appreciate how she engineers or creates her own loneliness and even abandonment in relationships. She may be led to develop insight into her own script decisions, "I don't need. I have to do it alone. If I need I will be despised and abandoned." Further, she can be helped to appreciate how these script decisions fuel the "games" that she plays, which repeatedly justify the reassertion of these basic life decisions. Though she typically offers love and nurtur-

ance and though she can typically deliver what she didn't receive for
a while, her undercharged and basically infantile nature will eventually
assert itself and cause the breakdown of any steady, solidly grounded,
adult giving. The consequent collapse, dependency, clinging, and essentially self-centered behavior will eventually wear down the patience and
affection of friends, colleagues, and lovers to the point where she will
be rejected, abandoned, and frustrated again. Her demands, usually
unconscious, for unconditional, total acceptance and love are inappropriate for mutual adult functioning. Just as she fears, the neediness and
the collapse associated with it bring abandonment. Inevitably, they lead
to a reassertion of the essential script decision and of the compensatory
moves to grow up in order to be acceptable. The flight to compensation, then, sets up the progression toward collapse, and so on.

Insight into the cycle will prove to be a very useful tool for the adult
oral character. As this is done, the therapist can begin to work to
dismantle those defenses which fuel the compensation: denial, projection, introjection, reversal, identification, turning against the self, and
displacement. Always keeping in mind the oral's need for continued
acceptance and support, you can explain, challenge, confront, interpret, or otherwise undermine the defensive systems which keep the pattern going. These cognitive strategies related to insight about the cycle
are particularly useful during the excited or manic phase of the oral's
process if combined with physical grounding strategies.

As all of this is done, and as these insights are complemented by affective and behavioral changes, the oral person will begin to be able
to see herself as she really is. She will be able to admit to her infantile
and needy nature, knowing that she came by it honestly and acknowledging that she does need to grow up. She will identify with her history
of abandonment and chronically unmet needs. Knowing that these are
the wounds to be healed, she can more realistically devote herself to
the growing-up process. She will then not attempt to override her
vulnerability, but realistically work within her limitations, building her
strength, reality relatedness, and instrumental abilities.

Throughout this entire process, it will be important to repeatedly
affirm the oral's right to need and to strengthen the identification of
the self with those needs. In simple affirmation terms, we hope for the
oral person to achieve this: "I have the right to need. I have the right
to ask that my needs be met. I have the right to reach out and take

what I need, respecting the rights of others. I can take care of myself. I can be alone. I have the right to mourn the losses I have sustained. I can be strong. I am whole in myself. I have the right to want love and to love another."

When any of us come from our true ground, there is a fundamental solidity and strength in that. Even when that ground is as infantile and despairing as it is in the case of the classic oral character, there emerges a certain peace at knowing just what we are dealing with. No more energy need be wasted in maintaining the illusions, the suppression of affect, the maintenance of false ideals and hopes, and the continuance of poorly integrated behaviors. It may take many years, and perhaps more than a lifetime to repair the damage and realize the potential that living affords, but there is no longer the despair of false hopes forever unrealized. There can then be reasonably steady movement, growth, and maturation. With the early disappointments worked through and accepted, the disappointments are no longer repetitive and unabating. Then one can reach out for what is available under the circumstances, however limiting they may be, and live life from one's own realistic ground, whatever that is. This does not constitute a resignation to life; rather it represents an acceptance of an resolution with reality—a rapprochement. From that position, one can really live and appreciate life's tender mercies.

Like the schizoid, the oral also suffers from the good-bad split in his representation of self and other. This split is, of course, exemplified by the polarities he exhibits in his representation and feelings toward himself and others. The good self is independent, nurturing, active, and in other ways compensatory, while the bad self is needy, longing, despairing, unenergized, hostile and afraid. The good other is accepting, nurturing, attention-giving, and praising, while the bad other is rejecting, abandoning, and out to persecute the weaknesses. As with the schizoid character, a central cognitive objective will be to affect the ambivalent experience of the self such that the client is aware of his real assets and similarly cognizant of the difficulties with which he must deal. A related objective, of course, is ambivalent experience of the other, who can then potentially be truly loved as a differentiated person rather than merely as a source of narcissistic supplies.

Here in list form are the cognitive therapeutic objectives for the oral character:

1) Identify, interpret, develop insight into, and change the ego ideal or false self ("I am sweet, soft, and entirely giving. I am needed.").
2) Identify, interpret, develop insight into, and change the script decisions ("I don't need. I have to do it alone. If I need, I will be despised and abandoned.").
3) Challenge, interpret, or explain the defenses (denial, projection, introjection, reversal, identification, turning against the self, and displacement) to effect their flexibility.
4) Assist in the recognition of the pattern of compensation and collapse. Assist the person in identifying and cutting off that repetitive pattern through the acceptance of responsibility for it.
5) Strengthen the identification of the self with one's needs, affirming the right to need and to have those needs met.
6) Strengthen the identification of the self with the history of abandonment or unmet need and the resulting vulnerability. Affirm the individual's right to the natural feelings engendered by the abandonment—rage, despair, and fear.
7) Strengthen the identification of the self with the natural aggression and assertion.

Though the objectives involving attitudes and beliefs are considerably different for the schizoid and oral characters, the cognitive ego ability objectives are essentially the same in both character structures where they share a disruption in the early period of attachment formation. These are:

1) Promote or teach self-soothing and self-nurturing.
2) Establish an ambivalent experience of the self and others and discrimination between the self and others.
3) Assess and repair construct formation: assimilation, accommodation, discrimination, integration, and generalization.
4) Strengthen the voluntary use of existing defenses to the extent that these are productive and useful.
5) Teach ego defenses not yet learned.
6) Reinforce, repair, or teach strategies for dealing with harsh or anxiety-provoking environments.

Behavioral-Social Objectives

The behavioral-social objectives for the oral character derive directly from the affective and cognitive objectives and in some ways are repetitive of what has earlier been described. The difference, of course, is that in addressing yourself to behavioral objectives, you work directly to change behavior both in and, particularly, outside of therapy. This may, in classic behavioral tradition, be effected by direct suggestion or prescription or, in hypnotic tradition, through more indirect suggestion.

A number of discrete objectives can be derived from the simple knowledge that the oral person needs to do whatever he can to get his needs met. Because he has not internalized the self-caring functions very well, it is usually necessary to suggest and even prescribe the learning of self-caring behaviors. It may be useful to help him experience the fact that his "adult part" can care for, soothe, and nurture his "child." Together with this, a number of techniques can be used to strengthen his ability to reach out and ask for help or for what he needs in all relevant social relationships. He will probably need to be encouraged to develop his aggressive and assertive nature so that he may set up his life in a way that serves him.

A part of his growing up may involve the direct learning of various instrumental behaviors, which will allow him to get more of what he wants. Thus, acknowledging that he needs, claiming the right to need and to have his needs met, may not be enough. Because his development has been retarded, there may be many areas in which he has been waiting and longing to be given what he wants. Once his assertiveness is mobilized to solve his own problems, he may need to actively learn the skills he needs in order to achieve such a set of solutions. As he takes real responsibility for himself and his adult functioning in work, family, and personal management, he may need to simply learn strategies for coping with realistic adult demands. One of those demands will be to really face his own aloneness. Behavioral strategies may be used to increase his tolerance for simply being alone and being enough for himself.

One fundamental ingredient of all of this will be an increased constancy of commitment to work, relationships, child-rearing, personal projects, etc. As the oral grows up, he will need to develop simple "stick-to-itiveness." With regard to relationships of all kinds, but particularly close love relationships, he will need to work on developing mutuality and adult-adult forms of relating, which are individuated as opposed to symbiotic. Thus, he may need to learn very discretely and behaviorally to give *and* take rather than to simply give *or* take.

The oral character will also typically need some assistance to smooth out the cyclic manic-depressive pattern. Thus, when he is feeling good he needs to be discouraged from overwork, overexercise, excessive drug use, exaggerated responsibility and nurturing of others, and all other manic-like behaviors which exhaust him and propel him to collapse. He needs to learn to stay in touch with himself and recognize the real signs of increased fatigue or vulnerability and then to rest. The self-administration of body or relaxation techniques may be useful to him in smoothing out the cycles, such that he moderates his activity when feeling good and enjoys peaceful relaxation when fatigued or at rest. Teaching him to use direct techniques to experience his real feelings rather than collapsing into illness or depression will also smooth out the cycle and reduce the severity of his down times. Though this is an affective objective, it may be realized by directly teaching him the techniques for emotional access and expression. Thus, the therapist may give him something to do in order to *feel* and eventually *feel better*. A program of physical exercise may be particularly important for an oral person and constitutes a strategy of self-care and strengthening; further, exercise will discourage the drivenness in manic periods and bring him back to life in depressive ones.

In list form, here are the behavioral-social objectives for the oral character:

1) Strengthen or teach self-care and self-soothing strategies.
2) Strengthen reaching out and asking for help directly in social relationships.
3) Strengthen aggressive, assertive, and instrumental behaviors.
4) Increase reality relatedness to the demands of adult functioning; strengthen the constancy of commitment to work, relationships, individual projects, etc. Develop stick-to-itiveness.
5) Strengthen mutuality, adult-adult contact, and individuated (as opposed to symbiotic) arrangements in love relationships.
6) Increase tolerance for being alone.
7) Discourage overwork, excessive drug use, exaggerated respon-

sibility and nurturing, and other manic, self-destructive behaviors in the compensatory phase of the cycle.

As with every character structure, the oral's existence is devoted to
preventing what has already happened—abandonment. The very maneuvers engaged in to prevent it often recreate it, together with strengthening the characterological defenses to deal with the loss. The oral must
learn to stop abandoning herself, denying her needs and her natural
reactions to needs unmet. When this happens, she begins to grow up
by acknowledging what is infantile in her and caring for her own abandoned child. By taking responsibility in this way, she stops looking for
the lost mother and is able to receive adult love.

CHAPTER VI

HEALING THE
ABANDONED CHILD:
PART I

THERAPEUTIC NEEDS OF THE ORAL PATIENT

WHERE THE SCHIZOID patient most requires the therapist's presence or availability, the oral patient requires his attention and sympathy. The oral is typically a very sensitive individual who fares best in a supportive, sympathetic, and comfortable setting. You will get furthest with him by hearing the justice in his complaints and the realness of his pain. Therapy as a "holding environment" (Langs, 1976) is of particular importance to the oral person. He needs to know that you are on his side and that you will not abandon him before he can own his own longing, hostility, and infantilely narcissistic nature. He usually needs to complain and will feel much better if you can just listen and show that you hear him and understand. Any premature effort to point out his responsibility for difficulty or failure will fall on deaf ears and engender resentment, disrupting the necessary initial attachment. Ultimately, such confrontation will be necessary and will most likely lead to the very same reaction, but without disrupting the attachment or the therapeutic alliance.

In the course of early history-taking, it will be useful to encourage the expression of frustration and disappointment and assure him that he has the right to these most natural feelings. To the extent that there is a serious oral issue, the person has been trying to live an adult life with the emotional maturity of a 12- to 18-month-old child. It has been a difficult struggle indeed and your sympathy is warranted.

To the extent that you are still denying your own neediness, you will find this difficult. The disgust or rejection that you feel at your patient's weakness will be a signal of your own countertransference on that issue. It will be difficult for you to lead this person in the direction he needs to go until you come to terms with your own denied need. Counseling and psychotherapy are natural draws for the compensated oral character due to the closeness and opportunity for nurturing which they provide. If orality is an issue for you, on the way to its healing, you will need to be aware of the expression of countertransference in your relationship with oral clients and seek some supervisory assistance in dealing with it. The oral therapist, in her compensated phase, will have difficulty in helping the client acknowledge and support his own level of neediness and vulnerability. In her collapsed phase, the oral therapist will tend to use the client for support and foster dependency, retarding the client's adult growth and individuation. To be a "good enough" therapist you must work on any oral issues you have in your own therapy and supervision.

Just as you can make great initial strides with the oral person by supporting his right to express disappointment and sorrow, you can further the process by supporting his resentment and frustration. Though it will always be difficult to ascertain the degree to which he is a victim of the fallibility in others, you can initially support the fact that he feels victimized and affirm that he has the right to his feelings. In this way, you provide the joining and sympathy he requires without inadvertently reinforcing the irresponsibility which is probably there as well. Your joining him will tend to facilitate his spontaneous consideration of his own responsibility. Even if it does not, this early and consistent alliance with his right to feel whatever he feels will allow you to introduce insights about responsibility at a later time.

EARLY AFFECTIVE WORK

In initial verbal contact with the oral person, I have often found it useful to employ what I call the "Gestalt therapy frame" for determining the therapeutic flow. In the discussion of historical, contemporary, and immediate events, I encourage affective expression and stay tuned for the emotion that seems to be just below the conscious surface. I then guide the flow of the interaction to pull for that affect, being careful to maintain the supportive nature of the therapeutic context. Spotting the affect in question may be as simple as noticing the instant when a feeling begins to emerge and is blocked—noticing, for example, a slight clenching of the jaw or of the muscles at the base of the neck, a disruption in the regular pattern of breathing, or a looking away as an emotion begins to surface. You may then gently redirect the person's attention to that moment, literally or figuratively "touch" him in an attempt to encourage his continuing with the flow of his feelings, or simply ask him to breathe and relax, allowing the feelings to emerge.

If these most gentle interventions do not work, there are basically two alternatives. First, with more highly defended and rigid individuals who have been in treatment for a while, it may be quite useful to "up the ante" and involve them in more vigorous body therapy techniques, which will more decidedly release the block and pull for the feelings. Alternatively, and often very productively, you may simply ask the client to identify with the resistance and give voice to that part which resists the recognition and expression of feeling. As outlined in the treatment of the schizoid, this technique of identifying with the resistance and giving it a voice will, over time, lead to its relaxation as well as enhance appreciation for its function. When the feeling which has been held back just below the surface of consciousness is expressed, there is movement and release. There is also greater freedom in the body and receptivity to insight. As a result, the person feels better, usually immediately. This is important to anyone in the painful process of psychotherapy, but it is particularly necessary for the oral personality.

The oral's rage may be initially tapped in this way by nurturing the resentment, pulling for the anger, and ultimately calling up the enraged infantile affect carried in the body. Some initial resistance may be reduced with an intervention as innocuous as, "How would you feel about that if you were a less understanding and compassionate person?" Once the affect is elicited, the opportunity presents itself to explore its familiarity and uncover or interpret its original origins, "I have a sense that this is not the first time you have experienced this feeling, not the first time that you have been treated this way, not the first time you have hidden your natural feelings about this kind of frustration, even from yourself." Or, "Who else treated you this way? When have you felt this way before? Who else often felt the way you're feeling now?" Thus begins the elicitation and analysis of the oral's hostility, which will continue at higher and higher levels of intensity and meaning thoughout the entire course of treatment, augmented by such procedures as the persistent problem exercise outlined earlier (see p. 87) and vigorous body work on this affect.

Even this initial and relatively superficial early work on anger and hostility may lead to other important affective experiences. When the oral is given a sympathetic ear and empathic encouragement, the resentment, frustration, and even rage will flourish and sooner or later the person will experience hostile reactions that even he will perceive as out of proportion to the triggering circumstances. One possible therapeutic response to this rather predictable occurrence in therapy is the adoption of another variant of the "Gestalt frame." In this frame or orientation to emotional work, you assume that any exaggerated feeling is a "racket" feeling or cover for another affect which is denied, suppressed, or repressed. The therapeutic effort is aimed, of course, at uncovering the hidden or real feelings. In her book, *Self-Therapy* (1967), Muriel Schiffman outlines a five-step process which has a good deal in common with Eugene Gendlin's (1978) focusing process, although Schiffman emphasizes a slightly different outcome. I will first outline this process for your own use and then present an example of its use with an oral issue.

Schiffman's Hidden Emotion Process

Step 1. Recognize an inappropriate reaction

In general, an inappropriate reaction is any which seems disproportionate to the circumstances or in some sense "overdetermined." It is the kind of reaction which prompts you to ask yourself, "Now why am I feeling so angry or hurt?" You may try to talk yourself out of the inappropriate emotion by explaining to yourself, "After all, he's only a child; she's just a stranger who doesn't know how to drive a car; they're doing the best they can," etc. Yet, somehow the explanations don't work and the apparently overdetermined emotion persists without completion or resolution. These "racket feelings" tend to be characteristic of you and lead to obsessive preoccupation rather than affective release and completion. The persistence of the emotion and its failure to listen to reason signal its "racket" nature and suggest it as a productive target for the kind of work outlined here.

Step 2. Feel or recreate the apparent emotion

Dismiss all the reasons you shouldn't feel what you are feeling or have felt, and experience all the sensations and thoughts which accompany it. Allow yourself to indulge in its exaggeration and vent in fantasy or physical work the full depth of the experience. Allow the anger, anxiety, or despair to build. Again, the avoidance of inappropriate feelings often contributes to their maintenance. The recreation of the exaggerated feeling may be enhanced by talking through the triggering event in some detail or by altered state work in which you recapture all of the sights, sounds, sensations, and emotions which occurred in the original situation.

Step 3. Ask yourself, "What else did I feel?"

Another feeling, which you have skipped over quickly and neglected to develop may be available to you now. Usually, that other feeling was fleeting and occurred just before the apparent feeling. Schiffman (1967, p. 7) writes: "If you try, you can remember it, just as you can recall something you saw out of the corner of your eye, hardly realizing at the time you were seeing it." Often, this will be a feeling you are loathe to admit to, something that would be "wrong" to feel or inconsistent with your own view of yourself. Often, it is a feeling you would be ashamed of experiencing.

Step 4. Ask, "What does this remind me of?"

Here, as in the persistent problem exercise, you are looking for similar previous reactions, other situations or individuals who have elicited this same emotion or cover for the real emotion you have just uncovered. The objective of this step is less to elicit the pattern than to assist in eliciting the real feeling. Schiffman suggests at this point that if you have difficulty uncovering the real feeling you take a more objective viewpoint and ask, "What do I seem to be doing?" What is suggested here is that you try to see yourself as another would see you and ask what hidden emotion seems to be covered by this behavior. As in Gendlin's focusing process, the validity of an idea will come not from its plausibility but from the emotional reaction it engenders. In other words, you look for a *physical* change, that is, a change in breathing, pulse, level of arousal, etc. Thus, the intellectual suggestions will be taken over by the body and felt as true or real. Ultimately, there will be a congruent registration of the feeling so that you will feel comfortable in saying "Yes, that is it." Schiffman (1967, p. 7) lists two criteria for confirming that you have discovered the hidden emotion. "1) It is as intense as the apparent emotion you began with, if not more so. 2) It displaces the apparent emotion. The feeling you began with is gone; it is really an unimportant thought now." You may ask yourself four discrete questions to help uncover the hidden feeling. Wherever the emotion involves another person or persons, and it usually does, ask yourself, "What about this person reminds me of myself? What about them reminds me of something in me which I dislike?" Second, ask, "What is my fantasy of their expectation of me?" Third, "Of what am I trying to convince myself in experiencing the apparent emotion?" And fourth, "Of what am I trying to convince others in experiencing this emotion that I do not yet fully believe myself?"

Step 5. Look for the pattern

The fifth step obviously overlaps with the fourth in that you are looking here for historical replications of this real-racket feeling connection. Undoubtedly there have been other times when the forbidden emotion has been elicited and covered by the selfsame racket feeling as in the current case. Recollection of these instances, particularly with recovered feeling of that real underlying emotion, will do much to heal the pattern in question. There have, for example, been other instances in which you have felt disapproval of another's self-centeredness while denying your own, anxiety at another's flirtatious sexual expression while denying your own sexual arousal, or desperate need to prove yourself right while denying your own doubt of judgment.

Though this process may be useful for anyone, the oral's particular propensity for reversal, displacement, and identification make it a natural for him. The oral persistently deceives himself with his feelings to maintain his denial and the believability, both to himself and others, of the false self which he presents. Once he knows he is safe with you as therapist, however, he often is willing to explore the catacombs of his intricate defensive structure. Thus, Schiffman's hidden feeling process may be executed with a client in a simple interview format or through the elicitation of an altered state which facilitates the client's ability to slow down the emotional reaction and perceive that often fleeting real feeling which was its antecedent. A trance or altered state will also facilitate the memory of earlier similar events and feelings.

A Case of Hidden Emotion

Carol was a 35-year-old small business executive who had recently broken up with her live-in boyfriend, Bob. Throughout the relationship, she had felt a chronic sense of emotional abandonment. Though she and her lover had a good deal in common and made a satisfying partnership, there was considerable sexual incompatibility. The relationship was somewhat symbiotic in that their ideas, values, friends, recreational and other activities were identical and they spent a good deal of time together. Yet, Carol was chronically dissatisfied because her boyfriend was not sexually aroused by her. He did not give her the kind of romantic or sentimental attention which she desired and would occasionally engage in flirtatious dalliances with other women. When they did make love, she found him to be unemotional, mechanical, and generally uninvolved. When he initiated lovemaking, she would often reject him because of his detached sexual behavior.

In large measure, these chronic sexual problems culminated in their separation. But, because of the mutuality of friends and interests, Carol and her former lover maintained a good deal of social contact. And, even though she developed another relationship which was in many ways superior to the earlier one, she became the victim of intense anger directed at Bob's new partner, Jeanette. She found it difficult even to be in the same room with this woman, of whom she completely disapproved. The "other woman" had a history of relative helplessness in the world. In contrast to Carol, with her long history of executive ability and self-support, Jeanette was a woman who had always been supported by men and who, according to Carol, received this support through the use of her "feminine wiles." To see Bob "duped" by such a woman infuriated Carol. She became particularly livid when she saw Bob "starry-eyed and following her around like a puppy dog."

It was not too difficult to help Carol realize the not-so-hidden feeling of envy that she experienced toward Jeanette. There was in Carol a very well-denied oral component. While maintaining a work history far superior to the collapsed oral character, she had several involvements in very symbiotic relationships with little sexuality. There was a well-denied longing to be totally enamored by a man and totally taken care of by him. When she observed Jeanette getting what she had always wanted, and getting it for nothing other than being a woman in need, she became instantly envious and secondarily furious. Though it was not necessary in this case, the question, "What about Jeanette reminds you of something in yourself you do not like?" might have been very useful.

The uncovering of this hidden feeling led to other memories of very similar occurrences. Carol became aware of her predictable fury at women who got what they wanted while breaking those rules which Carol had set for herself—responsibility, honesty, self-support. This, then, led to an ever-increasing awareness of her own need for attention and nurturance.

So, as in this case, the nurturing of the irritability or resentment in the oral can lead to the more free experience of the rage. This, in turn, can lead to the realization of the need which, for the oral, is the core of the personality. The same general sequence may occur with an initial awareness of sadness or anxiety. The strategies of focusing, Schiffman's hidden feeling process, and the persistent problem exercise with all their combinations and permutations present a wide range of verbal techniques to touch and move the oral person to discover and ultimately integrate his core life issue.

SELF-SOOTHING

Having begun the early affective work and illustrated how it can provide relief and beginning insight for the oral person, let us shuttle away from this area temporarily and consider some other forms of early intervention. As outlined in the previous chapter, the oral will welcome anything which is soothing or nurturing and can profit greatly from encouragement to soothe and nurture himself. At a conscious level, this may be accomplished by simply dicussing this concept, assessing the level of current self-soothing attitudes and behaviors, and suggesting or even prescribing self-soothing activities.

The oral needs to be introduced to the idea that she can really take care of herself and "baby her baby," as it were. She can, as an adult, introject and identify with nurturing skills which others possess but which were deficient in her early history. She may be assisted in this by simply realizing what kind of nurturing activities she engages in already and learning what other people do to provide themselves soothing release. Mild exercise such as a walk in the sunshine, a good meal, a warm bath, a break to listen to music or watch television, a nap, a warm fire — all are part of a self-soothing menu. Frequently, a good deal may be accomplished by simply shifting one's perspective about these activities. When we feel that they should be done *for* us, cooking the meal, drawing the bath, or building a fire is a resented chore. When, however, we see that they are a form of self-care which we can give freely to that part of us which only wants to receive, our experience can change dramatically. As adults, we do have the ability to do these things, or if we don't they can be readily learned. Even the most oral among us is more than a helpless infant. We can at once celebrate our ability to do things, while at the same time nurturing and soothing the undernourished child within us. And, when we do this, we are in a far better position to produce for and nurture others. An unripened fruit is not only bitter, but also hard and not very juicy. The more nourishment we get, the more juice we have for everything.

In addition to permission-giving and prescription, hypnotic skills are very useful in reprogramming attitudes around this central context. After a process of hypnotic induction, I typically use at least three strategies to indirectly suggest self-soothing. In an approximate text here they are:

It might be nice to remember a time when it was necessary to comfort and soothe another person. Perhaps there have been many times when you have done this, but perhaps one will stand out for you now. It was a time when you felt compassion, caring and empathy. You knew how it must have felt to the other person and you wanted to give what you could to help them feel better. You can remember how it felt and perhaps you can remember what you said and the tone in which you said it. You can remember what you did, how you reached out and perhaps you can remember how your nurturing and soothing were received. Now, as the experience becomes full, make one very minor change. Put yourself in the place of the one nurtured while continuing to be the nurturing one. Soothe and be soothed. Comfort and be comforted. Use the same words and the same tone of voice as before. Reach out in the same way, touching and being touched. Know that you have the right, the same right as any other, to this attention and support. Take it in as you give it. Feel the release as you feel the compassion. Let it all be.

* * * *

Now, as you allow the experience to deepen, take one hand and put it over your heart, just in the middle of your chest, and take your other hand and put it on your abdomen. Feel the warmth of your hands on your body. Feel the comfort, the reassurance of the warmth. If you were to hold a baby in your arms, your hands would be in about the position that they are now. Your lower hand would support the baby's bottom and legs, and your upper hand the baby's body and head. You would be holding the baby close to you, providing it the warmth of your body. It could hear the beat of your heart as it felt the security of your large hands supporting its entire body. There would be complete safety, security, comfort here. If the baby needed, you would move or walk or rock the baby. You would hold the baby as long as it would want to be held, and when the baby was ready to be put down, perhaps to go to sleep, you would put it down. If it needed you again, you would be there. You would hold the baby, support the baby, comfort the baby. It would feel good to do this. What it asked would be so little to you. You could do it so easily, so simply and with your nourishment and love, the baby would grow and mature yet still need guidance, still need support, still need love. You would enjoy the child as it grew up, but you could always remember and enjoy how to soothe, nurture, and satisfy the baby in the child.

* * * *

I wonder if, when you were a child, you ever lay on your back and looked up into the sky and watched the clouds. Perhaps you lay down in the grass, where you could feel the coolness of the earth and that prickly sensation of grass against the back of your body and legs. Looking up, you could see the marvelous patterns of the clouds, sometimes perhaps you saw in the shape of the cloud a familiar form, an animal perhaps, which would stay in that form for a while and then drift into another form. The clouds were changing and yet the change was often so slow that you could barely see it in the small movements. Yet if you looked away for a moment and then looked back again, there would be a definite change. You'd notice all the differences among the clouds, the big white billowy clouds, the wispy streaking clouds, the dark rumbling rain clouds. Some days there would be all these kinds of clouds one after another and it would seem that one form would change to another form and there would be sunshine and then darkness, blue skies and then nothing but grey and even impending blackness. And you learned what the clouds meant. Sometimes, in the middle of summer, you could feel the big rain clouds rolling in heavy with moisture almost dying to unburden themselves of the heavy rain, so full of fullness that they had to burst and shower everywhere giving their moisture to everything in sight, needing to give it, having to give it. Having no other choice than to shower and give away the mositure which burdened them. No pretty wisp of a white cloud against a blue sky could ever give such life to the earth. Fullness is needed to give. Such fullness that giving is a must, a release, an unburdening. Giving requires fullness and fullness demands giving . . .

The trance utilization would not, of course, end here but the foregoing is sufficient to illustrate the type of hypnotic work which I believe engenders enhanced self-soothing attitudes. The first process, involving the switch of nurturing to nurtured is based on neurolinguistic programming principles. I learned the self-holding pattern requested in the second process during my bioenergetic training experience and added the metaphor of holding the baby during a spontaneous trance induction with a client. The final metaphor, about the rain cloud which must unburden itself, was borrowed from a talk by the Bhagwan Shree Rajhneesh, in which he was lecturing on the same point: that to really give one must be full. This is a message, of course, which every oral character needs to hear. As outlined in the last chapter, the oral is prone to give from a position of wanting rather than from a position of fullness, thereby engendering not relief in the recipient but obligation and thus promoting further rejection and abandonment.

One basic problem with the oral character is that he is unable to enjoy nurturing from either himself or others or to relax uncompromisingly during his eventual collapse. Because he has contracted against his need and weakness, there is always a guilt associated with getting what he wants and there is never really a complete letting down. If he is not anxious about what he is doing, he is guilty about not doing it. As illustrated by the poignant example of the injured worker, he must pay for his support with pain. Any maneuver which will assist him in really relaxing and, more importantly, enjoying that relaxation will help him immeasurably, not only in satisfying the unmet needs but also in strengthening him to meet the responsibilities of adult living.

By way of review, we have essentially covered the need in the oral case to provide contact, attention, sympathy and support and to provide the client with the certainty that you are on his side and will not reject or abandon him. As indicated earlier, from this solid base you can go almost anywhere in the treatment, as dictated by the issues that present themselves and your judgment as to the client's ability to handle various forms of intervention. In the present hypothetical scenario, I have so far chosen to present relatively mild therapeutic techniques which give permission to the client to experience all his feelings. In particular, I have suggested nurturing him in the affect realm so that his resentment will lead to rage, his sadness to despair, and his anxiety to deep-seated fear around his core issue. The interview and other techniques which I have presented will typically yield some relief and insight and the beginnings of central therapeutic change. Finally, I have outlined some techniques to increase self-caring abilities and attitudes which will also serve to make the client more comfortable with himself and in himself.

ORALITY AND GRANDIOSITY

Somewhere along in here, especially as safety and relief from the collapse are experienced, it is common for the grandiosity and manic nature of the oral to take over. As he feels better, he will overextend and this overextension will lead to all of the grandiose and manic-like symptoms listed earlier for the compensated oral—poor self-care, overwork, excessive drug use, excessive nurturing and responsibility relative to what can be sustained, and the expenditure of ungrounded energy in plans and actions which may be described as optimistic to grandiose.

If you are not taken in by all this, you will probably find yourself cringing silently as you experience a person about whom you've begun to care set himself up for another fall. If you miss this the first time it happens, you will typically catch it the second or third time before he becomes aware of it. The ungrounded excitement which he feels may relate to a new work project, a new love affair, or a new personal endeavor which fuels the manic excitement.

If you have built sufficient trust at this point, it will be possible for you to begin to deflate the inflated ego gently and gracefully. Besides pointing out the pattern to him directly, you may gain even further ground by assisting him in discovering it himself. One method for doing this is to simply ask, either in or out of trance, for the recall of another time when this same level of excitement was experienced. As with other processes of this type, a complete recall, including feelings, sensations, attitudes, self-statements, visions, etc. will be useful. Then ask him to remember the sequence of events which followed this period of elation. Usually, what he will find is the pattern of elation and collapse outlined in the last chapter. Typically, the new love, project, or possession did not bring the hoped for salvation. More importantly, the elation and its attendant behaviors exhausted the person and he was unable to follow through with his responsibilities.

Some orals are unrealistically narcissistic and grandiose, but many do have plans which are realistic for a reasonably well functioning adult. The problem is that they are not reasonably well functioning and cannot follow through. They become better functioning as they even out the pattern of elation and depression and their realistic goals become correspondingly easier to attain. When things begin to go well in the oral's life, he will tend to set up that fall by responding in the ways already outlined. The fall is, in part, another bid for the nurturing and support which he has always missed. The oral, while consciously wanting to stand on his own two feet, is often afraid to do so, for that would, at an unconscious level, mean giving up the hope of ever getting what was missed. In every case, the oral must acknowledge and mourn his real loss and then move on from that "ground" to get what is possible. Until that is done, the cycle will persist.

One very useful strategy, when you see the manic phase preceding the fall, is to ask the client to explore the ways in which he might now sabotage the positive present. A cognitive rehearsal of the manic behaviors which precipitate the fall will tend to inoculate him from them or at least increase his awareness when he begins to act in a self-defeating manner. Because of the underlying dynamics just outlined, there may need to be many trials of this in the course of treatment before the pattern will begin to level out and become more mature. These manic periods also represent a time when you can profitably encourage him to expend his energy in maintaining his existing commitments to himself, his work, his family, etc. To the extent that you have already introduced the client to his own need and the denial of that need, it will be possible to integrate your interventions directed at the manic behaviors within this larger scheme. Then, you are not merely raining on his parade; rather, you are encouraging him to understand himself as he is and helping him get from life what is possible.

ACTIVE TECHNIQUES

A great deal can be done for the oral character with some very simple body exercises. Whether you encounter the oral person in his compensated or collapsed phase, he is out of touch with his real feelings and is ungrounded. Work with the body will increase his grounding in external reality and his connection with his real self. In his collapsed phase, the oral is depressed and/or ill and in that physical and mental depression he has buried his real feelings. In his elated stage, he is flying above the ground, as it were, and is similarly out of touch with reality and himself. The humble and humbling grounding exercises will tend to bring him down to earth and down to the experience of his real self.

The oral person will often resist the effort of body work and the consistency of commitment which it requires. There is in that a metaphor for his resistance to effort in general and that can be worked through in this context. You will, however, need to pay somewhat more attention with this personality to shaping his tolerance for effort, to providing him with contact which will ease the pain and effort, and to doing whatever you can to produce release and relief in the process.

Initial grounding exercises have been outlined for the schizoid character (see pp. 98–108). Those consist of the dowel work with the feet, the exercises to develop and release energy through the ankles, and especially the forward position to strengthen and bring charge into the legs. The typical oral character can profitably spend a good deal of time and energy on the simple forward position, increasing his grounding and strength in the legs. Though it may be difficult to get him to follow through, self-administered programs in grounding can be very useful to the oral, particularly during periods of manic excitement. Also, body work in general can be extremely useful to the oral in periods of collapse, when all of his affect is essentially depressed and there is little movement or life in the body. All of the basic warm-up exercises presented in chapter III for the schizoid person will be valuable for the oral as well. He is, however, somewhat less likely to require work on the eyes and ocular segment as outlined in that chapter. There are a few additional exercises which will help grounding and loosen the typical areas of contraction that the oral experiences.

Grounding Exercises

Standing on one leg

A number of variations of simply standing on one leg can be used to bring more energy and charge into the legs. The simplest variation involves a simple alternation such that you stand on one leg attending to the foot's contact with the ground and feeling the charge building in the leg. Then, after a time, shift to the other leg and repeat the process. A second variation brings more charge to the legs. Stand on one leg with the knee bent and extend the other leg behind you for support only, so that all of your weight is resting on one leg. Hold this until vibrations have been established for 15–30 seconds. Repeat this with the other leg. The third alternative involves the basic bow position outlined in chapter III. After assuming the bow position, shift the weight until it is over one leg. Hold this as long as possible. Then shift the weight to the other leg and repeat. Any of these exercises may be repeated several times to increase grounding, charge, or strength in the legs.

Putting the foot down

In this exercise, you simply stomp your feet alternatively on the floor. It is often useful to experiment with the way in which this is done, altering the angle of the blow, stomping with the heel only, etc. This action is also, obviously, of metaphoric value and can be used literally when the person needs to "put his foot down." When the exercise is used in this fashion, add appropriate verbalizations, such as, "No; I won't; stop it," etc.

Squatting against a wall

Stand against a wall and then go into a squat with your back flat against the wall. Cup your hands behind your head, keeping your breathing full and open. Sustain this posture at least to the point of vibration. This posture is particularly useful for building a good solid energy charge in the legs and for strengthening. It is a useful exercise to recommend for self-administration.

Jumping

Jumping may be used in any number of variations, not only in improving grounding but for other sensory experiences involved in this process. Some of the variations are as follows:

1) Jump up and down, banging the feet on the floor, like a protesting child.
2) Jump for height, but land flat-footed for a solid sense of the ground.
3) Lean back on the heels and try to jump from this position. This illustrates that the heel rest posture, typical of the oral character, is not only a "pushover" position, but also one from which one cannot very well "take a leap."
4) Jump from and return to the ground with the toes, giving the experience of springing up, "taking a leap," and returning lightly to the ground.
5) For a self-administered exercise, regularly use a jumprope or small trampoline for jumping. Concentrate attention on feet and legs.

Loosening Chronic Tension

The windmill

Stand in the usual position and place your right foot slightly forward of your left. Then, simply swing your arms from the shoulder in a backwards direction. Slowly increase the speed of this "windmill" motion until you are going as fast as you can. After a period of this, reverse direction so you are swinging your arm as a windmill in a forward direction. Now reverse your stance and repeat the process with your right arm. This exercise, of course, begins to loosen the chronic tension in the shoulder girdle.

Reaching up

To bring greater sensation and energy flow to the shoulders and upper body, simply ask the client to reach upward with both arms extended. Turning the palms upward with the arms at about a 45° angle from the neck will give the greatest stretch in the shoulders. This posture may lead directly to one pulling for anger if the client is asked to clench her fists and bend somewhat at the elbows.

The upper back stretch

This is a sequence of three yoga postures which brings a considerable stretch to the longitudinal muscles between the shoulder blades and up through those muscles in the base of the neck, all of which are particularly tight in the oral personality. To do these postures, get on your knees and put your head on the floor in the Muslim prayer position. Now turn your head to the right so that your left ear and cheek are on the floor. Relax and drop your shoulders so that you feel a considerable stretch in the neck and shoulder and into the upper back on the left side. Hold this position as long as you can. Now shift the position such that you put the top or crown of your head onto the floor, thereby pushing your head forward and stretching down the back of your neck into the upper back. Hold this position as long as you can. Now shift to the opposite side so that your right ear and cheek are against the floor and you are stretching the right side of your neck and muscles in the right shoulder and upper back.

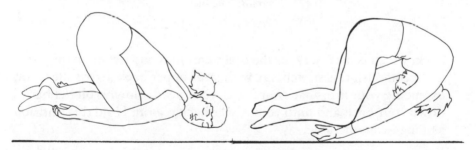

Figure 7. Upper back stretch

The barrel

The barrel, another bioenergetic therapy tool, is about the size of a small barrel but covered with foam and upholstery to make it more comfortable. It is useful for the same back stretch described with the stool, although it provides a more gentle stretch since it is closer to the ground and easier for the client to control. It has the additional advantage of providing a gentle and controllable stretch of the lower

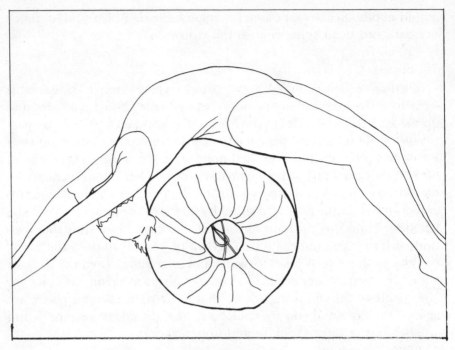

Figure 8. The barrel

back, which is necessary for the oral's chronic constriction in this area. To accomplish this stretch, lay with your upper back across the stool, extending your arms backward over your head. Slowly roll the barrel down your back and onto your lower back region. Hold this position as long as is tolerable.

The roll

The lower back stretch with the barrel will be too severe for some clients and a more subtle extension of the lower back will be useful for them, as well as for others when a less intrusive stretch is appropriate. In this exercise, the client extends his lower back over a rolled up towel or small blanket. To make the roll, simply fold a bath towel in half and roll it up. With the client seated upright on the floor or mat, simply push the roll up against his lower back. Ask him to recline over the roll, raising his knees with his feet flat on the floor or mat. When lying on the floor, his buttocks should still touch the floor, but he should experience a slight elevation and lessening of pressure there. Greater stretch can be accomplished by dropping the knees to the side. This more gradual stretch can usually be maintained for several minutes without any discomfort to the client. In cases where there is any acute back injury, of course, all these exercises for the lower back should be avoided, and where there is a serious chronic back problem, they should be approached with considerable caution.

With grounding accomplished and a systematic lessening of tension in these chronic trouble spots, you are in a much better position to achieve therapeutic gains with any number of bioenergetic, Gestalt, or even behavioral processes. Engaging in exercises of this kind for only 10 to 15 minutes will leave the client feeling more alive, grounded, and energized, breathing more fully and feeling more deeply. Any number of the affective and behavioral objectives outlined in the last chapter can be better achieved with the client in this state.

Opening the Need and Longing

You could, for example, go for the denied core feelings of need and longing following a basic warm-up, charge-building session. To do this, you might ask the client to lie down on his back on the mat or floor. You might then further build the charge by asking him to kick vigorously for a while. Following this, you could ask him to breathe deeply, relax, and feel his body. Then ask, "Now, very slowly, I would like you to reach upward as if reaching out to embrace someone. You might imagine who that would be. Begin slowly with your wrists and fingers in reaching and move into this reach slowly, breathing and feeling as you reach. Do this now."

In spite of this lengthy, careful instruction, many clients will reach quickly, holding their breath and stiffening their arms so as not to register the reach and the feeling of need which it engenders. If this happens, you can gently point it out and assist the client in recognizing his defensiveness. If the client seems ready, you can escalate the process by asking him to repeat the reach and verbally say the name of the person for whom he is reaching. Additionally, you may ask the client to say the words, "I need you," as he reaches.

Most clients with any appreciable oral issue will balk somewhere in this sequence. They will refuse to reach or to vocalize or they will defend at a less conscious level by tensing in the base of the neck and jaw, reducing their breathing, or moving quickly and rigidly to defend against the feeling. This, of course, provides the opportunity to recognize, point out, analyze, or interpret the resistance. By now, I needn't remind you, as you needn't often remind the client, that identifying with the resistance and giving it a voice can be instructive and ultimately relaxing of the defense. Uncovering the oral's typical decision, "I'd rather die than need you," can make for the most dramatic of therapeutic sessions.

When the feelings do connect or register, there is typically either great relief at their release or the uncovering of other feelings—namely, the despair at previous abandonment when needy, the rage at this abandonment, or the fear of future abandonment. In the work, there may emerge only a hint of these *hidden* feelings, but these flashes of feeling can be developed. Such is the progression of affective work. There is the opportunity for release, remembrance, and analysis.

For me, these are rewarding and intense sessions which, as with the schizoid character, lead to fundamental transformative changes. From them, the client can begin to realize who she really is. She may, for example, be able to say, "I do have a great need and that is all right. I was abandoned when I was needy and I am afraid of being abandoned again. I am still angry at having been deprived and I am still afraid that it will happen again. I am an adult but I have some childlike emotions which run my life." At this point, she begins to play the hand in life which she was dealt. While it may not be the best possible hand, she has a much better chance of winning the game if she plays the hand which she has rather than the hand she wishes she had. It is this "coming from one's own ground" which this kind of analytic therapy tries to achieve.

The foregoing scenario illustrates again how affective treatment in one area will elicit the opportunity for affective treatment in another. In this case, all of the primary affects are centered around the need and longing and pursuing any one will ultimately lead to the others. The strategies outlined in the previous chapters on treating the schizoid apply completely to the further elicitation of anger, fear, or sadness. Once the chronic tension has been reduced and the charge and deep breathing realized, actions and words which call up the emotions can be requested. Then, the client experiences the experience, or the resistance, or some combination of both. Where there is a release, the client will know it and the therapist's job is to help deepen the release as well as the insight around it. Where the resistance is experienced, the therapist's job is to help the client identify with that resistance, appreciate its function, and ultimately release its grip so that the actual experience can be had.

With these changes in affect and cognition, there will almost naturally be a change in behavior, though this can be nicely augmented by a therapist who knows how to accomplish behavioral change directly. After a succesful affective release session on need and its expression, you may do a number of things to strengthen the transfer of the direct expression of reaching out and asking for help into the person's social relationships. You may, for example, future pace this by simply asking the client to imagine herself reaching out, either literally or figuratively, to her friends or family. Or, similarly, future pace her asking for help in any relevant context. Alternatively, you may wish to engage in actual assertiveness training such that you assist the client in role playing direct expressions of affection or of asking for assistance.

Once a person knows that she wants, knowing exactly what she wants and how to get it are often not far behind. She may then begin to engage in very practical problem-solving. This may involve going directly after what is wanted, or it may involve acquiring the instrumental behaviors which will be necessary to do that. Once the original denial of the need is overcome, and the process of working through the associated affects is begun, the adult in the oral may begin to engage in some very real, no-nonsense discussions about how to grow up and make her life really work.

As outlined in the table in chapter V (see p. 180), when the oral collapses into her need and her longing, she begins to take responsibility by reaching for help. She is then motivated to change. This responsible position, albeit a needy one, is the place from which she can really move. The movement is toward maturation and does not involve any instant cure, yet there is a cure in the solidity of finally playing one own's hand. From this position, some remarkable things can begin to happen. There will always be a temptation at this point, short of the oral's enlightenment, to jump to ungrounded mania. The job of the therapist will be to continue the grounding process, muting the manic phase and steadying the step-by-step maturation process.

CHAPTER VII

HEALING THE
ABANDONED CHILD:
PART II

INTERPRETATION AND THE TWO TRIANGLES

PRIOR TO CONTINUING with specific issues and interventions for the oral character, I would like to introduce a very useful tool for understanding the basic structure of interpretive psychotherapy. This tool has been used most consistently by the short-term psychodynamic therapists (e.g., Davanloo, 1980; Malan, 1979) in teaching interpretive methods. The two *triangles of insight* illustrated in Figure 9 visually diagram the content of virtually all interpretations in psychodynamic psychotherapy. The triangle of feeling on the left stands on its apex because the hidden feeling is viewed as the underlying basis of defense and anxiety.

In the oral case, for example, extreme need, as well as rage and grief associated with chronically unmet needs, is hidden. Theoretically, it was the *anxiety* produced by these feelings which originally prompted the formation of the *defense*. Thus, when that defense is softened or threatened, anxiety results. Direct experience of the hidden feeling is the goal of affective therapy. An essential strategy of affective work is to 1) relax the defense; 2) increase the client's tolerance for the anxiety; and 3) assist the client in the direct experience and expression of the hidden feelings. Interpretation is one method among many for achieving this central purpose. When used most constructively, the interpretation will assist the client to feel as well as understand, helping him to experience the anxiety as the defense relaxes and to experience the hidden feeling as the anxiety is tolerated. Many of the active therapy techniques outlined in this volume are directed primarily toward realiz-

216

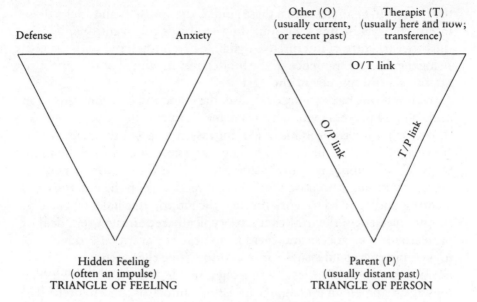

Figure 9. The Two Triangles of Insight

Adapted from Malan, 1979, p. 80.

ing this goal. They are designed, however, to achieve it not through therapist interpretation but through direct client experience. Interpretation may then add cognitive understanding to that process.

The triangle of person, presented on the right in Figure 9, details at whom the defense, anxiety, and hidden feelings may be directed. Once again, the triangle is on its apex with the parent figures, usually in the past, presumed to be the original target of the feelings in question. Through transference, the same feelings, with their associated anxiety and defense, may then be directed at other people in the client's environment or at the therapist in direct, here-and-now transference. In giving interpretations, a dynamic therapist will frequently link two points of the triangle of person. He will, for example, notice that the client's behavior, attitudes, or feelings are similar for another person and the therapist (the O/T link), for another person and parents in the past (the O/P link), or for the therapist and the parents in the past (the T/P link). With enhanced awareness of his defensive structure, the client will begin to notice these similarities himself, and make these interpretations or links without the therapist's interventions. This is the basic structure of interpretive dynamic psychotherapy, with the goal being the direct experience of the hidden feeling aimed at its appropriate target—the parent in the past.

To bring this back to the oral case, the client in both compensation and collapse presents you with his defenses in transference in relation to yourself and others in his life. Your task is to relax the defense and transference so that the hidden feelings are expressed toward their real target. The formula is really rather simple, but the execution is often extremely difficult because there is great resistance in the defenses and a corresponding need to work through the interpretive links repeatedly. In my experience, the oral character typically requires a great deal of patience in this process and there is no neat hierarchy of hidden feelings or interpersonal issues for resolution. The therapeutic process is more one of repetition, cycling through the defenses and hidden feelings again and again and again. In the remainder of this chapter I will present treatment strategies for a number of typical oral issues with the extensive use of one case study.

CASE EXAMPLE

When he entered therapy, Phil was a 48-year-old state government employee in the process of being divorced from his second wife. His presenting complaints were chronic depression, exhaustion, multiple physical ailments, and feelings of victimization. Through the 20 years of his marriage, Phil had not only maintained his state job, but also developed a constantly expanding small business involving such things as fast food franchises, laundromats, and small rental storage units. Though rich in holdings, Phil usually had little cash. Whenever he did have cash, he would, essentially on margin, invest in a new small business. He had worked days on his full-time state job and evenings and weekends on his other businesses. For his entire adult life, he had slept only three or four hours a night; further, when he was too busy or when cash was tight, he could go for two or three days without eating. Though there was a history of painful multiple injuries and illnesses through all of this, he typically kept going, building his career and paper fortune. His divorce and the economic depression of the early '80s coincided, and the breakup of his business holdings, mismanagement caused by his emotional depression, and the economic conditions of the times combined to lead to his eventual bankruptcy. In the course of therapy, his job tenure was threatened due to his repeated inability to do his work. In short, he lost almost everything important to him and the external circumstances of his life called for collapse.

Yet, the persistence of his compensation in the face of all this and more was almost unbelievable. He continued, for example, to deliberately get very little sleep; also, on many occasions, because money was tight, he would go without food or heat in his apartment. On the other hand, he would nurture others by taking them out to dinner, buying them flowers or gifts, or loaning them money. He was persistently drawn to women, friends, or business associates who were, in every sense of the word, "bankrupt." And, in any way that he could, Phil would support them. On one occasion, for example, he showed pity on a destitute couple, putting them in charge of one of his small businesses. Although Phil vaguely knew what they were doing, they were able to embezzle from the business to buy drugs and essentially ruined the business. Though he had been living for a time in a small, motel-like apartment, he had been planning to move to a small house which he still owned despite his bankruptcy. However, he began dating a poor, unemployed woman with three children who needed a home and he gave his home to her. Whenever complete collapse threatened, either physical or fianancial, Phil would typically find a new girl friend or a new scheme which would promise to pull him out of economic disaster. Almost every scheme, and certainly every relationship, failed, providing the opportunity for collapse anew and the stimulus for a new compensatory cycle. The story of this rather profound oral character was one of repetition with gradual improvement—two steps forward, one and one-half back. To every technique but sympathy and support, there was massive resistance. Let me share some therapeutic techniques used with him now, as well as their initial and cumulative result.

The history plus incidents recovered through the persistent problem exercise and other historical methods revealed an infancy and childhood marked by neglect on the part of a chronically ill mother and abuse on the part of a very narcissistic, perhaps at times psychotic, father. Phil remembered his mother as always sick in bed and his father often spending their last dollar on medicine for her. Revealing a history which included much more than simple oral etiology, Phil recovered many instances of being severely beaten by his father to the point of serious injury. In tracing loneliness, he repeatedly recovered instances of severe grieving for lost love and remembered promising himself to be good, not to be angry, and to give to others. During the initial months of therapy, Phil spent most of the 60- to 90-minute sessions recounting in detail the occurrences of the week, particularly instances in which he had experienced some losses or disappointments or instances which pointed to hope for some financial or personal gains. I got virtually nowhere by trying to intervene, but he seemed to appreciate listening a great deal. Only after a long initial period was some intervention possible.

There were, of course, many times when Phil was unable to cope, overwhelmed with responsibilities, suffering from multiple physical breakdowns, and essentially feeling beaten down by the circumstances of life. With Phil, as well as with most oral characters, this can be a useful time to encourage a complete collapse. The oral patient tends to resist the collapse while complaining about it. Encouraging the collapse may be done directly and consciously, of course, but it is also useful to do it hypnotically and physically. Natural metaphors for collapse are common and release or relaxation can be suggested as a concomitant to the collapse. In addition, a number of physical exercises are useful in making this metaphor concrete.

Exercises to Encourage Collapse

The forward squat position

One such exercise involves asking the client to come down into a squat posture from the forward position, as illustrated in Figure 10. In this posture, ask him to continue to breathe in as he bends his knees a little and to breathe out as he comes up, but to stay in the squat position. Ask him to hold this posture as long as possible, holding out with all his will before even-

Figure 10. The squat

tually falling forward. This exercise puts an extraordinary strain on the legs and it is very painful too sustain. Toward the end of the exercise, when the pain has built considerably, you may ask the client to reach out and to ask or yell for help. When the collapse comes, you might suggest that the client say as he collapses, "I give up." As he comes down to the ground, it is often useful to make some physical contact with him, particularly in the lower back region where a good deal of strain has been placed. At this point, it is useful to be silent for quite some time and to simply be with the client in whatever experience he has.

Standing on one leg

There are a number of other alternatives to achieve this holding up, reaching out, collapsing sequence, as illustrated in the accompanying figures. In one such variation, simply ask the client to bring his weight over to one leg, bending it considerably and standing on it for as long possible. If it seems advisable, you may add to this the step of reaching or asking for help in the strained position, but always end the process with the collapse. Again, make contact with the client physically and await the spontaneous flow of feelings or ideas.

Lifting both legs while prone

Another option is to have the client lying on his back on the floor or mat. Ask him to lift both legs in the air as high as possible, pointing his heels to the ceiling. Again, ask him to hold this posture as long as possible before collapsing. The collapse itself may initiate a flood of feeling, particularly sobbing, and result in the client's finally coming to his fully collapsed position, from which he can really feel himself and begin to responsibly ask for help. Short of this desired reaction, there is at least the concrete body experience and therapeutic suggestion of collapse and,

Figure 11. Extending both legs while supine

over time, you may get the desired effect. Particularly as these body
techniques are mixed with others of both a conscious and unconscious
nature, they will eventually erode the defenses.

INTERPRETATION AND COLLAPSE

In Phil's case, all but the hypnotic techniques aroused considerable
resistance. Yet, through the course of treatment, or perhaps through
the sheer weight of the burdens with which he was dealing, he began
to sleep eight to ten hours a night and to frequently collapse rather than
work on weekends. Together with the suggestions to really collapse,
I repeatedly worked on the concept of self-soothing, both consciously
and unconsciously. Here, there was more conscious acceptance, yet
repeated backsliding in his self-care functions. Over time, there was
gradual progress such that he was eating more regularly, cooking for
himself, and following various medical regimens more appropriately
as treatment progressed.

These simple strategies for encouraging the oral to really collapse
may constitute a large portion of the therapeutic intervention and lead
to core hidden feelings of despair at the loss, and ultimately, to the
oral's acceptance of the original loss. When that happens, there is no
longer a pull to recreation of loss through contemporary set-ups and
disasters involving new losses. After about 18 months of therapy, this
was, in fact, the interpretation I finally offered to Phil. I suggested that
the disasters, which by then he recognized having set up, were contemporary transference opportunities for him to experience the grief which
was within him. Though not fully understanding this interpretation
at a conscious level, Phil responded positively to it by saying, "My son
always has a tale of woe to get sympathy and help. And, you know,
my father always did the same thing—always a hard luck story. And
that's what I do. Always a story of grief." And, several times, I said
to him, "You don't need any more losses in your life to justify mourning the losses of your life."

Then, just as I knew I was beginning to get through, just as the collapse would begin to fully reach him, there would be a new love or
a new scheme on the horizon and the pace of the treatment would shift.
During these more manic times there would always be a "solution."
The most common type of "solution" would be his emotional and/or

business partnership with another who had been chronically deprived and unable to make it in the world. He would set his son up in a business that they would share, or his lover in the house which he was holding on to by a thread. The symbiosis of the personal or business union would then give way to the narcissism of the plans for success and fulfillment.

In each example, one interpretation was obvious. If Phil felt that he took care of the other, he could eventually get from them what he needed. In childhood, he had always hoped that if he could adequately take care of his mother, she would ultimately give him what he wanted. During one of these manic phases, he could not arrive for his 5:30 p.m. appointment and I allowed him to come at 6:30 p.m. As he rushed in, he announced that he had bought dinner for me because he thought I might be hungry and unable to provide my own dinner due to the delay he had caused. Here again is the inappropriate nurturing of the other amidst a pattern of poor self-nurturance. In taking care of others, Phil provided examples of the other/parent link, the other/therapist link, and the therapist/parent link in his triangle of person. These interpretations—Phil's reenactment of his original loss and gifts of nurturance given with the hope of receiving nurturance—were made wherever it seemed remotely possible that he might hear them and again, over time, he did. Yet, because of the great resistance in this case, hypnotically delivered interpretations were used with more frequency and more success than those delivered consciously and intellectually. I knew that I had gotten through when he began to tell me of situations in which he could have indiscriminately rushed to the aid of another or denied himself while nurturing another but resisted doing so. Again, however, the process was one of repetition requiring a great deal of patience. It was, indeed, like raising a child. It was important and sometimes difficult for me to keep my investment in the outcome under control.

The periods of collapse for any oral person are also times to encourage the experience and expression of the resentment felt at having to do what is really too much for the undernourished person. Such encouragement can be accomplished with simple interview technique, but this is another area in which the direct and concrete procedures of bioenergetic therapy can be particularly useful. The procedures are very simple and straightforward. After engaging in exercises or direct physical manipulations which relax the areas of chronic tension, simply schizoid are directly applicable. In this situation, however, you may wish to ask the client to shout some relevant short phrase such as, "It's too much" or "I won't!"

In the process of releasing the oral's resentment of demands, ask him to keep kicking or hitting to the point of exhaustion. When this process begins to work, there will be a complete breakdown, usually into tears, followed by a period of deep relaxation. The most therapeutic response at that point will be to silently stay with the client and support the collapse, the despair, and the eventual relaxation. There may be insights and an opportunity for interpretation at this point, but it is more imoprtant to stay with the feeling and to avoid rushing on to more cognitive interventions.

Because affective release therapy is new and unfamiliar to many therapists, it can be intimidating. It may be useful, therefore, to remember how really simple this form of therapy is conceptually. The basic affects which underlie a good deal of our complex psychopathology are few in number, primitive in nature, and most therapeutic when allowed a direct and primitive expression. Most of us are intimidated by affective therapy, I think, not by its complexity but by our own resistance to these primitive emotions. Because of this, we often tend to make this form of therapy overly complex and difficult when, in reality, it is incredibly simple. As therapists, we often need only to desensitize ourselves to witnessing and allowing this kind of experience in our clients. While to most therapists it will be initially threatening, it will ultimately become vicariously releasing.

Though I did not involve Phil in this more intense form of work, the content involved was repeatedly dealt with in the interview context and he was moved to experience the resentment rather than the pride of working from childhood on. Again, however, this work occurred after three years of therapy and is still progressing. It is clear that it will need to be repeated again and again, probably in the more intense forms described above, before the compensation will yield to the reality of the true self.

ELATION AND THE FALSE SELF

The reality for most oral characters who have any degree of compensation is that they put themselves into circumstances which are overly demanding and then resent those demands and are taken over by them. In Phil's case, for example, as soon as his bankruptcy was completed and he began to have the resources to adequately care for himself, he tried to embrace ventures which would "rebuild the empire." This involved new business ventures, which would require back-breaking work as well as the commitment of his meager financial resources to keep up with loan payments. At these points, Phil was able to hear that he was beginning to create demands for himself which he might be unable to sustain and come to resent. He began to appreciate the fact that just living out his real self was not, and never had been, "enough." His original narcissistic injuries compelled him to attempt to create a false self which he could not sustain and which, in any case, did not give him what he really desperately wanted in life. A good deal of the therapy was devoted to shortcutting the repetition of the destructive cycle. He could respond to gentle interpretations which questioned whether the current scheme was not really the reinitiation of the compensatory trap which had led him to financial, personal, and physical collapse. Beneath that understanding, he slowly and repeatedly came to the experience of himself as not enough and to deeper levels of the affective experience of that injury which propelled the life pattern. Yet, there is still more work to be done on that core realization after years of treatment.

Thus, the essential strategy for therapeutic response to the oral person in the manic phase is to develop grounding in reality. That grounding in reality can be both physical and cognitive. The development of "understanding" can refer both to development of a solid sense of support in one's body, particularly in one's legs, and to a cognitive understanding of one's situation. So, on a physical level, a therapeutic response to the elation would include suggesting such processes as the "I am" meditation, focusing, or those literally "grounding" exercises emphasizing the feet and legs presented in the last chapter and in chapter IV. When this literal, physical grounding is developed, you have a far better chance of helping the client "get down to earth" with respect to his goals, life plans, etc. In the reparenting process which is a good deal of the therapy for both the schizoid and oral characters, you can be of service by simply reassuring the person that his real self is enough for you. In addition, you can use any number of strategies to help him understand that the realization of the false self does not yield what he has really longed for. Most people who seek out therapy do so late enough in life to have had the disappointments of success — for example, direct experience of the fact that money can buy only things and accomplishment can buy only recognition. Reaccessing these disappointments of success relative to what the oral *really* needs can gradually facilitate his letting go of the false self.

For everyone, the essential choice in life is between the compensatory false self with the compromised gratification which it achieves and the real self which, though injured, is the only one capable of experiencing any real gratification. This universal dilemma is often more poignant for the oral character because he is so often cyclical in his ability to sustain the falsity. Yet, a real, felt collapse into the reality is too painful for this weakened and unsupported organism. Only when he is sufficiently strong and supported will he be able to make this courageous choice in the direction of reality and health. I have shared the case of Phil here primarily because the lines of this dilemma are so clearly drawn with him. To be "good enough" therapists for a seriously oral person, we need to appreciate the enormity of this dilemma. Only in this way can our compassion and support, which will be sorely tested, continue to be freely given rather than coerced.

ORAL GAMES

It is in the coercion of support that the oral plays one of his most destructive games. This will come out in therapy through requests to alter the frame or ground rules to gratify the dependency. The adherence to a reasonable set of ground rules is often more important with the oral person than with many other character types. The difficulty is that there is a very real need for sympathy and support with the oral person and a harsh and rigid response or interpretation will often be unfacilitative, particularly in the early phases of treatment. Thus, one needs to walk the very tricky line of standing one's ground while maintaining support.

For this reason, I have found it useful to give a good deal of therapeutic attention to these sorts of requests while usually denying them. My own strategy is to use a good deal of explanation for my rationale as well as employing interpretation to assist the client in understanding his pattern of the coercion of support. To do this, I may discuss with him my negative past experiences in breaking the ground rules, including the fact that when I have done so, or when I have observed my students doing so, a resentment builds which contaminates the therapy. Thus, I may share my own experience of resentment in order to soften the confrontation and disclose my own humanity in the process. By taking responsibility for my part of the interaction I not only provide a good model, but also pave the way for the O/T link interpretation in which I question or point out the resentment which others may have evidenced to the nurturing coercion of the client. In Phil's case, for example, I used these opportunities to harken back to instances of rejection he had experienced and even to point out the coercive quality of his pattern of giving gifts to others rather than eating himself and letting others know of his sacrifice. Obviously, this is an extremely ticklish area for the oral because it challenges an essential component of the false self ("I am giving but not needy"). Yet, done softly and repeatedly it can yield results, particularly when coupled with techniques which demand direct asking.

During therapy, the oral person will typically give you a number of opportunities to call for the direct expression of asking. Repeatedly, the typical oral character will come in with complaints of being unsupported, misunderstood, and persecuted, and will blame others for not caring or giving enough. Sometimes this will be directly and consciously stated and other times it will be more implicit. At these times, I often choose a particular bioenergetic technique involving the use of a large bath towel. After the typical warm-up period, I ask the client to stand in a well-grounded position and to grip the towel with both hands so that he is wringing it in front of him as depicted in Figure 12. I ask him to say, and then yell, the words, "Give it to me." I ask him to escalate this such that he is yelling these words louder and louder while wringing the towel. At its most successful, this exercise results in a breakdown or collapse into that demand, accessing rage and then despair. Over time, this sort of process results in an ever-widening awareness of the oral character's own demanding nature, against which he typically defends with a vengeance.

Thus far, through Phil's case, I have illustrated three of the most characteristic presentations of the oral character in therapy with suggestions for therapeutic response. These have been the presentations of collapse, elation, and the perceived failure of social or therapeutic support. In each case, I have recommended procedures which, among build a charge in the body and then call for a discharge. In this case, simple hitting or kicking as outlined explicitly in chapter IV for the

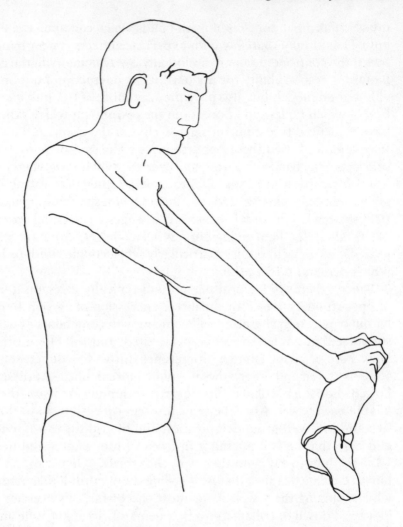

Figure 12. Wringing the towel

other things, bring the client down to his ground, strengthen him in both his body and cognitive understanding, and most importantly, give him the deepest experience of the underlying feelings which sustain the pattern.

LONELINESS, JEALOUSY AND FEAR OF ABANDONMENT

A fourth characteristic pattern for the oral person is the repeated experience of intolerable loneliness, jealousy, and fear of abandonment. Typically, the client's request is to "make it go away." My response, of course, is just the opposite. I am guided by one of the essential insights provided to me through Werner Erhardt's est training, "What you resist persists, what you experience disappears."

In the panic of loneliness, jealousy, or abandonment anxiety, the oral is really closer to his core than in any of the aforementioned patterns. The essential problem is the resistance to that core experience.

As a way of beginning treatment on this issue, which I consider a variant of classic separation anxiety, I frequently employ object relations theory. I explain that child development can be used as an analogue for adult problems and that we can learn from the ways in which children first master some of life's basic issues. In optimal development, the child enjoys a sense of solid unity with his mother from about two to eight months of life. At that point, the realization begins to dawn that he and mother are separate and for the next year and a half he will be working on the many ramifications of that realization. At that time, the real or threatened loss of the mother's presence may be experienced as traumatic or life-threatening in that he has seen the mother and himself as one, with all security and meaning in life associated with that oneness. The more secure the symbiosis, the more confident will be his expectation of the future and the less traumatic will be that separation.

To deal with the anxiety created by the necessary separations, the child will typically develop transitional objects such as blankets or teddy bears to soothe himself from the anxiety. Through repeated occurrences of separation and reunion, he will learn to manage the anxiety and realize that mother does come back. Further, as he becomes more mature and autonomous, he will learn to take better care of himself and reach out to others for what he needs. With a confident self intact, he will delight in his own abilities to deal with the world and become more and more involved with it. Finally, he will take into himself the nurturing functions of both his mother and his transitional objects so that he can soothe himself mentally in the absence of both. Developing a solid sense of who he is and who his mother is, he can experience himself as separate and complete, yet appreciate and rely on the constant cycle of love which exists between them.

With this brief overview of the developmental process, I may then offer explanations as to the likely antecedents of the current presenting problem in light of the client's history and symptomatology. This represents only a lightly held working hypothesis which can assist the client in orienting to the difficulty with which he must work. At this point, it may be useful to reassure the client that, in many areas, he is a responsible and well functioning adult. But, in this area of difficulty, he is in some meaningful respect a very young and frightened child who must work on an emotional problem which he has never completely mastered. This explanation provides an orientation to working on the problem and a rationale for many of the methods used in dealing with it. For example, it may lead directly to consideration of existing psychological defenses, useful and harmful transitional objects, the need for experiencing emotions around separation, further discussion or direct work on historical antecedents of the problem, or to developing self-soothing abilities and the capacity to reach out. With this menu of therapeutic alternatives, you may then move to a many-pronged attack on the problem with a shared view of its etiology and projected treatment course.

Explicit outlines of the many techniques which may be applied to this problem have already been presented in this volume in one context or another. At this point, we may briefly review these strategies in the current context.

To further explore the etiology and to access and even abreact the core terror, the persistent problem exercise as outlined in chapter IV may be very helpful. In this case, the persistent problem would be instances of anxiety at being alone or episodes of jealous panic or rage. With appreciation of the intensity of the emotion that the exercise will give, the client may even be more amenable to the interpretation of his defenses. Very commonly, the oral character will be overly ingratiating and nurturing in order to avoid the possibility of separation and in so doing build up resentment and irritability. The interpretation of this pattern both with a therapist and with significant others can be particularly useful as the O/P link and the P/T link are elaborated with the developing understanding of etiology. Together with this, a critical interpretive look at the individual's transitional objects can provide a contextualized understanding of their function and suggest possible changes.

With this background and context, direct bioenergetic or gestalt methods may then be used to access and release the held-in emotions around this issue. After building sufficient "understanding" at both a cognitive and body level, for example, one may begin to pull for the fear with the methods already outlined in chapter V. Ask the client to engage in deep and perhaps paradoxical breathing and then call for the verbal expression of fear. In this case, for example, you might ask the person to breathe deeply, open the eyes wide, loosen the jaw, and scream at higher and higher pitches the words, "Don't leave me." Typically, this process will lead not only to the experience and expression of fear but will ping-pong to the other associated affects of rage and grief. As in every case, patient and repeated affective working-through will be required for the transformation.

Another alternative sequence for this process involves having the client assume the posture of squatting against the wall as described in chapter VI. This posture grounds the client but is a stress posture which serves a purpose in the affective objective of the exercise. Have the client maintain the posture for some time until there is vibration. Then ask him to reach out with his arms, imagine a significant person leaving him and cry out repeatedly, "Don't leave me." In the latter stages of the working-through of this issue, you may wish to be the person walking away, though it would be well to have established his ability to experience the affect and stay with himself before playing this active role. The objective of this process, of course, is for the person to experience his abandonment, staying with rather than defending against his feelings.

Eventually, the oral person must realize both cognitively and affectively that he is and, in an essential way always has been, alone. He has supported himself and can do so even better. There is support available, though he can never undo what was done nor recapture what was lost.

To concretely reinforce some of this learning, you can literally call for self-soothing after experiencing the terror and you can give him your support and contact. You may, for example, when he is lying prone, instruct him to reach out and take your hand, moving it slowly down to his heart and holding it there. Alternatively, you may ask that he bring his arms down slowly from their outreached position and place one hand on his abdomen and one hand over his heart. In this position, you may ask him to quietly and repeatedly say the word "me."

Throughout exercises of this type, it is important for you as therapist to be comfortable with the role of witness. You need not make anything happen. Every session need not be a catharsis of emotion and a flood of insight. Your clients are learning the language of feeling and the lessons of life and unless you are very far along, you are learning all this with them. The learning may be neither swift nor error-free, but it will usually progress at the rate it can if you simply trust the process in yourself, in the other, and in the interaction. When an exercise like this is most effective, the client will experience release and relief and simply feel better. She will have insight into the current relationship with you, relationships in her current life, and the relationships of the past. Frequently, you or she will begin to interrelate these insights and the hidden feelings will increasingly be directed at their original targets. Over time, the client's responses in her current environment will lose their overdetermined quality. The past will be removed from the present and behavior will become more appropriate to the here and now.

As therapy progresses, you may feel the client is strong enough to recommend that he engage in these affective release and soothing procedures on his own. Thus, the next time separation panic or jealousy attacks he may breathe deeply and feel freely rather than try to ward off the uncomfortable emotions. After the feelings have peaked and settled, it is usually very useful to recommend a conscious movement to self-soothing or deliberate reaching out to others, if only by telephone.

The diminution of anxiety around abandonment may or may not automatically occasion greater self-sufficiency. Because of the long-established dependent orientation, the oral may need to be gradually phased into more and more instrumental activities, which will render him more independent. Since this kind of learning is often done better in classes devoted to direct instruction, it can be a real waste of time to use individual or even group psychotherapy to perform instruction in instrumental skills. Yet, I believe assistance in life planning is quite appropriate in the oral's therapy as he begins to come into his own and requires the strengthening of certain skills to realize his full potential in the world.

STANDING ONE'S GROUND

Another typical set of presenting situations for the oral are those in which he is being taken advantage of or pushed around. At these times, it is useful to attempt to set up a situation in which you can give him the direct experience of "putting his foot down" or "standing his ground." In my study of the work of Milton Erickson, it seems obvious that one very salient feature of his creative work was that he provided the client, in or out of hypnosis, with the exact experience he needed in order to dramatically learn what he needed to learn. Erickson's ingenuity and skill were extraordinary but this guiding principle of providing the needed experience can be extremely useful even to those of us who are a bit less imaginative than he.

In the instance of a client who is being pushed around, the very concrete maneuvers of bioenergetic therapy can be usefully engineered to follow this principle. After developing a sense of grounding and some charge in the body, you might ask the client to stand up, face you, and engage in a simple exchange in which he stands his ground. You might, for example, take the role of someone insisting that he do something and request that he take the role of one resisting that. You might say, yell, or cajole repeatedly, "Yes, you will," while he responds repeatedly, "No, I won't." It can also be useful to reverse roles in this process; in any case, it is important to attempt a number of variations in the requesting and refusing (e.g., "Pretty please?" "Absolutely not," etc.). Alternatively, this therapeutic situation is one in which it can be very useful to demand that the client repeatedly put his foot down in the stomping exercise outlined in the last chapter. Again, appropriate verbalizations accompanying this exercise will be useful (e.g., "I won't," "Never," "No").

Another variation in response to this presenting situation can involve a classic form of "Indian wrestling." In this exercise, you face the client and extend your hand as in a handshake. You then place your right foot adjacent to his. The object of this wrestling contest is to hold your right foot where it is while throwing your opponent off balance. Your left foot may move, but your right foot must stay stationary. This process is particularly useful when the client has some realistic chance of winning. His reactions to knocking you off your ground while holding his own can be very enlightening.

You probably know, or can create for yourself, any number of other exercises which require the client to stand his ground. The sessions including this kind of work are usually fun, light, and often more productive than they might appear. To enhance transfer outside of treatment, it can be useful to future pace the expression of such assertiveness in the client's life.

These exercises and others like them are good for direct strengthening and behavior change in the client's day-to-day life. Further, by accessing these often taboo forms of self-expression, directed at the therapist, you may elicit the T/P link. The client may then begin to recall the parental prohibitions against such expression—instances in which self-assertion was cut off or in which the client was manipulated or overpowered. Any resistance he experiences to standing up to or beating you will be particularly likely to elicit these kinds of memories.

Similarly, the oral character will typically present you with repeated instances of being let down or disappointed by others. Also, there probably will be instances in which she feels let down by you when you are forced to change an appointment or are unable to see her on the spur of the moment. These situations will trigger very significant replays of the oral's abandonment script. I was once seeing a fairly well compensated man who worked as an emergency room physician. He brought in one of those life incidents in which it was obvious, even to him, that his emotional response was exaggerated and overdetermined. On a moderately busy evening shift at the emergency room, his x-ray technicians had "let him down," delaying the x-ray turnaround time to over an hour, thereby clogging the normal flow of patients through his service. This resulted in his falling behind for the entire evening. Yet, he admitted that he had handled many more cases on other evenings and had certainly gotten further behind on a number of other occasions. Still, he was enraged by this failure of support and held on to his resentment for days thereafter. These kinds of overdetermined, somewhat irrational, emotional reactions are often signals of an opportunity to discover the O/P link in the analytic therapy.

In this case, a variation of a classic bioenergetic treatment strategy was used. Initially, exercises were employed to strengthen grounding and effect relaxation of chronic tension so that the patient experienced movement through those areas typically blocked. With grounding established and energy moving through the body, I asked the client to simply stand on one leg with his knee bent and waited for the expected vibrations and signs of pain to occur. I then made an interpretive leap by asking him to reach out from this pained position for his father, saying the words, "Help me." From earlier work, I knew that he was aware of many of the difficulties he had had with his somewhat rigid and affectively cold mother, but that he was unaware of the hostility he felt toward his father for his lack of paternal support. I watched carefully for any sign of anger or hostility in his facial expression. When I saw it, I requested the client to stand in front of the bed and hit it with both fists. This hitting led spontaneously to an awareness of his hostility and disappointment with his father for being insufficiently supportive in dealing with his mother, a recall of the script decision, "Men disappoint me and aren't ever there to help," and the realization of his persistent expectation, "I will be let down." When I asked him the question, "In how much of your life do you expect to be let down or disappointed?" he was somewhat stunned as he realized that his whole interpersonal life was centered around that expectation. The session was then ended.

This example illustrates the kind of interpretation often offered through bioenergetic work. Rather than armchair speculation, questioning, or direct interpretation, the client is asked to essentially act out the hypothesized affective sequence; often, as in this case, the hypothesized original target is introduced as well. If this action is not taken prematurely, there will usually be some level of insightful awareness occurring at both affective and cognitive levels. Even when the interpretation is somewhat premature or the affective energy in the body not completely mobilized, there is often delayed insight. The combined features of increased energy flow in the body and direct expression of the affective content enhance the emotional effectiveness of the experience and the insight realized.

INTEGRATING COLLAPSE AND COMPENSATION

A final oral issue is one which must be resolved by all character types, but it is more obvious in the oral case. That is the integration of the collapsed and the compensated selves, the "good" self and the "bad" self, the false self and the real self. This integration of polarities in the representation of self for the purpose of accomplishing a superordinate self-construct is the objective of any characterological transformation. There is a process originating in Gestalt therapy and more explicitly outlined in neurolinguistic programming which provides a "quick reading" of many of the essential ingredients of this integration. A derivative of the Gestalt "empty chair" technique, it is labeled in NLP terms the "two-part reframe," as it incorporates all the basic ingredients of the reframe process outlined in chapter III with the addition of a second, opposing part. Like the simple reframe, the two-part reframe relies on the useful fiction of dividing the self into parts. The table in chapter V (p. 180) was devoted to delineating characteristics of the oral's two opposing parts—the collapsed and compensated ego states.

Any truly oral character will be able to readily identify those times when he has been collapsed into loneliness, despair, and longing or times when he has been depressed, withdrawn, and helpless. Similarly, he will be able to recall times of compensation when he felt good or elated and competently engaged in those real, adult-like behaviors of which he is justifiably proud. The two-part reframe begins by having him access each of these two parts. This is often best done in an altered state, though that is not absolutely necessary. As with the other processes described in this book, it is most useful to assist the client in developing a complete auditory, visual, and kinesthetic representation of each part, including such things as a self-image, behaviors, postures, facial expressions, attitudes, beliefs, physical sensations, emotions and feelings, etc. In this process, you can ask the client to imagine the collapsed self existing on his right side, for example, and the compensated self on the left.

Once one side has been completely developed, ask the client to be aware of the beneficial intention or purpose of that side of the polarity. Typically, the positive intention of the compensated part is to make it in the world, attract love and admiration, and give to others what they need. Typically, the intention of the collapsed part is to get needed rest and escape the exaggerated demands of the compensated part.

At bottom, the collapsed part wants to rest and play and protect the self from the exhaustion and self-denial which the compensated part will impose. Finally, and even more basic, the collapsed part wishes to be taken care of and in lieu of that to express the resentment and rage of the original loss.

Once the intentions of both sides have been elicited, each part is asked to look at the other directly and see if he or she can develop an appreciation for the *intention* of the other part. A good deal of processing may be necessary at this point to flush out the initial opposition, which has typically existed for years. Usually, a mutual appreciation of intention can be achieved. At this point, the two parts may be asked if they could begin to work together to achieve the purposes which are in the best interests of the whole self. To the extent that this may be done, you may wish to ask the client to allow the visual images of the two conflicting parts to move together. If there is sufficient agreement between the two polar parts, you may suggest the two images fuse and the person take some time to experience the full impact of that fusion — to be aware of all the feelings and images and attitudes which accompany this fusion of polarities. Finally, you may ask the client to future pace the result of this integration by imagining the fused self as it deals with the salient situations in current life. Here, in outline form, are the steps of the process.

Two-Part Reframe

1) Identify the essential features of two conflicitng "parts."
2) Establish an altered state.
3) Establish a complete representation of each opposing part locating the representation of one on the client's right side and the other on the client's left.
4) Elicit the positive intentions of each part.
5) Work toward the acceptance of each part of the basic *intention* of the conflicting part.
6) As the basic intentions of the other side are accepted, ask both parts to agree to cooperate on the realization of the mutually accepted purposes.
7) Request the visual representations of the two parts to come closer together and, when appropriate, instruct the union or

fusion of these two formerly opposing parts. Instruct the client to fully experience the fusion of polarities in images, attitudes and feelings.

8) Future pace the experience of fusion in the client's relevant life situations.

As with all similar processes, it is important to remember that this is an oversimplified outline of a more complex process, which can be accomplished in many, many ways. One of the many benefits of doing it in this prescribed way, however, is the seeding of the principles for integration of polarities and forming the superordinate construct of the self. Like the reframe itself, the two-part reframe calls for acceptance and integration of the split-off aspects of oneself. As such, it implicitly but powerfully suggests that those aspects may not be eliminated but are the expression of some positive intention and must be appreciated and integrated. Further, to the extent that the altered state aspects of the work are realized, the process bypasses or utilizes constructively the long-standing resistance to such acceptance and integration. As an analogue to a longer therapeutic process, the exercise reminds all those involved of what is essentially going on in the therapeutic process.

I have had considerable difficulty in completing this chapter on the treatment of the oral character because of a nagging sense that something has been left out—that somehow what is here is not enough. I allowed the chapter to lay unfinished for several months waiting for the final piece to come. Then it dawned on me: In the treatment of every oral character one has to deal with being unable to meet all the client's needs—in short, with *not being enough*. This is a rather obvious component of the transference situation for an individual whose needs have been tragically and chronically unmet. No one *can* meet all the needs of the oral character. His experiencing the depth of his deprivation and discovering which of his needs can now be met is really the point of the therapy. Yet, the client's very real disappointment in therapy—and therefore in the therapist—will stimulate our own necessary awareness of our limitations so dramatically portrayed in the book *Psychoanalysis: The Impossible Profession* (Malcolm, 1981). To the extent that we are ungrounded in and unaccepting of these limitations, we will have great difficulty in productively dealing with this predictable oral issue. Relative to the massive personal damage which we are forced to confront in our work, our contribution to healing that damage will often seem trivial. This can be very discouraging and threatening. The limits of our helpfulness is an issue that we must work out for ourselves before we can really be of assistance to others. I am still in the process of working it out. I am still disappointed that the work takes so long, that it can be so stalled by ego deficit and resistance, and that it can sometimes be so tedious. As indicated earlier, I have found these obstacles to be particularly strong in serious cases of oral character expression.

Fortunately, I have been involved in a good deal of psychotherapy as a patient and have dealt at some length with this issue in myself. As a therapist, I welcome the expression of disappointment as a very important door into the eventual transformation of the oral issue. I take a deep breath and, remembering to stay with myself, encourage the client to elaborate about her disappointment. The trick is not to condescendingly, and thereby defensively, ask the client, "Show me all your anger." Rather, it is necessary to really hear and empathize with the person's very understandable disappointment and frustration. Then, it is often necessary to provide some contact or reassurance in order to let the client know you will not leave her in response to her feelings. Some clients, in anticipation of your desertion, will become very anxious or frozen after sharing these very necessary feelings. Following this, there are two essential therapeutic responses, the order of which may vary depending on the circumstances: 1) deal with the immediate disappointments and frustrations of the therapeutic relationship, and 2) deal with the historical roots of the current transference. Often, it may be most useful to deal with the second objective first, while the affect is still available and not diffused by an immediate resolution of conflict. At the same time, it is important not to ignore, and thereby condescend towards, the client's legitimate concerns about the limitations of the therapy she is receiving from you.

To elicit and interpret the transference, I often ask the client to simply look at me and say the words, "You don't give me enough." I may ask for a repetition of this phrase or for an elaboration on it. As the feelings expand and find expression, I will then ask the client to imagine a parental or other significant figure in another location and say the same words to him or her. This Gestalt technique for interpreting and working through the transference may then provide the impetus for affective release, abreaction, insight, and an eventual rapprochement with the reality of what one can and cannot get from others. This issue really represents the essential drama of the oral's choice in relation to love. She can stubbornly hold on to the infantile need for complete and unconditional love, caring and fusion, looking for it, clinging to it, and demanding that the illusion be realized. In so doing, she will set up reabandonment. Or, she can experience the devastation of the original loss, accept it, and move on to get what is possible in loving relationships. This will be less than she wants but will be much, much more than she has ever had. And, what is wanted will come from within as well as from without.

To deal with the very real here-and-now disappointment in the therapeutic relationship, I usually acknowledge and respect its reality. I often tell the client how I truly feel about the work we have been doing, and though this is frequently a much more positive assessment than that of the client, I will also acknowledge the disappointments I have suffered both in my own therapy and in coming to terms with my own limitations as a healer and helper. I often wish that I could be a psychic surgeon and simply cut out the torment in people's lives, sending them home whole and happy. But, I have had to face my own grandiose and messianic self-expectations and come to terms with reality in this respect. However I have not had to face my disappointment alone and quietly. I have had help with this and I assure the client that he too will not have to face his disappointment alone, that he can come to understand it, work it through, and accept it. Powerful sessions have occurred in this sharing of mutual disappointment; the oral and others find solace in learning that disappointment, frustration, and anger can be shared and the target of those negative emotions will not desert them or retaliate. For the oral character, this is a transforming and healing experience.

THE HEALED ORAL

As each person discovers the real self, he or she experiences some unique advantages in that discovery. The oral initially finds in herself someone who is needy, and though that discovery is threatening at first, there will eventually be increasing joy in that experience. Over time,

the oral will discover that patent need is the ticket she has always wanted to the satisfactions of life. Surrender, particularly to the longing for
another, will eventually become a treasured and transporting experience. In order to experience the profound depths of such longing, the
oral person needs to become stronger in herself. There must be a solidity of self to reexperience the all encompassing yearning for another,
which was not satisfied initially and which may continue to be unsatis-
fied in the present. Thus, the oral must experience herself as powerful enough to be vulnerable. She is needy *and* strong, no longer needy
or strong.

The clear experience and expression of the need will be achieved
because of the repeated affective work which cleans out the contamination of the need by other affects — rage, terror, and grief. In everyone
with an oral issue, the experience of need will elicit rage. As a consequence, the need cannot be simply and clearly experienced as a profound feeling that is a natural part of living. This changes when the
accompanying rage, associated with past disappointments, has been
worked through or cleaned out. Then, need is experienced as a part
of living and the feeling of need as an exquisite part of the human condition. As the schizoid begins to know life in the freer movement of
his body and breathing, the oral regains his life in experiencing clearly
the need within him. He is strong enough to experience the need without having to have it immediately satisfied. Also, he knows the need
will never be satisfied if it is never experienced. Need is a passport to
satisfaction, but in adulthood it is not a guarantee of immediate gratification. Satisfaction requires the strength and assertiveness to which
the therapy for the oral should be equally devoted. If it is not, the therapy will yield only someone who is able to need, but unable to act to
have his needs met.

As the oral person begins to improve, he will be more and more able
to completely relax and to surrender to his need for collapse. There
will be an increasing tendency to accept the rest and relaxation without the need for pulling up out of it to do something or be somebody.
As the oral lets go of his compensation in this way, he will be more
accepting of his limitations and arrange his life to compensate for them.
He may, for example, work less than full-time or cut back in other
commitments to nurture himself. The oral is an undercharged, and
therefore weakened, organism and will usually carry some of that vul-

nerability throughout his life. Acceptance of this, at both an intellectual and practical level, is evidence of his healing. With increased strength and acceptance, the oral person will realize that to a great extent he has made it alone in life and is capable of doing so even though he desires a greater sense of attachment and belonging. Thus, he will be more and more free of anxiety about abandonment, panic at being alone, or grief about his prior losses. He will enjoy his time alone. Concomitant with that, one of the great joys of oral healing exists in repeated discoveries of his ability to function autonomously and meet the responsibilities of adult living calmly and competently. Discrete behavioral programs to that end can be very useful and I have written extensively on methods and sources for this kind of programmatic learning of autonomy (Johnson, 1977).

In relationships with others, the oral will be increasingly able to give *and* take rather than to give *or* take. She will become less invested in nurturing the helpless or in being helplessly nurtured. She will be able to be a member of the group or community without always assuming the role of the all-giving nurturer or, alternatively, the role of the recipient of others' welfare. As in all character transformations, her love relationships will either evolve or be replaced by new ones which are more reciprocally adult in character.

In general, of course, all of the changes outlined above will take place gradually rather than suddenly. In the oral case, particularly, there tends to be a pattern of improvement and backsliding and a good deal of patience is required. As issues are worked through, there will be a deepening in the achievement of therapeutic goals with repeated wins and losses along the way. In the oral case, perhaps more than any other, healing will come with the integration of the key polarities—weak-strong, nurturing-collapsed, and give-take. With this integration accomplished, living a realistically rewarding adult life becomes possible.

CHAPTER VIII

THE EGO REPAIR SHOP:
STRATEGIES FOR SUPPORTIVE THERAPY

Analytical work needs hundreds of different fantasies — not techniques, not methods — but fantasies within which one can work. It can be baseball or bullfighting or cooking or farming or military strategy or weaving or shell collecting or sculpting. . . . Unless you have a fantasy of work, there is only work as collectively conceived, a kind of literalism that is either Marxist or psychoanalytic "working through" — very heavy, very dull, very resentment producing. One needs a fantasy that gives a body feeling, a manual feeling to the job you are engaged in. And it helps in therapy to mention casually along the way which fantasy you are working with, because one of the things therapy has to do is to work on the problem of work itself in the patient, help the patient learn in therapy how to imagine the act of working. So, if I can say what fantasy we are in now: encircling the city of high walls or turning up the heat a little or trying to get more rose-madder and aquamarine and Naples yellow into the picture, then these fantasies keep the analytic work from becoming literalized into a "what-we-are-supposed-to-be-doing," some abstract concept, some idol called "analysis."

— James Hillman (1983, pp. 175–176)

I HAVE BEEN immensely helped in my own practice of psychotherapy by expanding the models I use for envisoning the activity. Among those models are nurse, parent, family therapist, high school coach, analyst, teacher, business consultant, listener and Zen master. It is important to remember that each hour of psychotherapy is an hour devoted to improving the quality of the client's life in either the short or long run. Any fixed notion concerning what that hour must be about constrains flexibility and limits potential. Different clients require us to play different roles and the same client may very well require different roles at different times. We must do whatever we can to legitimize the

243

freedom we can have as psychotherapists to flow with the client rather than fit him into our preconceived notions of psychotherapy. So often, the fixed and confining notions we have about psychotherapy come out of the insecurity of our trainers and the insecurity in ourselves over a process which severely challenges the limits of our intellectual and emotional understanding of life itself.

This chapter will highlight the integrative thrust of this book perhaps more directly than any other. This is so because "supportive therapy," so often misunderstood, requires an underlying theory which indicates what is to be "supported" and specifies what should happen if adequate "support" is given. Ego psychology does this very well. The "descriptive developmental diagnosis" advocated by Blanck and Blanck (1974, 1979) offers a comprehensive reading of a client's ego functioning and suggests what elements of ego functioning might be acknowledged, bolstered, redirected, etc. A knowledge of object relations theory helps in this endeavor through outlining how the normal human infant develops the relevant ego functions. Psychoanalytic psychotherapy contributes a well-thought-out menu of classical verbal therapy methods which have been used in supportive or ego-building therapy. Finally, the therapeutic schools which advocate more active, here-and-now approaches to human problems contribute a myriad of strategies aimed at better ego functioning. But, to integrate all this, not only in your head but in your behavior, requires many different "fantasies" of therapeutic work. The theoretical underpinning of object relations and ego psychology will render the fantasies consistent though radically different. In this way, you can be eclectic without being completely confused.

THE DEFICIT MODEL AND THE CONFLICT MODEL

Throughout this volume, I have presented an approach to psychotherapy which balances the objective of eroding the client's destructive defenses and compromises against the objective of strengthening those adaptive abilities and defensive functions which help the client cope with internal demands and deficiencies as well as meet the external requirements of reality. Without this balance, therapy for many individuals may risk decompensation on the one hand or be no more than superficial counseling for coping on the other. I am convinced that the vast majority of psychotherapy clients require this continually balanced approach, which utilizes both the deficit model and the conflict model to explain and treat psychopathology. Most clients observed in general outpatient treatment fortunately do not suffer the kind of severe ego deficits characteristic of the dramatically borderline or narcissistic characters described by Kernberg, Kohut, and others. By the same token, most psychotherapy clients today do not possess that solid level of ego organization which would entitle them to be called "neurotic" in the classic psychoanalytic meaning of that term. In other words, most clients in psychotherapy today have deficiencies in preoedipal development such that they are dealing with more than simply a malfunctioning defense structure against the emergence of "id" impulses. Much of the psychoanalytic literature misses the point, it seems to me, in concentrating on these two extremes, when most people who require psychotherapy are somewhere in the middle. They have the ego structure to function in the world, earn a living, sustain some level of human, sexual, and intimate relationships, and acquire some pleasure in living. Yet their lives may be plagued by essentially preoedipal psychological issues rendering ego functioning deficient in cognitive abilities, behavioral execution, and affective regulation. So, for most psychotherapy clients, treatment must be much more than ego reconstruction and, at the same time, more than working through the resistance provided by an ego defense to an id impulse. For psychotherapists, knowing when to do how much of what in this balancing act is an essential ingredient of the art. The insights of object relations theory and character analysis, therefore, are of very great utility to the practicing therapist, for they apply to most if not all of the therapist's clientele, even when ego functioning appears intact.

Throughout the discussion of the schizoid and oral characters, I have emphasized a continuum of functioning, with the highly compensated, well-functioning individual at one end of that continuum and the undefended, collapsed, or borderline individual at the other. On the face of it, it would appear that the less compensated individual would require more ego-building therapy while the more compensated character would require more of those techniques which bring to his attention the great cost of his compromises and adaptations. While there is some truth to this, particularly in the initial stages of treatment, the underlying theory is helpful in alerting us to the fact that an individual who *appears* to be very adaptive may really be covering some very severe deficiencies in ego development. Similarly, the client whose ego abilities are overwhelmed by panic, for example, may possess some fairly highly evolved functions which have been temporarily overwhelmed. In the first case the treatment may be far more protracted and reparative than would initially be suggested, while in the latter case the prognosis for treatment may be more favorable than is indicated by the initial evaluation. A deep appreciation of the client's level of ego functioning requires time and experience with the client's coping mechanisms over the course of treatment. Usually, inexperienced therapists tend to overestimate rather than underestimate the client's level of emotional development.

The developmental theory outlined here provides a reorientation to the classical concept of resistance. The client's negativism, reluctance, and stubborn holding on to maladaptive patterns are not merely resistance to giving up defensive maneuvers which control id impulses. Rather, they often represent the person's clinging to a primitive ego adaptation which covers a serious ego deficiency and literally allows him to function. If that primitive adaptation were taken away before the underlying ego dysfunctions were repaired, or another more evolved adaptation reached, a decompensation could well occur. On occasion, this does occur, particularly with therapies and transformational group procedures which do not take these factors into account and overwhelm the precarious adaptive functions.

A commonly seen example of this kind of primitive ego adaptation exists with those individuals who hold rigidly and defensively to an inflexible, moralistic, fundamentalist, often religious position. Typically, these people have swallowed whole a very simplistic, dogmatic, and punitive moral position which is obviously low in the hierarchical development of moral sense. Frequently, they believe that when people do not hold similar views, they are possessed by evil and threaten the very fabric of society. Essentially, this is a projection. These people need such a belief system in order to control their own primitive impulses, and their defense of this position is completely in the interest of themselves and the community. This is not to say, of course, that these individuals cannot achieve a higher level of moral development. It is merely to illustrate the point being made here and to caution against attempts to remove primitive adaptations before the underlying deficits are repaired.

The objective of this chapter is to reemphasize and elaborate on the value of "descriptive developmental diagnosis" (Blanck & Blanck, 1974) and more exclusively and self-consciously than in prior chapters to address the problem of ego repair from the point of view of the integration of therapeutic technique that seems necessary at this time. I do not intend to provide extensive descriptions of the specific techniques of classical verbal supportive therapy. This has been done extensively by those who have far more experience with it than I; in this regard, I refer you to those books which have been of most use to me (Langs, 1973; Blanck & Blanck, 1974, 1979). Rather, I will outline the kinds of questions to ask regarding ego functioning, and catalogue the verbal techniques. I will then elaborate on the very real contributions to be made by adopting a cognitive-behavioral-systems perspective in addressing the problem of ego repair. By attending to the contributions of the behavioral, family, and strategic therapists, I believe we can greatly assist the client's ego development well beyond the therapeutic hour. By directing our own and our client's attention to the outside world, we can strengthen ego function through the basic principle of "exercise of function" in day-to-day living. By collaborating with the functioning "adult observing ego" of the client, we can formulate agreements with him for work in the outside world which will provide both the assessment and exercise of ego functioning. His execution of the agreed-upon intervention will serve a diagnostic purpose by revealing his level of ego functioning and the nature of resistances, thereby suggesting further interventions. The execution of the agreed-upon intervention will exercise the function of the ego and begin to establish more evolved and autonomous functioning.

AUTONOMY AND EGO FUNCTIONING

It is extremely important in executing these more active, prescriptive techniques to do so in the context of an adult-adult therapeutic alliance rather than in the context of a parent-child milieu that would pull for the client's resistance in the interest of his own autonomy. When I introduce this orientation to clients, I often use the metaphor of piano lessons. One function of the piano teacher is, of course, to introduce the student to new material and directly teach new technique. Yet perhaps the teacher's most important function is to simply work out a suggested lesson for the student to practice and use each lesson as a catalyst to encourage that practice. In employing this kind of prescriptive psychotherapy, I am careful to point out to the client that, at some level, it doesn't matter whether he accomplishes the agreed-upon task or not. If he succeeds, he will be moving along in the direction we both agree he wants to move. If he does not, this will be feedback concerning the block to completion, which we may then explore with many other methods.

The collaborative, adult-adult milieu is perhaps the most important component of this kind of treatment from an ego-building standpoint. This is so because the "guardianship of autonomy" (Greenacre, 1959) should be the therapist's guiding principle in conducting supportive therapy. Thus, anything that will protect or enhance the client's autonomous ego functioning may, other things being equal, be confidently employed. However, anything that will erode autonomy or infantilize the client is to be avoided.

The application of this autonomy principle gets sticky, of course, in those situations where therapy involves the creation of symbiotic matrix within which grounded ego functioning can be truly achieved. In these cases, the therapist walks a tightrope in which the moment-to-moment balance between immediate necessity for attachment and eventual achievement of autonomy must be continually kept in sight.

In addition to integrating some of the approaches of behavioral, strategic, and family therapy for their "outreach" function, I also wish to devote some of this chapter to further integration of cognitive approaches to psychotherapy. Here I wish to elaborate further on what I consider to be the key cognitive therapy contribution: the value of detailed attention to the precise sequencing of mental representations in an adaptive or maladaptive thought process. One may ask, for example, "What is your internal mental strategy for becoming depressed, anxious, suspicious, overwhelmed, or your strategy for feeling competent, secure, and loved? What do you do internally with auditory, kinesthetic, and visual representations to manipulate your state of mind? Further, what are your internal cognitive strategies for instrumental sequences such as fixing breakfast, cleaning your house, or selling your car? How can these outlines of adaptive and maladaptive internal sequencing be used to assist in the diagnosis and repair of adaptive ego function?"

In the application of this cognitive metastrategy, the objective is to nurture the development of the client's autonomy, to enable the client's observing ego to see how his cognitive strategies work and to determine where they are adaptive and maladaptive. Frequently, in the use of this strategy, one can find a content area in which the client's cognitive strategies are functional and bring that sequence to bear in areas where functioning is dysfunctional. Further, it is clearly in line with the therapist's supportive function to assist the client in experiencing where his functioning is adaptive and useful to himself and others. It should be remembered, however, that where this kind of therapy is simply a demonstration of the therapist's exercise of function, it may be minimally useful as modeling but runs the risk of being demoralizing and fostering dependency. To remedy this, I have often found self-disclosure useful in presenting what I have learned about the value of examining and repairing my own cognitive strategies.

In sum, this chapter is somewhat of a potpourri of strategies for ego assessment and repair presented within the rubric of a comprehensive developmental theory which can easily incorporate everything from psychoanalytic psychotherapy to behavior modification.

ASSESSMENT OF EGO FUNCTION

Perhaps the overwhelming advantage of an object relations or ego psychology perspective is that it attunes the therapist, and ultimately the client, to the developmental level of ego functioning and offers something of a road map for the further development of that functioning. Thus, an accurate diagnosis leads one to have at least a general idea about what to support and what to ignore, what to confront and what to leave alone, what kind of advice will be within the client's capacity to follow and what will not, which forms of exercise of ego function are possible and which are beyond the client's capacity, what current ego functions may be used to increase adaptation and which are still to be developed. With this more sophisticated knowledge, then, supportive therapy becomes much more than just being nice to people, teaching them what they do not know, or attempting to remove maladaptive behaviors and attitudes which are absolutely essential to shore up a faulty ego structure.

What follows is a still-incomplete list of questions which a therapist may ask concerning any client to establish some general understanding regarding his level of ego functioning. In reviewing this list, it may be well to consider the fact that while there is a general tendency for the level of ego development to be consistent at a certain level across categories, this is not always the case. It is still quite common, particularly in reasonably well-functioning adults, to find a person who has "missed a stitch" in some pocket of ego functioning, such that his level of development is very primitive in that area while much more developed in others. It is possible, for example, for a schizoid client to respond with a great deal of anxiety to situations of personal threat, almost as if reactivating an early schizoid fear of annihilation, while at the same time possessing a very intact level of ego functioning. Where there is a full-blown and clear-cut borderline or narcissistic adjustment, however, there is frequently a surprisingly consistent profile in terms of the analogue developmental level of the ego functioning in question. In formulating the questions that follow, I wish to acknowledge my considerable debt to Gertrude and Reuben Blanck who have so well synthesized a good deal of this material in *Ego Psychology: Theory and Practice* (1974), chapter 7, and *Ego Psychology II: Developmental Psychology* (1979), chapters 5 and 12. Most of the questions outlined below are attributable to the work of Blanck and Blanck though this specific elaboration is my own.

1) *Self-representation*: Is there a firm representation of the self? Does this self-representation include a clear self-image, a kinesthetic sense of self identified with the body, and a cognitive understanding of "who I am"? Is the self-representation clearly differentiated from the representation of others, such that one knows what is coming from inside and what is coming from outside? Is this differentiation stable or fluctuating? If it fluctuates, what triggers that fluctuation? Is there splitting in the self-representation such that the client experiences himself as all good at certain points in time and all bad at others? Does the client expect you or others to read his mind and fulfill his wishes on the basis of only his having that wish? Does the person continuously seek union with another and feel incomplete outside that merger? Does the self-representation include a solid sense of gender identity? Does the individual desire in a significant other someone who is "just like me"?

2) *Object-representations and relations*: Does the client perceive others as they really are or as he wishes or fears them to be? Are others valued beyond their need-gratifying abilities and is there a relative "constant" value placed on others which does not fluctuate with the person's need level or mood state? Can the person maintain a relatively stable visual, kinesthetic, and auditory representation of the other? Are others self objects or real objects? What is the nature of transference in therapy—distrust, merger, dependency, twinship, idealization, placating, manipulative, challenging? Is the desire for merger, if present, conscious, denied, or defended against in some other fashion? What is the quality of the person's outside relationships in love, work, and friendship?

3) *Anxiety*: What is the primary anxiety—fear of annihilation, fear of loss of the object, fear of loss of the love of the object, "castration anxiety" (fear of retaliation), or fear of the superego? How does the client handle anxiety? Can an anxiety-provoking situation serve to enhance performance, indicating that it serves a signal function, or does it consistently overwhelm the individual's ability to function, indicating that signal anxiety has not been achieved? With respect to anxiety or distress, what is the extent of self-soothing capacities and to what extent can the individual be externally soothed? To what extent does the level of anxiety fluctuate and to what extent is anxiety situation-specific? What situations elicit anxiety and what situations elicit relaxation?

When anxiety is overwhelming in one or a few areas, this does not necessarily indicate that signal anxiety is not operative. It may simply mean that, in that area of functioning, there is some internal conflict which seriously debilitates performance in that area. Blanck and Blanck (1979, p. 223) write:

The patient whose anxiety does not abate, who cannot employ competent defenses nor tolerate the small doses of anxiety that we all live with, who is in terror most of the time, who does not have self-soothing mechanisms but needs to be soothed, or the one who cannot even accept soothing, is living with levels of anxiety that have not diminished to a signal.

4) *Defensive functions*: How well can the individual defend? What is the developmental level of the defensive function? Are the defenses primarily so primitive in nature as to be characteristic of the earliest

kind of developmental arrest, which we have labeled schizoid—denial, introjection, projection? Or are defenses more characteristic of the oral period, including turning against the self, reversal, displacement, and identification? Or do the defenses more characterize those later phases of separation-individuation so as to include undoing, reaction formation, isolation or splitting, intellectualization, and even regression? Or is the defensive structure primarily oriented around repression and suppression of id impulses, characterizing the more highly developed ego structures? Which mechanisms of defense are ego-syntonic and which ego-dystonic?

5) *Regulation or containment*: Is the person capable of regulating or containing anger or grief in response to frustration, loss, or disappointment? How is the containment accomplished both cognitively and energetically? Does the containment require withdrawal or elicit paranoid ideation?

6) *Adaptive functioning*: What is the quality of the individual's overall external perception (reality-testing)? What is his ability to delay gratification? To what extent can the client formulate intentions and follow through on them? What is the quality of abstract thought, the ability to synthesize and integrate? What is the level of functioning of memory? Are deficits in memory content-specific? Where adaptive functions are adequate, what are the properties of the adaptive strategies involved? Where the adaptive functions are impaired, where is the deficiency in the adaptive strategy?

7) *Internalization*: To what extent has the individual internalized parental and societal values to formulate a "superego" or cohesive value structure? What is the developmental level of the person's moral sense and is there consistency between belief and behavior? Is the value or moral structure cohesive and unified or does it exist in unintegrated components? Does the primary anxiety involve fear of the superego and experience of true guilt or does it involve developmentally lower levels of anxiety? Who were the primary figures for identification? Were there difficulties in development which would have precluded or interfered with identification or prompted a refusal to identify? To what extent were the identificatory figures adequate from the point of view of developing a mature moral sense?

8) *Affect; range and differentiation*: How much can the person feel and how subtle are the differentiations among feelings? Are particular or all affects muted or out of proportion to the eliciting situation? How does the client stand in relation to the ability to experience and express the primary colors in the affective range: anger, grief, fear or anxiety, love, joy, personal power, etc. What is the extent of mood swings? What is the preponderant affective state?

9) *Regression*: Can the individual regress and maintain ego control of that regression? In what areas does such regression occur — in regulation or containment, object relations, adaptive functions, anxiety level, defensive functions? Is such regression engaged in for pleasure or creativity? This ability to regress while maintaining ego control is essential for the successful completion of much of the Gestalt, affect release, bioenergetic, and certain forms of hypnotic processes outlined here. When these abilities are not intact, the client may be seriously retraumatized in the process, further stiffening the resistance to change.

10) *Oedipal complex*: Is there evidence from the client's material that the oedipal situation was confronted in the family of origin? To what extent did preoedipal issues and the failure of their resolution affect the nature and eventual resolution of the oedipal complex? What were the attitudes of the parents to the love and sexual reaching out of the child? What were the patterns, if any, of parental seduction, rejection, threat, etc.?

With the answers to these and other related questions coming out of psychoanalytic developmental theory, the therapist will be armed with an ego profile of the client. This profile, when timely shared and adequately delivered, can provide the client's adult observing ego with a very useful tool. Operating with this shared profile perspective, the clinician and client can enter a true therapeutic alliance aimed at repair of function and eventually resolution of conflict.

As indicated earlier, I believe that such a combination of the deficit and conflict models and associated therapeutic function is necessary in almost every case of outpatient psychotherapy. The dichotomy of oedipal versus preoedipal personality seems to exist rarely in nature and, I think, even more rarely in therapy. As a dichotomy it is generally false; as a continuum, it can be incredibly useful.

TECHNIQUES OF VERBAL PSYCHOTHERAPY

It is helpful at this point to briefly outline and define the most commonly used techniques in classic verbal psychotherapy that have been used in the context of "supportive therapy." Most, though not all, of these techniques come from the literature on psychoanalytic psychotherapy—an activity characterized by far more active techniques than psychoanalysis proper. This verbal and usually face-to-face form of psychotherapy has been created to respond to the ever-greater proportion of clients who do not possess the ego structure for classical analysis. This outline provides a sort of "baseline" of active psychotherapy technique to which I will add by the integration of some other models— namely, behavior modification, cognitive psychotherapy, strategic and family therapy. Psychoanalytic psychotherapists generally agree that these techniques should be used primarily in the context of encouraging the client's exercise of his own ego function following the guiding principle of "guardianship of autonomy" (Greenacre, 1959).

1) *Ego support*: Acknowledgment, encouragement, or praise of the client's existing or evolving ego functions. Ego support is technically most useful when it is specifically directed toward assisting the client in appreciating the ego resources which he does have and does exercise. Alternatively, it is used to reinforce and thereby encourage ego development in those areas on which the client is working. Supportive comments can be used in the context of *reframing*, such that the therapist may find positive ego functioning even in the client's negative experiences. In any case, ego support is most constructive when it relates to specific life experiences and is directed from the adult ego state of the therapist to the adult in the client to acknowledge and encourage further development and exercise of such things as reality-testing, synthetic functions, moral development, consciously used psychological defenses, differentiation, initiative, etc.

2) *Confrontation*: A presentation to the client of an external view of his behavior, attitudes, conflicts, and defenses as they relate to cur-

rent situations. In confrontation, the therapist simply directs the client's attention to an aspect of his behavior of which he is already aware, and invites him to take a look at what he is doing from the perspective of his observing ego. As distinct from interpretation, confrontation focuses on current situations or real conflicts rather than being directed at unconscious or intrapsychic conflicts or historical antecedents of current patterns. Where the therapist is more active, confrontation may involve the therapist's offering the client a "snapshot" of himself. At a more surface level, this may assist the client to see himself as others see him or, at a deeper level, become aware of his own behavioral and thought processes. Where the therapist is less active, he may simply direct the client's attention to an observed pattern of thought or behavior and promote the exercise of ego function by inviting him to take a critical look at it.

Confrontations are technically most helpful when they are adult-adult communications completely free of judgmental content or tone. In some circles, the confrontation label has been used to justify castigating clients in hopes of changing their more destructive behavior patterns. This use of confrontation has been generally disapproved of in the psychotherapy literature because it is not believed to encourage the development of autonomous ego and superego functioning. Further, it tends to disrupt the therapeutic alliance and, in fact, encourage a more infantile level of ego adaptation.

3) *Explanation*: The therapist shares her knowledge of human psychological processes and indicates how this general knowledge may apply to the client's current situation. Explanation is a very explicit exercise of the therapist's educative function, which engages the client's adult, observing ego and encourages exercise of cognitive functioning. Explanation may lay the groundwork for the client's own use of reconstruction and interpretation.

4) *Interpretation*: Cognitive restructuring by the therapist of the client's behavior, attitudes, or feelings designed to render conscious previously unconscious conflicts and/or transference concerning the therapist or others. As indicated in the last chapter, most if not all interpretations involve some connection between points along the triangle of conflict and/or the triangle of person. Interpretations are believed most effective when they are experienced by the client as both cognitive-

ly meaningful and affectively contactful. Dreams, fantasies, and real world reactions which seem overdetermined are common subjects for interpretation, as is transference or resistance in therapy.

5) *Reconstructions*: The therapist's attempt to build a historical scenario for the client which explains the client's current level of functioning, fantasies, affective reactions, or associational content. These verbal interventions lie somewhere between explanations and interpretations and are used to hypothetically construct a historical understanding of the kind of psychological trauma which would produce the current level of the patient's dysfunction or conflict. Reconstructions are particularly useful where the etiological trauma appears to be preverbal and therefore difficult if not impossible to recall, or where that trauma has been so effectively repressed that interpretive efforts do not release it. Though reconstructions do not typically have the affective impact associated with a well-placed interpretation, they can result in the client's general understanding of his own trauma-based functioning and even pave the way for eventual traumatic recall. It is often important for clients to realize that whatever problems they have in living were natural and expectable given their history and genetic endowment. In other words, it is important that clients appreciate that they are not bad and evil people but rather people who suffer the natural consequences of early injury. To give the adult, observing ego some cause-effect construction of the likely etiology promotes organization and encourages further exercise of this organizational ego function. As one of my clients said to me rather abruptly but appropriately, "In other words, what you are saying is that if I'm pregnant I must have been fucked."

6) *Questions and clarifications*: Questions and requests for clarification are attempts by the therapist to resolve ambiguity and bring greater specificity to the client's communications regarding behaviors, attitudes, and feelings. Because people use words differently, these verbal procedures are particularly crucial to assure that the therapist is fully understanding the client's experience or "deep structure" (Dilts et al., 1980). One person's depression is another person's anxiety, etc. It is essential, particularly as a therapist attempts to intervene in the client's cognitive functioning, that he know as precisely as possible the nature

of that functioning. Further, questions and requests for clarification are ego-building in that they require the client to exercise the ego functions involved in responding—perception, affect differentiation, reality-testing, synthesis, etc. Clients with certain forms of ego dysfunction will expect or at least hope that the therapist will read their minds and that verbalization will not be necessary. Thus, questions and requests for clarification challenge this dysfunctional illusion and begin its working-through process.

7) *Encouragement of verbalization*: The client's verbalization of his experiences, feelings, and conflicts is ego-building and conflict-resolving in several respects. First, as the client talks about reactions, states of mind, or beliefs that have been either preverbal or unconscious, he renders them more available for ego processing through assimilation, accommodation, synthesis, etc. In effect, verbalization is exercise of ego function and encourages further exercise. Second, verbalization serves to regulate drive and affect in providing a more evolved set of functions than simply acting on impulse or feeling. Third, verbalization confronts the more primitively organized individual with the necessity for communicating clearly and specifically, challenging the wish to be understood without the need for verbal communication. Finally, tolerance of frustration may be developed through verbalization, thus building the capacity to delay gratification. It is important, for example, for the client to realize and then state, "It really feels as if you disappear once I leave your office." Or, "I feel like killing you when you say that."

8) *Silence*: The meaning and impact of silence on the part of the therapist are always contextual. Silence can be highly traumatizing or the most effective of interventions. Used appropriately, silence can communicate respect, listening, acceptance, or encouragement of greater ego autonomy. Particularly where the client's history includes severe absence of preverbal symbiotic union, developing the client's ability to tolerate and even enjoy long periods of silence with the therapist can be very reparative. In other contexts, silence and the nonverbal communication which accompanies it can be used as a method to discourage lines of thought or behavior. Alternatively, silence in the proper context can build frustration tolerance and demand that the

client use his own devices to resolve that condition. For further elaboration on the use of silence, see Langs (1973).

9) *Advice-giving*: Advice in the present context refers to the sharing of the therapist's opinion concerning what the client should do or how he should think about a particular situation in his life. In general, of course, psychotherapists give much less advice than many patients initially expect; in fact, in the field of psychoanalytic psychotherapy, offering advice is generally viewed as a rather primitive and ill-advised technique, except in extreme emergency situations. The very sound reason behind this eschewing of advice-giving revolves primarily around the concern for ego-building and guardianship of autonomy. The object of psychotherapy should be the ever-greater reliance of the client on his own resources. And, in any case, advice-giving invites the inappropriate projection of the therapist's value structure and erroneous perceptions onto the client's life. For the most part, people tend to need to make their own mistakes and learn directly from them.

On the other hand, I think it is incorrect to take a rigid position on this. Certainly, when a client's behavior or situation endangers himself or others, advice is appropriate. Beyond this, there are probably occasions in which advice-giving will further autonomy rather than discourage it. There are often those situations in the client's life which put her under so much external stress that substantial or lasting therapeutic progress is all but precluded. In these situations, it is obviously necessary to initially confront the client with this reality and attempt to elicit and support her ego mechanisms in dealing with it. Sometimes these efforts fail and not infrequently this failure is caused by simple cognitive rules, often preconscious or unconscious, which restrict the individual's ability to problem solve. When this is the case, it is once again important to detect and then confront the client with this reality. This kind of work is close to advice-giving and may on rare occasions become advice when confrontation and the encouragement of autonomous functioning fail. In this rare situation, advice-giving is truly in the service of the ego as it is aimed at relieving the stress which makes further adaptation impossible.

10) *Behavioral prescription*: Though prescribing particular behavior to a client does tell him what to do, it can be very different from advice-

giving. It prescribes a course of action to work through a problem rather than directly advising a resolution to it. It is a therapeutic task guided by the concept of guardianship of autonomy. When best executed, it involves a collaborative alliance with the client in determining the exact nature of the prescription itself. Though definitional of much behavior modification, this technique is widely used in many forms of counseling and psychotherapy.

11) *Persuasion*: In the most general sense, persuasion is clearly a part of all forms of psychotherapy. Though the form of persuasion may be subtle, all therapies implicitly offer the hope of an improved quality of life, and each therapist, in his own way, persuades the client that this hope is at least somewhat justified. Even where such persuasion is paradoxical, it still exists—perhaps even more powerfully so. I believe it is incumbent on the therapist, a professional communicator, to be very cognizant of the effects of his communications and structure them with this responsibility in mind. As the therapist is more active and prescriptive, he will need to be more facile with both direct and strategic methods of persuasion. However, whatever the orientation, all forms of therapy are essentially selling a world view and a way to deal with human suffering. Once therapists are clear about this, they may then take more fully conscious responsibility for the effects of their communications.

LEVELS OF SUPPORTIVE THERAPY

In integrating verbal and other strategies for supportive therapy I have found it useful to distinguish the following levels of ego support. These cut across all techniques of whatever origin.

The first category is *simple human support* and refers to those activities which one human being can do for another to be supportive by simple availability and presence. These include such things as attentive and active listening, personal congruence, empathic response, and contact, both physical and emotional. Frequently, and especially in periods of crisis, an individual's ego functioning may simply be overwhelmed by anxiety and adequate functioning may be achieved with the simple reassurance provided by the true presence of another involved human being. Even where more needs to be done, this simple human supportiveness is often prerequisite to the other more involved processes.

The second level of supportive therapy I have labeled *auxiliary ego support*. This refers to those instances in which the therapist almost literally loans his ego abilities to the client, assisting with the client's judgment, reality-testing, cognitive structuring of experience, etc. In this category of activity, the therapist is primarily counseling, sharing perceptions, or even advising.

The third level of supportive therapy I have labeled *instructional support* or *ego-building*. This refers to therapist activities or strategies which are self-consciously aimed at strengthening a client's ego function. Here we are referring to techniques which help develop the client's ability to make decisions, test reality, structure his cognitive understanding of the world, manage personal and interpersonal affairs, etc. The objective is to leave the client with skills which render her more instrumental or functional in life. Like most categorizations of this kind, this one is primarily of heuristic value. Therapeutic activities overlap these categories, and even simple human support, for example, creates that human matrix wherein the lost self of the schizoid or oral client may be found and developed. The categories are useful, however, in legitimizing all levels of supportive psychotherapy and orienting the clinician to what is being done and why.

Having now reviewed the assessment of ego function, the common forms of ego supportive verbal therapy, and the levels of ego support, we may turn to more active strategies for supportive therapy. A case study will begin this process.

A CASE OF SUPPORTIVE THERAPY

Melissa is a 31-year-old woman whom I have seen in essentially supportive psychotherapy for over four years. Her history is one of extreme early deprivation and abuse yielding a powerfully schizoid character with a developmentally low level of ego functioning. Though she is still unable to remember a good deal of her history or to confide all of what she does remember, extreme maternal deprivation and hostility are evident. She remembers that her mother refused to feed her as a child and she has been told that this refusal went back to infancy. She was dependent for food on her father, a marginally functioning alcoholic who was alternately nurturing and verbally abusive to her. Melissa's mother was psychologically torturing toward her. She remembers many instances of abusive criticism, withholding of food, and bizarre acts of hostility aimed at her by both her mother and older sister.

The father left the home when Melissa was eight years of age, moving into a shack nearby. Melissa remembers that when her mother and sister were particularly cruel to her she would go to her father, who would initially offer support but eventually deliver malicious verbal attacks. Later analysis revealed an atypical symbiotic characterological issue developed in response to her father's behavior towards her.

Melissa developed a brittle and fragile "as if" personality to cover the deep early trauma suffered in the family. For periods of time, she had been able to maintain a very superficial yet ambulatory level of functioning. Periodically, however, she would be overwhelmed by panic, possessed by a demonic, self-destructive force, lose track of time for hours in a twilight fugue state, become seriously suicidal, experience relatively constant terror, and be unable to eat or sleep. These episodes lasted for several days at a time and provided the most painful part of her symptomatology. In therapy, she has often been unable to tell me any details of her present or past life for fear of being punished by the demonic force. Until the last year of treatment, she frequently spoke in code words which had meaning to her but which she could not define for me. Nearly every therapy session begins with her being unable to talk about anything as she struggles for and resists human contact.

In the early years of therapy, she had no real sense of self, relating almost completely through the "as if" self. Now, a sense of self and realness comes and goes. In keeping with this, she has changed from living a fairly solitary life to being rather deeply involved with a small group of female friends. Attachment in therapy has progressed from a situation in which I was barely recognized to a deep and very symbiotic attachment. As this was developing, it was necessary to deal with and work through dependency issues which arose as the attachment was being formed. Gentle but firm limits were established and now Melissa is a regular, biweekly client with whom there is occasional brief telephone contact. My vacations still provide a problem with which she deals more and more constructively.

In the sections which follow, I will discuss a number of general principles involved in the treatment of the less well compensated schizoid and oral clients. In each section, Melissa's treatment will provide exemplary illustrations of the general topic under discussion, knitting this diverse discourse together with a single human thread.

The Holding Environment

Melissa's case is one of those in which the provision of simple human support is instructional and ego-building. This is so because it repairs the severe early damage and recreates that symbiotic matrix of the self and other in which an identity can be established. Melissa was especially challenging, however, because her inability to really talk to me at the beginning of each session necessitated discovery of other forms in which to provide a holding environment. Relaxation methods, meditation, and hypnotic induction procedures all failed to calm or reassure her; instead, they served only to make her even more mentally active and fearful. In the course of the work, however, I learned that some very brief and simple bioenergetic grounding exercises as described in chapters III and VI comforted her and enabled her to begin to make contact and communicate. Second, I learned that my talking to her about my own life, feelings, intentions for our therapeutic work, etc., brought her into reality contact with me. Finally, I discovered that some very minimal physical contact would break through the barrier. Initially this amounted to a mere touch in the context of the bioenergetic work. Eventually, I learned that holding her feet would calm and ground her.

While I believe it is very important to take great care in respecting the client's boundaries regarding touching and to be very clear about what one's own boundaries are in this regard, physical contact is essential for many clients. The injury is preverbal and the repair will be best done at a concrete physical level. I think it is important to ask the client's permission before any touching is begun and for the therapist to be particularly sensitive to the effects it has. Establishing and working within boundaries established at a physical level provide just one more way of working with the self-other boundary issue. The simple relaxation exercises of bioenergetics provide a particularly useful context within which to introduce contact. Placing the therapist's hands on the client's lower back while she is in the forward position, for example, provides a relatively innocuous touch. Similarly, the whole issue of accepting support may be addressed in the simple concrete act of asking the client to stand and lean backward against the therapist, who provides support. Another alternative which gives supportive contact while minimizing the threat of contact involves the therapist and client sitting on the floor back-to-back, mutually supporting one another.

In Melissa's treatment, I have explored the effects of a number of such physical interventions. Through them she has come to know what level of contact and intimacy is reassuring and what level is threatening. A whole segment of therapy had to do with exploring these boundaries of social distance and assisting her in initiating and terminating contact or in distancing or closing the gap between us. These precedents established, she or I will now initiate some very simple contact which can have the effect of grounding her and, as such, laying the groundwork for an entirely productive hour of verbal interchange. I may, for example, sit on the floor in front of her with her feet resting in my lap, literally providing the kind of grounding that a mother provides a child. Another posture which is far more intimate but which she is now able to tolerate involves her sitting on the floor in front of me and leaning back so that her back rests on my chest. This classic bioenergetic holding posture provides perhaps the most literal holding environment for the client. It does, of course, carry transference and countertransference risk, particularly in cases where there is any sexual charge between the participants. The therapist's job is not to avoid these risks, but to manage them, giving the client the sense of solid, firm boundaries in the interaction. In Melissa's case, this simple human physical support has been absolutely essential before much auxiliary ego support or instructional ego-building support could be attempted.

Auxiliary Instructional Support

As our relationship began to build, Melissa found the courage to confront her self-punitive demonic part by talking with me about some concrete life stressors. She had, for example, fearfully avoided renewing her driver's license for over a year. Because of her delay, she had to take both the written and driving test over again and was terrified of failure. She had been driving with an expired license for over a year when she confessed this and said that her demonic self-punishment was often centered on this situation. In the next session, at my request, she began to bring the driver's manual and I spent about 10 minutes of every session constructing sample questions for her. After four to six weeks of this work, Melissa was able to go to the Department of Motor Vehicles and rather smoothly pass both written and performance aspects of the test.

With the successful completion of this task, Melissa came in and confessed that she had also failed to pay her income taxes for the last three years out of the same kind of fear — self-punishment pattern. As with the driver's license situation, she expected some dire consequences from this failure even though her income had been rather minimal over those years due to her inability to sustain employment. Thus, her tax situation was fairly simple but she was finding it impossible to complete her return. I suggested that she get the simple forms that she needed, work on them as much as she could, and then bring them in for us to work on together. Given this minimal support, Melissa did her own tax returns for the first two years, needing me only to go over them for her and check their accuracy. She was able to complete the final year's tax return without my assistance.

During one particularly difficult period of breakdown, I believed it necessary to send her to a psychiatrist for psychotropic drug treatment. She found herself unable to report to him on the symptoms or the effects of various treatment regimens. As a result, I rehearsed with her the kind of verbal dialogue she would have with the psychiatrist and made notes on her responses. I then suggested that on seeing the psychiatrist she could speak to him as she had to me or, if that were not possible, read to him from the notes I provided or, if that were not possible, simply hand him the notes I had made. From this work, she was able to go into the psychiatrist's office and verbally present him with the information he needed for her treatment.

All of the foregoing are examples of the kind of auxiliary and instrumental support that a therapist can and should give a client who requires it. The guidelines for such work, of course, are to require as much of an instrumental response on the client's part as possible while being available to fill in whatever is necessary. The idea is to assist and support the client in meeting her responsibilities rather than meeting them for her. Where the damage has been early and severe, as in Melissa's case, it may be essential on at least a few occasions to extend support into the client's real outside life while preparing her for more and more autonomous functioning.

Explanation: Signal Anxiety and Traumatic Anxiety

I consider most of my efforts at explanation as lying somewhere between auxiliary ego support and instructional, ego-building support. The objective is to introduce the client to a new way of understanding his experience, which will hopefully assist him in adapting better to it. This is auxiliary in the sense that I am simply handing over my theoretical structure for adoption, but instructional to the extent that he is able to accommodate his existing structure and actively use the model adaptively. Sometimes explanation alone will have this effect, while at other times more explicit instructional or ego-building methods must be used.

Melissa, for example, exhibits a relatively high level of ongoing anticipatory anxiety about the world and what it will bring. This is true of almost all schizoid and oral clients. I have often found it useful to distinguish for these clients between traumatic anxiety and signal anxiety. In object relations theory, signal anxiety develops in the child at about 12 months of age. It refers to the infant's emerging ability to use anxiety as a signal to behave in order to avoid some aversive consequence. Thus, even at this early age, anxiety begins to serve as an internal, affective signal to do something instrumental, just as hunger serves as a signal to eat and fatigue a signal to rest.

Traumatic anxiety, on the other hand, is anxiety which results from trauma in the past, particularly the infantile past, and occasions an expectation of future trauma. Anxiety does not signal an adaptive response; rather, it leaves the individual in a hyperaroused yet frozen state. Those of us who have been seriously traumatized in the early years of life typically carry traumatic anxiety and suffer disruption in our ability to use anxiety as a signal. There exists a more or less continuous state of foreboding which can be dramatically increased when outside stimuli are perceived, either consciously or unconsciously, to be related to a recurrence of the original trauma. For the schizoid, this may involve any perception of hostility, threat, or rejection in the world, while for the oral this may involve any hint of abandonment or withdrawal of support. When experiencing traumatic anxiety, we tend to feel relatively helpless to do anything to avoid the retraumatization. And, because we are used to anxiety of this type, the signaling functions of anxiety have often been diminished or lost.

It is useful to appreciate this distinction so that we may determine in which circumstances anxiety may have a signalling function for here-

and-now behavior, as opposed to situations in which it is simply a trauma alarm which relates not so much to the here-and-now as to the there-and-then. This also provides a "reframe" for anxiety itself, so that certain types of anxiety are just as functional as hunger and fatigue for their signal properties. This can be of immediate instrumental value if the client can incorporate this knowledge and begin to ask, in any situation of anxiety, whether there is a signal in it for instrumental behavior. If anxiety continues beyond its signal function, this itself signals that the resources provided by therapy and the therapist may be used to deal with this historically based traumatic affect.

In any protracted psychotherapy with a person who suffers historical trauma and therefore traumatic anxiety, there will probably be instances of retraumatization both inside and outside therapy. Though a therapist will not deliberately arrange such circumstances, they can have a beneficial effect if they can be worked through in the course of treatment and serve to assist the client in making the here-and-now versus there-and-then discrimination. One such occurrence happened in the course of Melissa's treatment when I inadvertently left my outside office door locked so that she was required to knock on that door, interrupting a session and requiring me to come out and open the door. She did not, however, view this as an inadvertent mistake. Indeed, she experienced it as a deliberate, cruel, and rejecting act. By working this incident through, accepting her and understanding her anger, accepting responsibility for the mistake, and apologizing, I assisted her in making the discrimination between myself and her parents. In the course of treatment, other circumstances of this kind have occurred, and in the last year of treatment, she has responded to such occurrences as the need to wait longer than usual or the rescheduling of an appointment as relatively irrelevant events.

On another occasion, Melissa was retraumatized by a psychiatrist's remark that the major tranquilizer he gave her during one of her episodes could cause blindness in higher doses. After leaving his office, she panicked at this remark and was afraid to take the medication, to question the doctor about it, or to confidently stop taking it. She was afraid the doctor would criticize her for her concerns, belittle her, refuse her future treatment, etc. I agreed with her that the doctor appeared to have made an error in rather off-handedly making this remark about blindness as a medication side effect. I reminded her of

the discussion we had previously had about signal versus traumatic anxiety, the instances where I had inadvertently retraumatized her, and
reassured her again, "Our intention is not to retraumatize you. I think
the doctor has inadvertently done that, and I think he knows enough
to repair it. If the doctor does any of the things that you are afraid of,
we will find you another doctor. But, if you give him the chance, I think
he will repair the damage." Then, we rehearsed the way Melissa would
approach and deal with the doctor while I reassured her that I would
deal with him myself if that proved necessary and find her another
physician if that were required. As I expected, the psychiatrist did repair
the damage and provided another useful experience for Melissa in the
working-through of a retraumatization episode.

Building the Sense of Self

The most essential ego-building task of psychotherapy for the schizoid client, particularly for one like Melissa, is the development of a
sense of self—a direct kinesthetic experience of self and of the world
as related but separate. This sense of self is so fundamental, so nonverbal, that it is difficult to describe it or its absence in words. When this
sense of self and of the boundaries which help define it is incompletely
developed, the patient often does not experience incompleteness until
the work enhances a more solid sense of self. Several of the processes
described in chapter III are devoted to such enhancement, for example
the "I am" meditation, the visual and auditory clearing exercises, and
the simple awareness and relaxation exercises. For the most part,
however, these processes are intrapersonal as opposed to interpersonal
and their expansion to the interpersonal matrix will usually be necessary. One such process, which is deceptively simple, involves your placing your hand on various parts of the client's body and almost ritualistically asking, for example, "Do you feel my hand on your shoulder?"
You then ask the client to shift his awareness completely to the experience of your hand on his shoulder and say back to you, again
somewhat ritualistically, "Yes, I feel your hand on my shoulder." You
then repeat this process with your hand, for example, on the client's
hand, thigh, top of the head, etc. If the client has physical contact with
others, it is often useful in the context of this work to request that he
pay particular attention to how much of that contact he is able to ex-

perience and let in. Typically the schizoid client will block off awareness of the contact in any real sense. Since he does not allow himself
to feel it, he cannot be nurtured or soothed by it, nor can he concretely
appreciate the reality of the physical boundaries between himself and
others.

Another set of exercises which facilitate the kinesthetic experience
of self and of boundaries involves literal pushing and pulling between
the therapist and client. You may, for example, recreate the child's
game in which you sit directly across from the client on the floor, both
of your legs spread out and your hands joined together. You ask the
client to pull you toward him while you fully relax and allow yourself
to be pulled completely forward. Then, you pull the client toward you
in the same manner. Alternatively, you may engage in a simple "tug
of war" with the client using a bath towel. The object is to allow the
client to experience himself kinesthetically and feel the resistance you
provide. This particular "tug of war" exercise was so effective with
Melissa in establishing contact that frequently we simply continued our
discussion with one another holding the towel between us with some
minimal resistance. This kind of "umbilical cord" between us concretely
symbolized the symbiotic attachment which was being formed and had
the effect of helping Melissa feel "connected" to me and thereby safe
to talk meaningfully with me.

Eye contact represents the most common way in which we hold and
maintain contact with one another in ordinary social discourse. Thus,
eye contact is the vehicle through which we can explore our ability to
let others in while maintaining our boundaries and the integrity of self.
Eye contact exercises may well be too threatening for lower functioning or borderline clients until well into treatment and should be delayed
until it is clear that all of the foregoing processes presented are well
within the client's ability.

Before beginning an eye contact exercise, it is usually important to
help the client center and ground within herself. To do this, I often
use the "I am" meditation outlined in chapter III in which the client
simply closes her eyes, focuses inward and identifies with the physical
sensations of which she is aware. After a few minutes, when some
centering has been achieved, I ask the client to open her eyes, to look
around at the objects in the room while maintaining the centering or
enhanced sense of self. Then I request her to make eye contact with

me. At that point, I ask her to pay exquisite attention to her experience and when she feels like it to share or free associate. If the client begins to "go away" or dissociate from herself at this point, I instruct her to return to the meditation until she feels centered again and can reestablish eye contact. Typically, this exercise will assist the client in realizing how and when she is available and present and when she is closed or her awareness is elsewhere. These sessions may then be augmented by asking her to be aware of this same sort of fluctuation in her accessibility in daily life. She may then begin to develop, for example, an enhanced awareness as to when she "goes away" in social interaction, or when she becomes unaware of the physical contact which is being given to her. Additionally, it may assist her in being aware of and respecting her own boundaries.

Hypnotic procedures may also be used to further the development of a sense of self, boundaries, and relatedness. In my own work, I have found it useful to ask the client to visualize a core or center of self which she may experience visually and kinesthetically from the top of her head to the bottom of her feet. I will ask for a complete representation of this core sense, including its shape, size, texture, volume, etc. I will then ask the client to begin to imagine that the core extends outward in a loop into the external environment. The loop may be visualized as coming out the eyes or top of the head and in through the base of the feet. The loop completely joins the person with the environment or any object within it. Typically, I ask the client to begin to visualize familiar objects included in the loop which moves from her to and through the objects and back to her again. Where there is a boundary issue, I may suggest that the loop be different in some way where it is part of the core as opposed to where it extends to the environment. This may be a difference in visualized color or texture. After one or more hypnotic sessions involving the loop, I will ask the client to take periods throughout her daily life and imagine the core and its extending loop in her day-to-day life. I may very well also recommend a meditation once or more daily in which the loop is the psychological device or mantra. In all of this, of course, the process emphasizes 1) the existence and solidity of the core; 2) the client's connection, interaction, or oneness with the environment; and 3) the reality of the boundaries between her solid core and objects in the world.

All of the foregoing techniques have been used repeatedly with

Melissa, with the exception of the eye contact process, which is still too threatening for her. As a result of all the hard work in her case, there is often the miracle of her experiencing herself and the world in a new and real way. At these times, she will say, "I just can't tell you how different this is. I can't tell you how much it means to me. I just wasn't alive before. I am now, sometimes. It's completely different, but I can't find the words to tell you how." In writing this, I know now exactly what she means.

OBJECT CONSTANCY

Melissa expressed directly the most concrete manifestation of the lack of object constancy. She said, "It feels as though you cease to exist when I leave you." She could produce no image of my independent existence apart from her. In exploring this, she also reported similar experiences with other objects. For example, she had to move a plant which she treasured in order to care for it and when she saw the empty space where it had been she became anxious and was unable to retain a sense of constancy concerning it.

In addition to using this opportunity to explain the concept of object constancy to her and its interrupted evolution in her case, I began a program of instruction to develop this capacity. At the simplest level, I asked her to look about the room and find an object which she liked. I then asked her to look at the object and to be aware of its visual form, to notice the feeling inside herself when viewing the object, and to state a name for the object. I then asked her to take a mental snapshot of the object, to close her eyes, and to make an image of the object while reproducing the feeling and the name. It was important to assure her that the picture she saw with her eyes closed need not absolutely replicate the external reality in order to be adequate. I reassured her that practice would increase her ability to reproduce the object and during this practice it became clear that attention to lighting and the texture of the object was particularly facilitative.

As this ability became better established, I asked her to take a picture of me and to develop the internal representation of me more fully. During the course of treatment, I shared with her my work schedule so that she would have some idea about what I was doing at other times during the week. I then asked her during sessions, and later between sessions, to visualize me in other activities. I also assisted her in developing the ability to imagine herself as others see her, to use a mirror image as a point of departure and then to develop her ability to see herself in various contexts and postures. These higher level exercises are still in process with her, though with respect to the therapeutic relationship she is now able to see me as a real object with a life independent but interconnecting with her own. During the earlier phases of treatment, I was careful to provide transitional objects for her such as a telephone number where I could be reached when traveling.

Differentiation: Interpersonal and Intrapsychic

For all clients with a serious schizoid or oral issue, one central task of the therapeutic process will be to assist the ego in the process of differentiation—inside versus outside, self versus other, present versus past, etc. As these more primitive qualities are differentiated, it will be useful to help the client differentiate affects and their subtle combinations—anxiety, anger, sadness, jealousy, concern, love, pleasure, etc. Until the observing ego makes some present-past differentiation, there will be anxiety at the prospect of replicating the original trauma going well beyond neurotic transference. For this reason, it is more important with more borderline structures to maintain a consistently benign therapeutic milieu to assist the beginning differentiation of here-and-now from there-and-then. For the same reason, it is useful for the therapist to repeatedly be a source of comfort and to be associated with a reduction in anxiety.

To this end, I rely on all of the techniques developed for stress reduction—bioenergetic, stretch or yoga exercises, relaxation techniques, meditative practices, etc. Within limits, I allow clients to telephone me for brief periods of external soothing and then may remind them of the regimen of relaxation which has worked for them previously. Frequently, this also includes my encouraging them to reach out to other significant people in their environment who can provide support and another pairing of comfort with social contact. Then, with regard to that and the therapeutic contact, I am careful to provide continuing auxiliary ego support, particularly around the issue of retraumatization and discrimination of past and present.

More concretely, I assist the client in avoiding those people and those experiences which will provide replication of trauma, as well as in differentiating between reality and projection. With Melissa, for example, I would repeatedly say, "I am not your mother; she is not your sister; we do not want to hurt you." On other occasions, however, it would be clear that Melissa, like so many traumatized people, was drawn to others who would be abusive or at least insensitive to her. On those occasions, I would not hesitate to recommend that she avoid those contacts if at all possible. I might say to her, for example, "The world is not loaded with evil and hurt for you, but you can find it if you look for it." A real giant step in Melissa's work came when she had the courage to cut off relationships with two individuals who were repeating the kind of early trauma which was underlying her basic difficulty.

It was also necessary to assist Melissa in differentiating at a more intrapsychic level the nature of the demonic force which possessed her and the nature of the resources which she possessed to deal with it. Whenever she was taken over by the demonic force, I asked her to observe the nature of any visual, auditory, or kinesthetic experience she was having at that time. She would hear either me or the demonic force itself criticizing or castigating her. Repeatedly, I would ask if she was reminded of anyone from the past on the basis of the content, voice tone, etc., of the messages she heard. Through many repetitions of this process, she began to differentiate the demonic force as a composite of her mother and older sister who had treated her in the way she now treated herself. A breakthrough in her therapy came when she solidly made this differentiation and the power of that differentiating breakthrough is signaled by her repeated reference to her work "before the separation" and "after the separation" of herself from this demonic force understood through its origins.

Subsequent to differentiation at this level, I employed the explanatory device of the popular Dramatic Triangle outlined by the transactional analysts (James & Jongeward, 1971; Karpman, 1968). I likened her demonic force, which had now been solidly attached to her history with mother and sister, to the persecutor in that triangle. When she was overwhelmed by the persecutor and unable to function and feeling "beaten and torn apart" she became the victim of the persecutor. When, however, she was able to function and to analyze the persecutor, she was in the rescuer ego state, rescuing herself through her adult ego functioning from the persecutor.

Many sessions have been devoted since that construction was offered to simply assisting her in discriminating "who is on" at any point
in a therapeutic session. Melissa is more and more able to discriminate
when her persecutor is active, when she is overwhelmed by the persecutor, or when she is functioning appropriately or in spite of the
persecution. On several occasions, when victimized she will say to me,
"I want you to say something; I want you to tell me something." At
these times I have often given the interpretation that she wants my adult
ego to rescue her. While I will do that and have done it, I have also
demanded at these times that her own adult ego begin to function in
this rescuing capacity. On several occasions, she has been able to do
this while I have asked repeatedly, "Who is on now?" and occasionally
offered an interpretation of "who is on." This kind of intrapsychic differentiation, in which the observing ego is brought to bear repeatedly on the intrapsychic process, is, of course, a central feature of all
analytic psychotherapy. Where ego functioning is marginal, this intrapsychic differentiation may need to be done more explicitly and repeatedly than when the ego functioning is more intact.

One organizing "vision" for Melissa's treatment has been a "parent
transplant" in which the negative introjects are replaced by more constructive and benign ones available from others with whom she now
interacts. I have shared this vision with her and self-consciously engaged
in maneuvers which should enhance this outcome.

The remainder of this chapter is devoted to various instructional, ego-
building support strategies which are derived primarily from behavior
modification, neurolinguistic programming, and cognitive therapy approaches to various instrumental problems of living. As such, what
remains of this chapter is a kind of sampler of ego-building strategies,
with emphasis on those which would be particularly useful for individuals facing typical schizoid and oral issues. The attempt, then,
is not to be exhaustive but to illustrate the practical utility of these approaches, acknowledge their value within a more characterological and
object relations view of therapy, and legitimize and integrate their use
in this context. As opposed to the strategies outlined in the context
of Melissa's case, the ones that follow are often more applicable to better functioning individuals who have specific areas of dysfunction.
These special topics focus largely on social involvement issues which
are primary for all schizoid and oral structures, beginning with simple

strategies for increasing social involvement and treating social anxiety and moving to strategies for relationship and marital therapy. In addition, cognitive therapeutic strategies will be presented in the context of ego-building.

STRATEGIES FOR SOCIAL INTERACTION

Every individual with a serious schizoid or oral issue will have difficulty in reaching out. "Confident expectation" has been damaged or is nonexistent and due to the fear of rejection or abandonment, reaching and asking have been inhibited. I have had a good deal of personal experience, for example, with attractive, intelligent, relatively high-functioning men who tend to overwork, isolate themselves, and complain of loneliness, but who stubbornly resist, while bemoaning that resistance, any concerted effort to reach out for contact and support. From an affective therapy side, it is critical in these cases to help the man get in touch with how really lonely, unhappy, and personally unfulfilled he is. Typically, obsessive thinking or compulsive behavior, often in the work area, will defend him against the experience of the necessary deep despair which will motivate him to do what is necessary. Without that critical emotional work, simple cognitive or behavioral strategies to accomplish social contact will often have no lasting impact. By the same token, however, emotional work only will often not be enough and may unnecessarily postpone the social involvement which could provide rich material for the therapeutic process. So, once again, a combination of these approaches is often called for.

Social interaction begins, of course, with initiation. In my book, *First Person Singular* (1977), I devoted an entire chapter to cognitive reframing and behavioral strategies to facilitate the process of social initiation. I often refer my clients to this chapter as a part of addressing this issue in an educative, supportive therapy context. A central component of most direct learning approaches to the initiation problem involves teaching the basic principles underlying shaping and desensitization. It is, for example, simply easier to initiate to some people than others. It is less threatening to most of us to initiate to an old friend than a new one, easier to ask for time with a friend than call and ask for a date with someone barely known, and easier to initiate at a party than on a street corner. A review of the clients' life circumstances will readily yield the existing opportunities for social initiation and reveal areas of opportunity deficit.

To get the ball rolling on this problem, it may often be useful to set weekly objectives with the client regarding the number and nature of social initiations to be made. In doing this, it is better to err in the direction of asking for too little than too much and to frame the eventual outcome as either success or feedback. It is important not to get into a power struggle on these issues or establish a parent-child relationship concerning them. If the client fails to complete the agreement or has difficulty in carrying it out, this can provide very useful therapeutic material concerning the nature of the difficulty or block. If he succeeds, the effort is reinforced and together you may move forward in the hierarchical set of tasks. It is important in doing this kind of work to be very explicit concerning the exact agreement made from week to week, so that both client and therapist have concrete feedback as to how the agreements are being kept. This kind of straightforward behavioral process can be extremely useful, particularly when it is not viewed as "the therapy" for the socially anxious or withdrawn client. When it is an adjunct in the way outlined it has the effect of improving the client's social life while providing valuable therapeutic material for the affective and characterological work.

Various internal processes may also be used to facilitate social initiation. In particular, I have had success in using the V-K dissociation process outlined in chapter III (see p. 119). In this application, I simply ask the comfortable and relaxed client to watch himself in various contexts initiating and carrying on conversations with others. It is important in this process to maintain the dissociation such that he watches himself from an external vantage point rather than collapsing into the direct experience of these imagined activities. He may, for example, see himself calling a friend to make a lunch date, initiating an activity with a new acquaintance met at a party, asking for a date, or initiating conversation with a stranger in a public place. In some of these imaginings, it will often be important to incorporate social anxiety, frustration, and even failure into the observed experiences. While maintaining the external focus of the client watching himself, you may ask that he see himself displaying socially anxious behavior or watch himself being unable to maintain a conversation after an initiation or seeing himself being rejected. Through all this, of course, it is important to maintain both the external viewpoint and the relaxed state.

In many cases, even more directive procedures will be necessary. In addition to direct instruction, it may be useful to role-play initiation situations with the client in a variety of social situations, giving him feedback and encouragement. Detailed instructions for how to do this are provided in the assertiveness training literature (e.g., Liberman et al., 1975). A final step of actually accompanying the client out into the world on an initiation "field trip" may be most beneficial. I may propose to the client, for example, that we go together to a potentially high contact area such as a college campus cafeteria or a public market where it is generally more appropriate to initiate contact with strangers. I will review with him or her the strategies for this kind of initiation and then propose an official therapeutic appointment at that location in which I will ask him to have at least three five-minute interactions. It is important to time-limit these interactions so that the individual can have control not only of initiating but terminating the interaction. In outlining this procedure, it is important to highlight the importance of frustration and perhaps even prescribe that there be at least one frustrating experience or failure. The rationale for this is that it is important to learn that one can survive rejection and frustration.

In order to affect the natural inhibition about this assertive activity, I commonly tell of the delightful success stories that other socially anxious or reticent people have experienced in completing this task. Indeed, some people have gotten so elated at their success and newfound freedom that they gleefully continue the assignment for several days beyond its completion. This takes therapy outside of the consulting room, provides support in the real world, and may be absolutely necessary when the resistance to engaging in this activity is very high. It is important not to turn this into a social event, but to structure it as a paid therapeutic interaction. If the client is otherwise psychologically ready, breaking the logjam in the inhibition of social initiation may very well lead to a marked change in the individual's social life and allow him to approach that ultimate discrimination: He is no longer hated and alone; his script decision which was understandable and appropriate at an earlier time is no longer valid. Acceptance, community, and love are available now if he will but reach for them.

In some cases it may be appropriate in the context of increasing social contact to give auxiliary and instructional support around the client's management of time. In considering workaholic, socially phobic individuals, for example, I recall a case in which the client and I both agreed on a system to require at least two hours a day of rest and relaxation which may or may not include recreation or social contact. A computer programmer, this client would typically spend hours on a home terminal, avoiding his internal emotional state and the depressing sparseness of his social life. Using the Premack principle (Premack, 1965), I suggested that he commit to a program in which he must have two hours of rest and relaxation on one day in order to have access to the computer terminal on the next. This program resulted not only in an increase in rest, relaxation, and social contact, but an increase in his uncomfortable experience of the isolation he had created in his life. This simple program introduced him not only to what he was missing but to the deep feelings he had about that loss. Increasingly, work could no longer serve as an unconscious escape from the painful reality of the life he had engineered. Occasionally, he would take that escape, but he would know just what he was doing. As his therapy progressed to deal with ever more profound affective and historical issues, I religiously monitored his external social involvement to effectively block the workaholic defense. As with many skillfully compensated individuals, it was essential to maintain the pressure of self-confrontation both in and outside of the therapeutic hour to sustain progress.

Whatever techniques are used to affect it, the schizoid or oral client's increased and varied social involvement in the world will typically stimulate the issues that he needs to confront. Among other things, this kind of involvement will heighten the probability of affect differentiation. With variety in social stimulation, it will be more and more difficult for the evolving client to maintain rigid patterns of relationships and beliefs concerning them. Different objects will inevitably pull for slightly differentiated affective responses and in this there will be a tool to assist ego development. For these and other reasons, strategies that speak to the development of social skills, particularly social initiation and ordinary interaction, can be particularly useful in encouraging the evolving client with attachment issues.

ANXIETY, AGGRESSION, AND SOCIAL SUPPORT

As indicated repeatedly throughout this volume, anxiety from troublesome to decompensating is a pervasive problem for both oral and schizoid structures. From an object relations point of view, this can be understood to be the result of the fact that the person could not internalize the anxiety-relieving functions of a good enough mother. The rejecting, unstable, anxious, or overwhelmed mothering parent could not provide the external soothing to be internalized as self-soothing ability. As a result, anxiety as signal could not be fully developed. Consequently, anxiety cannot be well tolerated and it overwhelms or threatens to overwhelm whatever coping mechanisms the individual may have. The objectives of treatment are to increase the ability of the client to tolerate and cope with anxiety. Further, the objective is to eventually allow anxiety to have a signal function triggering any number of ego defenses and adaptive mechanisms.

Throughout this volume, I have discussed a number of techniques aimed at these objectives, including self-soothing processes, anxiety-coping processes such as meditation, V-K dissociation, and various forms of exercise, as well as the curative power of explanation. Yet, from an object relations point of view, the specific content of the anti-anxiety maneuver is less important than the client's real experience of the therapist's intention and ability to help him relieve, tolerate, and cope with anxiety. It is perhaps most essential for the client to get that he has the "right to be soothed" (Blanck & Blanck, 1979). If he gets that, he will then begin to internalize not only the therapist's methods but, more importantly, the therapist's intention to relieve, soothe, and help him cope. When this occurs, he can then begin to employ the observing ego to determine and then utilize those things which allow him to ease, tolerate, and cope with anxiety. In addition to the therapist, he may then begin to use other external human sources for anxiety relief and coping and begin to internalize their helping functions as well. As he develops a more nurturing social support system, he may find, for example, that others will be happy to hold him either metaphorically or physically when he is anxious and provide the interpersonal matrix within which he can develop ego abilities to better deal with anxiety.

In every case, there will ultimately be a connection between anxiety and aggression. The schizoid or oral person will fear annihilation, abandonment, or rejection in response to his own aggressiveness. Even that aggression which has an individuating function, such as the "no" of the 18-month-old, will often prompt an exaggerated anxiety response. The therapeutic task is, of course, to disconnect the aggression-anxiety link. You may do this by encouraging the assertive response in all the ways suggested in this volume, being sure to stay with and support the client's expression. This experience can then be replicated again and again in the individual's regular social environment to the extent that this environment can be nurturing and supportive.

A principal task of good supportive therapy for schizoid and oral characters is assistance in establishing, maintaining, and dealing with the inevitable difficulties of a good reparative social group. The schizoid character is inclined to isolate himself altogether from such a group, while the oral is inclined to try to find it in one person—the perfect mother. In both cases, of course, there will be little repair and a good deal of frustration. The client with attachment difficulties really needs to interact with and bump up against real and solid objects in the world. He needs to learn to absorb the bumps and he needs to learn to bump back, working through his fear of annihilation, rejection, or abandonment. The therapist can offer direct instructional ego support in these activities, as well as providing auxiliary support in reality-testing, judgment, and other functions where necessary. Of course, it is always better to allow the client to do that rather than take over these functions for him, but some auxiliary support is often required.

Direct assertiveness training as practiced by the behaviorists may be very useful in helping the client deal with the vicissitudes of day-to-day interaction with others. However, whenever possible, I attempt to augment traditional behavioral assertiveness training with affective release therapy, thereby separating out and releasing more infantile destructive impulses in the therapy setting before going to more ego-syntonic assertiveness training. For example, I may ask the client to kick or hit, releasing infantile rage in a bioenergetic session, prior to asking him to role-play with me an assertiveness situation with a boss, spouse, or some other person in his social world, On many occasions, I have seen the client's tension dissipate so thoroughly from the bioenergetic work that he was able to very calmly, appropriately, and assertively engage his adult ego functions in the role-play and then in the extratherapy situation. In this way, too, the therapist gives permission for primitive affective release in a therapeutic setting while modeling and calling for more socially appropriate assertion in the external world.

A therapist attuned to the support of emerging ego functions will always be willing to support the client's assertive behavior, whether it is directed toward the client's external social environment or toward the therapist himself. Any attempt to differ with the object encourages differentiation in the subject. The encouragement of the subject's "no," both in affective release and in appropriate assertive social behavior, can rarely be overdone as long as there is a consistent attempt to differentiate between primitive affective dumping and more evolved assertive and differentiating behavior. I believe that traditional behavioral assertiveness training often misses the treatment of the underlying affective state which gives the individual trouble, while the unfettered expression of aggressive affect may only encourage its undisciplined expression in the client's real world. A combination of behavioral and affective strategies is often optimally useful in assisting the client's emerging ego abilities.

PARADOXICAL STRATEGIES AND SOCIAL INVOLVEMENT

One extremely important contribution of object relations theory to clinical practice is in the understanding it provides of the developmental level of the client's ego and therefore of the necessity of the defenses and resistance employed for the very survival of the self as presently constituted. As Blanck and Blanck (1979, p. 240) put it, "A fundamental premise is that patients are 'entitled' to their resistance by virtue of their level of development." This developmental view allows the therapist to really appreciate the beneficent intent of resistance and defense and to honestly communicate that appreciation to the client both directly and indirectly. The theory makes such acceptance congruent for the therapist even though it is often her objective to eventually melt the defense and the resistance.

The strategic approach to therapy, introduced by Milton Erickson and delineated so well by Haley (1973), relies most consistently on this principle of acceptance. Yet, in practice, strategic therapy often appears manipulative and seems to be used to "put something over on" the client. When grounded in the theoretical understanding of object relations, however, I believe that strategic therapy techniques can often be very beneficial because the acceptance underlying the technique is real and accompanied by a real appreciation of the client's limitations.

Particularly in the schizoid case, the defenses and resistance are very powerfully mobilized against attachment. Both in and out of the therapeutic relationship, the client will most generally engage in automatic and often extremely stubborn patterns of behavior that preclude attachment. Among the patterns of such resistance are defensive detachment, unintegrated multiple attachments, and attachment through the false self (Horner, 1979). Defensive detachment occurs in those situations in which the client adopts an "I don't care" attitude in regard to attachment objects or the entire attachment process itself. Multiple unintegrated defensive attachment occurs when the client plays the "safety in numbers" game. Here the use of multiple or serial therapists or multiple or serial lovers serves the defensive purpose of preventing any deep level of continuing attachment. Attachment through the false self refers to that situation in which the person relates to the primary attachment figure or figures only through that false structure used to protect the vulnerable real self. As indicated earlier, this false self attachment may be unconscious, semiconscious, or reasonably conscious. In each of these adjustments, the function is to protect the real and vulnerable self from re-injury by rejection or abandonment.

In each case, explanation, reconstruction, confrontation, or interpretation may be useful to the client to increase his cognitive hold on the pattern. It is often the case, however, particularly with the schizoid individual, that this intellectual awareness may be split from any healing affective awareness of the personal price paid for this protection. In other words, the client may know but doesn't feel what he is missing. Concomitantly, he does not fully feel the vengeful satisfaction of his demonic side derived from the clever withholding which he executes in primary relationships. Strategic or paradoxical assignments can often be useful in assisting him in feeling both the price of detachment and the power of withholding. Such assignments can be curative rather than retraumatizing to the extent that the therapeutic alliance is solid, the therapist can be congruent and caring in his intervention, and the client's ego is sufficiently differentiated to absorb the impact of the work.

Strategic or paradoxical intervention in these situations may involve the prescription of the defensive maneuver. This may be done with or without a rationale, though I believe it potentially very destructive to present a paradoxical assignment to a client with a rationale which the therapist knows is false. When engaged in a therapy which is essentially reparative of a disturbed attachment, it is very ill advised to engage in anything which may be experienced as manipulative, sadistic, or less than forthright.

Charles was a 42-year-old college professor separated from his wife of 20 years. The separation was occasioned by his awareness of the extremely symbiotic nature of the marriage relationship and his awareness of the extent to which it kept both him and his wife stuck in a chronically unsatisfying relationship of turmoil and melodrama. Yet after two-and-a-half years of separation Charles still could not separate. He had developed a relationship with another woman but maintained his relationship with his wife, not letting either person know of the other. In this way, he understood that he kept himself detached from each one.

After a good deal of work with Charles from many angles, I decided to take a strategic tack. I seconded his own interpretation of the defensive nature of this adjustment but asked that he "up the ante" of the drama by increasing his contact with both women simultaneously while continuing to keep his secret. I asked that he pay a good deal of attention to his own experience as he did this. As a consequence, Charles became even more aware of the price he was paying for this adjustment. His tension about keeping his activities a secret increased, and he became aware of how much energy was expended in that preoccupation. As a result, he could not really be present in either relationship. This awareness led to some very profound sadness, one of the few deeply affective experiences in his therapeutic course to that point.

It is not necessary that a paradoxical intervention of this type result in sudden change. If this is the only technique which one can practice, then a relatively quick response may be necessary for the therapist's satisfaction, but impossible for the client to deliver. If, on the other hand, this is a technique aimed at moving the client to another level of experience in relation to the problem, then other techniques of counseling and psychotherapy may be used at that level. The strategic or paradoxical strategies can be particularly useful to get some leverage on a very stubbornly resistant problem.

An alternate paradoxical strategy often used for the most resistant cases has been termed the "why change paradox." In this strategy, the client is told that his current level of adaptation is the best compromise to be made between the existing reality and the demands of his psyche. He is told further that any change in the problematic pattern would result in tremendous psychic problems and that he might better appreciate and keep the troublesome behavior or attitude than face the difficult consequences which would ensue if he were to give them up.

There is a good deal of truth in that interpretation for many clients and it is completely consistent with the theoretical structure formulated here. In the strategic therapy literature, however, it is often presented in a rather manipulative way and without the theoretical underlying structure which makes it truly tenable. In addition, the more or less blind application of this kind of strategy assumes that every client so challenged has the resources to resist the therapist's interpretation and give up the symptom, finding some better adaptation. This assumption is often totally unwarranted and a challenge of this kind to a patient who is incapable of dramatic change can provide him only with another failure experience and retraumatization.

On the other hand, the same message delivered from a solid theoretical base which engenders understanding and acceptance may provide the client with a therapeutic reframe of his problem. It may suggest that the symptomatic behavior is indeed the best compromise solution available at the present time. It may assist him in getting in touch with the many benefits of the adaptation and to experience more directly and consciously any hostile expression that the symptom represents. It may further provide him with the rationale for why the diminution of the symptom will confront him with some very real objective pain and suffering and thereby prepare him to deal with it. And finally, when the client is capable of doing so, it may propel him by enhancing his motivation to change as it was originally intended to do by the strategic therapists. This intervention may be useful, for example, in cases of defensive detachment. Also, it may be coupled with efforts to prescribe and thereby enhance the awareness of the client's pattern of detachment in interpersonal situations.

An additional advantage of this paradoxical approach is that it helps the therapist become legitimately less invested in the necessity for the client to change. Particularly when the client comes from a situation in which his own identity had to be established by resistance to parental demands and expectations, his transference in therapy may be unproductively stimulated when the therapist *needs* him to change. When the therapist does not have that need and can be congruently comfortable with the maintenance of whatever pattern the client needs, there is a much greater chance of a therapeutic alliance and eventual progress. I believe that this is a central factor accounting for some of the very rapid changes produced with paradoxical interventions. When the client does have the resources for more immediate change, and where his resistance is of the type outlined above, a paradoxical intervention may well produce fast results. However, a therapist who believes that this will happen on every or almost every occasion will be sorely disillusioned.

COGNITIVE STRATEGIES FOR EGO-BUILDING

Throughout this volume, particularly in chapters III and VII, I've outlined a number of cognitive strategies for ego-building, most of which derive from neurolinguistic programming. These include reframing, resource accessing, V-K dissociation, self-soothing and other strategies for anxiety management. For the most part, however, these strategies assist in the development of defensive or coping functions. At this point, I will develop more fully the cognitive therapy notion of strategies per se and elaborate how these concepts can be used for greater understanding and control of internal thought process, as well as providing assistance in developing effective external behavior.

To elicit a cognitive strategy, you simply invite the client to observe his own internal process, while you provide him with some new tools for examining that process. I recall, for example, the treatment of John, a young man with a series of fairly profound oral-schizoid issues who was continuing to suffer several months after a separation from his live-in lover. She had rejected and left him, moving to a nearby city to which he traveled frequently on business. He was still plagued by protracted depressive episodes associated with the separation; his depression was particularly troublesome when he visited the city to which his former lover had moved. There he was continually preoccupied by her, expecting to see her around every corner and feeling more depressed and self-depreciating.

I assisted him in recreating this affective state through hypnotic work so that he could slow down the cognitive sequence and take a look at his own thought processes. In addition, I supplemented this by asking him to further observe his process when visiting the city or when otherwise depressed about the separation. What we learned was this: John, upon seeing or remembering various locales in the other city, would begin to visualize his former lover having a good time with another man. This initial fantasy might be quite brief or protracted. Then he would essentially talk to himself and decide that he was inadequate because he was unable to keep his lover happy while another man could succeed in that role. Finally, he would feel sad, lonely, and depressed.

Putting aside any interpretive reflexes that you may be feeling at this moment, I would like to ask that you simply concentrate your attention on the sequencing of the thought process. Essentially, John would make up a visual image, make negative self-judgments in response to this made-up image, and then feel bad. In short, John's *strategy* for depression involved his creating a visual image, engaging in negative self-talk, thereby producing bad feelings. John was helped simply by getting access to this sequential process, which before intervention was so quick and automatic that it was outside his conscious awareness. In pursuing this form of self-exploration, John learned a general strategy for internal cognitive exploration, as well as gaining insight into his particular response in this situation. Armed with this knowledge, he could decide to abort or interrupt the sequence by, for example, stopping his initial visual fantasies or changing the verbal decision that he made on the basis of them. For example, he could decide to feel good about the possibility of his former lover being happy. In any case, providing the ego with access to the internal fantasy and thought process is useful. This general approach may be taken with any cognitive, affective, or behavioral target to, for example, explore one's strategy for creating anxiety, guilt, shyness, joy, love, or competence.

It is often the case that a person may have developed some very effective cognitive-behavioral strategies in one content area or context but be unable to generalize them to another, usually because the latter is a conflict-ridden area. In this case, the exploration of both the effective and ineffective strategies in the two areas will be useful. The nature of the discrepancy in the two strategies may very well signal the nature of the disrupting conflict. Providing the client's observing ego with this kind of detailed, comparative information may very well begin to remedy the deficient strategy or at least repair it enough for somewhat improved functioning.

Another obvious advantage of the strategy approach is the handle that it gives for mastering many of life's little problems. For the borderline client, in particular, this is no small matter, since anything which will increase his ability to organize and master the environment will render life much easier. Frequently, borderline individuals live in a relatively disorganized state and the effects of this disorganization increase the level of frustration, anxiety, and personal chaos with which they must deal. Practical strategies for organizing their lives, if followed, can substantially reduce the disquieting background noise, releasing more energy for adaptive functioning.

Particularly with schizoid, oral, symbiotic, and many narcissistic individuals, there is a failure to really grow up and take responsibility for adult functioning. As a consequence, the more borderline of these structures will tend to have difficulty remembering things, taking care of ordinary life matters such as keeping enough food in the refrigerator, planning free time, and knowing where to find the pliers when they're required. All these things can be directly and often very easily taught and their mastery demonstrates exercise of ego function and concretely reinforces it. Because of my earlier work in divorce research and counseling the newly single, I've had a great deal of experience with individuals who have had to reestablish or learn from scratch these very practical life management strategies. I and they never cease to be amazed by the extent to which the mastery of some very simple tasks has contributed to a sense of power and increased self-esteem. What follows is a brief sampler of some of these simple strategies to provide examples for what might be done in this ego-building area.

In dealing with a continually frazzled client who had the problem of frequently losing her personal possessions as she went through life, I examined my own strategies for hanging on to my stuff. Like my client, I tend to be a fairly mental person and could, without a strategy for remembering, lose a great many personal belongings, creating a great deal of frustration for myself. In examining my own strategy, I found that I allow myself to be as preoccupied as I wish to be—except in times of transition from place to place. Then I go through a rather quick but elaborate checking procedure. First, I ask myself, "Do you have everything?" I then do a visual check of the place I'm leaving to see if I've left anything behind. Where there are a number of items to remember, as at the beginning of a complex day, I may make a mental or even written list of the things needed. I check visually to see that I have what I need. Then I do a kinesthetic check, feeling, for example, the warmth and weight of the coat I'm wearing, the umbrella in one hand, the briefcase in the other, and my keys in my pocket. Finally, I do a sort of intuitive kinesthetic check to see whether I feel complete closure in the situation or experience that nagging feeling that I have forgotten something. Where any of these checks yield a negative, I will cycle back and run quickly through the strategy again. Though this elaborate exposition may seem lengthy and complicated, like all ingrained strategies it occurs very rapidly on most occasions and often is outside conscious awareness.

I shared this strategy with my client, who seemed highly interested and motivated to use it. I then ran her through the strategy in imagination in several relevant contexts, and prescribed her conscious use of the strategy in the days and weeks ahead. In this particular case, the procedure "took" particularly well and she now reports that she rarely leaves things behind and notices the decrease in frustration as a consequence.

In general, every borderline character who is not too tightly wrapped could profit from some compulsivity to bring better external structure to his life. Most well-compensated individuals in our society utilize some compulsive maneuvers to survive and many of the more damaged of us use them both as structuring devices and defensive maneuvers. So, compulsivity is well-developed in our culture and there are many experts on how to be constructively compulsive (see e.g., *How to Get Control of Your Time and Your Life* by Alan Lakein, 1974). The experts emphasize a few key points in these strategies for life organization. These include the utility of making activity lists, prioritizing activities, scheduling time, and keeping a schedule book for that purpose. To organize a home or office, the basic underlying principle seems to be, "A place for everything, and everything in its place." Thus, the disorganized client may be assisted by any arrangements, agreements, or instructions which facilitate the organization of his kitchen, office, or shop. For these organizational tasks, the resources of those shops specializing in each of these areas can be readily and inexpensively employed. The creative compulsives of our culture have already done a good deal of work on the problems of efficiently and attractively organizing offices, kitchens, and shops. Considerable improvement in

Melissa's functioning came when I began to share cooking and other homemaking strategies with her. Up to that time she had rarely cooked for herself, repeating her mother's own failure to feed her. Her preparation of food for herself using some simple recipes I suggested began to repair this deficit and yielded a more mature functioning based in part on identification.

One final exemplary cognitive-behavioral strategy may be mentioned before moving on to less mundane matters. In counseling the newly single, I have found it very useful to have a strategy for recreational planning. When people are married, a great deal of their social interaction is preprogrammed and the rest of it is often delegated to one spouse. When one is single, the responsibility for recreational and social planning becomes much greater if one wishes to maintain an active involvement with other people, and the responsibility for arranging that falls squarely on the single person's shoulders. To make this new task easier, I have shared the following strategies of one of my friends. First, a greater amount of social contact may be preprogrammed by regularly scheduled commitments to social events such as luncheons, dinners, classes, regularly occurring symphony presentations, etc. Second, a large monthly calendar is a useful tool for this purpose. For 10 or 15 minutes each week, one can review a good deal of potential upcoming social, recreational, and community events and enter any such events which one might conceivably find interesting on that calendar. With this limited time investment, one creates an easily accessed visual map which can be used simply as a list of *options*. The constant availability of the potential schedule also prompts social initiations.

Dilts et al. (1980) have outlined the properties of an effective internal cognitive strategy to provide guidelines for strategy construction or repair. First in this outline is the requirement that the strategy have a well-defined desired outcome. In order to know whether the strategy is working or not, you need a well-defined criterion of success. And, of course, this determination will always be easier if the criterion is more concrete or observable. I know, for example, that my strategy for remembering outlined earlier is successful since I am able to hold on to my umbrella, produce my lecture notes for my 3:30 class, and see that my sport coat for the dry cleaners is in the car when I need it. Though I could define the criterion in more negative terms (i.e., I never experience the frustration of having forgotten anything), it is generally more effective to state the criterion in positive terms. Among other things, this gives me repeated opportunities to reward or reinforce myself for executing the effective strategy as I see the concrete evidence of its working. Each instance of having what I need at the time is then a reinforcer, and those rare instances of forgetting can provide feedback about repair of the strategy, rather than being experienced as failure because all of the positive instances have been overlooked.

The second desirable property of an effective strategy requires that all three of the major representational systems which humans use in their cognitive process be represented in the strategy — auditory, visual, and kinesthetic. In the remembering strategy, for example, I say to myself, "Do I have everything I need?" and check my mental list to provide the auditory component. I do a visual check to see that I have left nothing behind or that I have with me everything that is on my mental or written list for the day. Then I do a kinesthetic or feeling check to feel the coat on my back, the keys in my pocket, the briefcase and umbrella in my hand. And finally, I do more of a global, intuitive kinesthetic check to determine a feeling of closure in the situation. Although some problems require far greater reliance on one of these methods of representation than others, it makes sense in designing an overall strategy for oneself or another to utilize all of the cognitive equipment at our disposal.

The third criterion for an effective strategy involves a requirement that we not get stuck in a sort of obsessive-compulsive loop in the strategy before coming to that point when we can make a well-informed decision as to whether to repeat a certain aspect of the strategy or leave it and get on with life. In the remembering strategy, for example, the decision point comes at the time when I decide that what I have seen, heard, and felt around the question of remembering everything does or does not correspond to the other times when I have successfully remembered everything. If the answer at that decision point is "no," it is appropriate for me to cycle back through some or all parts of the strategy. Prior to that time, however, I could get stuck in a loop in which I might, for example, say to myself, "Have I got my keys?" feel for them, say "yes," and then cycle through a number of other questions and answers, then cycling back to the keys again and so on, perhaps indefinitely. This obviously is an ineffective strategy and the point of repair is obvious. In most cases of this kind of loop, however, there is a psychopathological component which needs to be addressed apart from the technical strategy of repair ordinarily envisioned by many neurolinguistic programmers.

The fourth requirement for an effective strategy involves having some way of knowing when to stop engaging in it to solve a problem. Even though a strategy is effective in every other way and even if it has been supremely effective in many instances in the past, one may run up against a situation or particular time when it repeatedly fails to work. It is useful at these times to have some criterion of when to give up, at least temporarily. I remember times, for example, when I have misplaced something and run through a very effective strategy for finding it. On occasion, the strategy doesn't work and I have had times when I would seemingly blindly refuse to quit looking even though I was wasting time. Once I got the notion of putting some sort of time limit on the process or a limit on the number of times that I would run through the finding strategy, I have found a more sensible time to give up. If I come back to the same strategy at a later time, I may well solve the problem very quickly or I may need to develop a new strategy. But all strategies need an exit point. Any good strategy will have some reasonable limit on the time and effort given it before one moves on in spite of not solving the problem at that time.

Of course, the individual with serious preoedipal disruptions in ego functioning will resist the execution of many of these strategies. The schizoid refuses to reach out, the oral refuses to take care of himself, the symbiotic is threatened by any emergence of autonomy, etc. But, wherever this occurs it is simply more grist for the mill of the characterological and analytic work. If handled properly, I see no reason why this kind of cognitive-behavioral intervention cannot be made to mesh with and nicely complement deeper, more analytic interventions. I have chosen for illustration these examples of time and practical life management because of their simplicity in the first place and their relevance for more borderline individuals in the second. But what I really want to convey here is the metastrategy which these cognitive-behavioral examples illustrate. Where one human being has devised a strategy to do something, another human being can, other things being equal, copy that strategy and produce results with it. There are, of course, many instances where things are not equal and the differences in talent, in-

telligence, or motivation will yield different results. In most of the areas
of personal life management which we consider for therapeutic intervention, however, these differences do not produce the greatest variability. Rather, the characterological issues produce the variability and
we have other tactics for dealing with those issues. The metastrategy
can, therefore, serve as a general method for assisting clients in improving the quality of their lives *and* as a catalytic agent for stimulating
characterological issues in a relatively circumscribed and easily observed
arena. If the therapist can keep in mind the overriding objective of
"guardianship of autonomy," he can engage in these activities to build
the client's level of ego functioning.

CHARACTEROLOGICAL FAMILY THERAPY

In my own work, particularly with ego-building psychotherapy, I
have found it very useful to integrate some of the insights and procedures of family therapy with those of characterological and object
relations theory. The family therapists are essentially correct in their
primary criticism of psychoanalysis, just as the psychoanalysts are
essentially correct in their primary criticism of family therapy. Covering
the first criticism first, it is true that most adults live in a familial context of some sort, usually involving some contact with the family of
origin and some with a current family or its facsimile. It is in this current family or its approximation that the person's ego deficiencies and
intrapsychic conflicts are probably most played out. Particularly where
there is a consistent lover or spouse, this relationship will pull most
deeply for the client's transference reactions. Further, that environment
will contribute greatly in either encouraging or discouraging ego evolution and resolution of conflict. We do not live in an intrapsychic
vacuum. Isolating one part of a close familial system and repairing it
independently may well lead to a good deal of frustration. To the extent that that repair is successful, it may also disrupt the ecology of
the social system, thereby creating more stress in that system and/or
perpetuating the breakdown of the system or individuals within it.
Therapists do need to be cognizant of the ecological impact of their
interventions and use that existing ecology to further those interventions where possible.

Yet, the analytic position is also fundamentally correct. Most severe and persistent problems that one has are characterological or historically based. Surface manipulation of the power structure or the quality of communication within the family will usually not produce any lasting change in these deep-seated difficulties. While such interventions may cause things to run more smoothly for a while, these interventions do not speak to more fundamental human problems.

My synthesis of this conflict is as follows: As with behavioral, cognitive, and strategic approaches to therapy, a family therapy approach can be extraordinarily contributive if it is not expected to do any more than it can. If it is practiced from this realistic position, as indeed it often is, it may be utilized either alone or in conjunction with other more characterological approaches to improve quality of life. In the present context, we will view it in its application as an adjunct to characterological transformation, keeping in mind that it may make many other useful contributions; at the same time its contribution is limited by the fact that characterological difficulties do not yield to surface manipulations.

From this perspective, the goal of family intervention is to provide an optimal context within which the evolution of ego functioning and conflict resolution may proceed. Assuming an existing family for the moment, this will require some diagnosis of family process and some general assessment of the developmental functioning level of at least the adults within the system. It may also involve the therapist in an educative role concerning the results of these diagnostic observations and at least some short-term goal-setting in terms of desired family process.

Together with this, and particularly in the context of marital counseling, I believe it is useful to thoroughly tap the insights of the characterological, object relations approach to understanding people and their relations to one another. In my own practice, I am involved in marital counseling per se, individual counseling secondary to marital work, and marital work secondary to individual psychotherapy. In this work, I generally use and share with clients, at varying levels of complexity, the basic tenets of the characterological approach. At a level which appears to me constructive, I will do a bit of explanation concerning object relations, character analysis, script decisions, etc., and share with the couple those characterological issues with which I see each of them dealing. Again, gauging this presentation to the ego and intellectual functioning of the clients, I will then outline, in general, the ways in which I see the family structure contributing to or detracting from the ego evolution and conflict resolution of each of the partners. Frequently this formulation leads to a therapeutic reframe of the problems found within the family. Often, it seems to me, we select those situations in life which present us with the opportunity to learn those lessons which we still must learn. This often looks like a repetition compulsion because we tend to be drawn to the same sort of people, the same sort of problems, and the same sort of choices again and again until the basic underlying characterological issue is resolved. We keep working things through until we needn't work them through any longer.

This central concept explains a good deal of mating choice and marital conflict. As a consequence, the most serious of relationship problems may be interpreted as providing an opportunity for the transformation of character. A relationship can be transformed, at least at a cognitive level, if this formulation of the issue can be shared, thus providing a constructive basis from which the couple can join ego forces against the family problem. As a consequence, the surface interventions of family therapy are contextualized within a framework of characterological healing where no one is to blame and everyone is responsible. This releases a good deal of psychic energy for problem-solving and personal growth.

This approach to marriage and family counseling calls for a book in itself. Elucidating all the possibilities of characterological family therapy goes well beyond the scope of this book, let alone this particular chapter. What is possible here, however, is the offering of some examples of procedures and cases in which family intervention served ego supportive functions to the members of the family system.

My most commonly used strategy for this more narrow objective has involved intervention aimed at promoting impulse regulation for out-of-control marital fighting. My first step in this type of intervention involves an attempt to restructure or reframe the problem such that both individuals begin to take responsibility for it. In my experience, wherever persistent marital outbursts are characteristic of the relationship, both partners have some serious preoedipal ego deficits to work out in their adult life. In several of the couples I have treated where this has been a problem, the characterological makeup of the partners has been strikingly similar. One partner, the woman in all

three cases which come to mind, possessed an oral or symbiotic character structure leading to serious problems with jealousy and separation anxiety. Often she would become panicky at separation or sus-
piciously jealous at the slightest provocation. In an infantile attempt
to deal with this separation anxiety, she would become enraged, accusatory, or clingingly dependent. In cases of clinging dependency,
when this did not produce the sought after reassurance and nurturance,
she would then become enraged and accusatory.

For their part, the men in this repeating melodrama displayed a more
narcissistic structure. In general, they tended to be gratified, at least
unconsciously, by the dependency of their partners and accepted responsibility for taking care of their mate's feelings. Yet, there was a
concomitant resentment of this responsibility and a tendency to do as
they pleased while verbally placating their partner. They often assumed
that their partner should trust and understand them without the kind
of verbal reassurance sought after. Their partner's rage and accusations triggered the narcissistic injury in at least two ways. First, it directly challenged their adequacy to provide satisfaction in the relationship,
saying in effect, "You're not doing enough, you're not doing it right,
you can't make me happy. You must give up more of yourself to satisfy
me." Second, and perhaps most essential in understanding the internal
experience of the man, the unremitting panic, jealousy, and accusations
of the partner rendered the narcissist *helpless* in the situation. If there
is one affect narcissists cannot accept, it is helplessness. In an attempt
to avoid this real but character-threatening emotion, they often jump
to outrage. This result, in these otherwise oft satisfying relationships,
was an almost complete ego regulatory breakdown in both parties so
that an emotional two-year-old began beating up on an emotional one-
year-old. No adults were in sight. These episodes led, at best, to out-
of-control, irrational screaming matches and, at worst, to instances
of physical assault and police intervention.

The acceptance of mutual responsibility in these cases was somewhat
easier because such loss of emotional control was ego-dystonic to both
partners. Further, each partner could see that, while the behavior of
the partner was inconvenient, disconcerting or even pathological, it
did not necessarily warrant rage; nor was that response likely to be
of great assistance in remedying the partner's behavior. Once I was able
to get each party to begin to accept responsibility and to essentially

buy the characterological formulation outlined above, a basis was available from which to make behavioral prescriptions which could lead to character growth, at least within the area of impulse regulation. With this formulation, every instance of the problem provides an opportunity to work through the characterological issue.

The objective is to *own* that issue and not blatantly discharge or "dump" the feelings in an attempt to coerce the other to stop stimulating one's central life concern. This gets one to the point of realizing that learning to cope with and work through separation anxiety or distrust is part of one's responsibility to mature. Similarly, dealing with one's limitations and accepting one's helplessness is a necessary rapprochement with reality for complete maturation. Demanding that the other stop stimulating these issues is only adding to the problem. Indeed, in the higher order of things, it may well be the responsibility of the other to stimulate one's life issue until it is resolved. So, whenever the problem occurs the solution is to experience and take responsibility for the feelings as fully and completely as possible without dumping them on the partner. In couples such as these, this will often require them to briefly separate from one another to remove the possibility of dumping and encourage the experiencing. The oral-symbiotic partner needs to be encouraged to experience and otherwise soothe the loss and anxiety, learning eventually to tolerate it and experience repeatedly the return of the lost object. The narcissistic partner needs to experience and come to terms with his own limitations: his inability to control the feelings of others or make others behave as he wants them to. All of the techniques outlined in this book for affective experience and expression both in and out of therapy can be useful in this experiencing mode of the therapeutic strategy.

In making these behavioral prescriptions for separation or isolation, I have found it necessary to be extraordinarily explicit concerning the ground rules for either party to cut off a rapidly escalating fight. Both parties agree to a contract regarding these rules. They may, for example, agree that when either party becomes aware of the escalation he or she may, with a word or prearranged signal, completely terminate the interaction, leaving the room or even the home to eliminate the possibility of further escalation. It may be further agreed that implicit in this termination of contact is a promise to get together at a later time when both parties are more calm and rational to discuss the issue in question. A time limit for this discussion may also be agreed upon and it may even be specified that a certain time and place be designated to be sure that dialogue is completed. In this connection, regularly scheduled communication sessions are often useful in systematically and regularly clearing the air and providing communication opportunities. Training in and prescription of various forms of active listening are often a useful adjunct to this work, as is a discussion of the distinction between problem-solving communication and expressive communication (Johnson, 1977). In this connection, the narcissistic partner, in particular, may often be urged to completely refrain from problem-solving attempts with his partner unless explicitly requested to render such assistance. His responses—both instrumental and affective—to this instruction will yield a good deal of information about his flexibility and the areas in which further work needs to be done.

Finally, I have often used a strategic therapy intervention with couples who have this and other interactional problems. In this intervention, I essentially prescribe the symptom by requesting that the couple *consciously* play out their persistent interactional game. In the case being considered here, that would mean that the narcissistic partner deliberately and subtly stimulate his partner's insecurity and jealousy by failing to call when expected or by coming home a little later than usual, etc. In response to this, the oral-symbiotic partner would *consciously* fly off the handle and berate and accuse the mate. As always, the narcissistic partner would then be asked to do what he always does —defend his actions and eventually become enraged at his mate's incomprehensible distrust and jealousy. The oral-symbiotic partner would do as she always does—continue to escalate the jealousy, paranoid accusations, etc. Somewhere in this process, one partner is to look at the other and say something to the effect, "Is this for real, or are we doing this because Steve (Dr. Johnson in the East) asked us to?" Whoever was *conscious* of this game as it proceeded is a winner of the game, yielding the possibility of zero, one, or two winners.

Whatever else it does, this prescription enhances ego awareness of the disruptive pattern and introduces a potentially powerful uncertainty in the process whenever it recurs. Results with this behavioral prescription can be very dramatic, particularly when it is placed well temporally—that is, when the clients have done other cognitive and behavioral work on the problem, making them ready for this powerful level of intervention. Often, the prescription is followed few if any times, but the effect is still quite profound. Among other things, the prescription seems to remove a good deal of the secondary gain or payoff the game provided and, in a sense, "takes all the fun out of it."

WORKING THROUGH AND TRANSFORMATION

It is no small task to keep all of these visions of psychotherapy in mind. Indeed, to do that continually and consciously is impossible. In my own evolution as a therapist, I threw myself into one individual model after another to eventually develop the kind of integration I experience now. This is not the most efficient way to do it. It was necessary for me because no teacher could offer the integration I wanted, and no theoretical underpinning was apparent until I neared the end of the journey.

Now, however, we are entering a period in the culture generally and in psychotherapy specifically during which there will be much more integration of polarities. In many schools of psychotherapy, for example, there seems to be a gathering trend toward acknowledging the limitations of one's model without throwing it away. With this acknowledgment of limitation, there seems to be an ever-greater openness to recognize the contributions as well as the limitations of another approach to the problem. Inevitable in this opening is the confusion of not knowing. In that confusion there is the essence of the beginner's mind and the doorway to knowing what was heretofore unknown.

A central, confusing polarity for my beginner's mind has been that reflected in this book's subtitle: *The Hard Work Miracle*. Given the current state of our consciousness and our art, psychotherapy for characterological issues often involves years of hard work. Yet, miracles occur. People do transcend spontaneously and quickly. How can this polarity be resolved?

Psychotherapy is hard work until it isn't. Ego-building is fundamental work which may set the stage for transcendence, but it is not transformational. Psychotherapy to resolve conflict involves working through the resistance to the necessary experience. This experiencing needs to be affective, cognitive, and behavioral in order to fully *release* the experience. Release is therapeutic and, though it is often hard won, it makes people feel better. Release is healing but it too is not transformational.

The final, necessary step for the miracle is *forgiveness* — forgiveness of what happened, forgiveness of what is happening, forgiveness of what may still happen. It is acceptance of what was, what is, and what may be.

Many of the case histories summarized in this book are tragic in the extreme. These people are entitled to a lifetime of suffering as a natural consequence of horrible rejection and abandonment when they were open, needy, and helpless. But some of them have had the courage to release enough of the pain to pave the way for a real forgiveness.

Our job as psychotherapists is to guide this process of release and forgiveness and our privilege is to witness it. A sensitive balance is required to complete the process. It seems to me that traditional, dynamic therapists often get stuck with their clients in the therapeutic cycle of working through to release. This helps, but it falls short of transformation. By contrast, the "transformers" often err by encouraging a premature forgiveness that is purely cognitive and not heartfelt. As a consequence, it is maintained with great effort and eventually collapses in disillusionment.

When the natural timing of the release-forgiveness process is respected and encouraged, a transformation is possible. Hugh Prather (1980, p. 76) has written: "Forgiveness and the willingness to be happy are the same." When the hated and abandoned children of this world are willing to let go of suffering — to get better rather than get even — a transformation is close at hand. If you can forgive being rejected and abandoned and if you can feel that forgiveness and act upon it, you are transformed and that is a miracle. Such miracles, large ones and small ones, occur in psychotherapy. That is why we do it.

REFERENCES

Abraham, K. (1921). Contributions to the theory of the anal character. Reprinted in *Selected Papers on Psychoanalysis I* (1953). New York: Basic Books.

Bandler, R., & Grinder, J. (1982). *Reframing*. Moab, Utah: Real People Press.

Bandler, R., & Grinder, J. (1979). *Frogs into princes*. Moab, Utah: Real People Press.

Benson, H. (1975). *The relaxation response*. New York: Arion.

Beres, D. (1956). Ego deviation and the concept of schizophrenia. *The Psychoanalytic Study of the Child, 11,* 164–235.

Berne, E. (1964). *Games people play*. New York: Grove Press.

Blanck, G., & Blanck, R. (1974). *Ego psychology. Theory and practice*. New York: Columbia University Press.

Blanck, G., & Blanck, R. (1979). *Ego psychology II: Psychoanalytic developmental psychology*. New York: Columbia University Press.

Boadella, D. (1977). *In the wake of Reich*. Ashley Books.

Bowlby, J. (1969). *Attachment and loss. Vol. I: Attachment*. New York: Basic Books.

Bowlby, J. (1973). *Attachment and loss. Vol. II: Separation: Anxiety and anger*. New York: Basic Books.

Bowlby, J. (1960). Grief and mourning in infancy and early childhood. *Psychoanalytic Study of the Child, 15,* 9–52.

Davanloo, H. (1980). A method of short-term dynamic psychotherapy. In H. Davanloo (ed.) *Short-term dynamic psychotherapy*. New York: Aronson.

Dilts, R., Grinder, J., Bandler, R., Bandler, L., & DeLozier, J. (1980). *Neuro-linguistic programming Vol. I: The study of the structure of subjective experience*. Cupertino, CA: Meta.

Freud, A. (1936). *The ego and the mechanisms of defense*. New York: International Universities Press, 1967.

Freud, S. (1913). On beginning the treatment. *The Standard Edition, 12,* 121–144. New York: W. W. Norton.

Freud, S. (1915). Instincts and their vicissitudes. *Standard Edition, 14.* New York: W. W. Norton.

Gendlin, E. T. (1978). *Focusing*. New York: Everest House.

Gerber, M. (1958). The psycho-motor development of African children in the first year and the influence of maternal behavior. *Journal of Social Psychology, 47,* 185–195.

Giovacchini, P. (1975). *Psychoanalysis of character disorders*. New York: Jason Aronson.

Giovacchini, P., & Boyer, L. B. (1975). The psychoanalytic impasse. *International Journal of Psychoanalytic Psychotherapy, 4,* 25–47.

Greenacre, P. (1959). Certain technical problems in the transference relationship. *Journal of the American Psychoanalytic Association, 7,* 484–502.

Greenacre, P. (1957). The childhood of the artist. *Psychoanalytic Study of the Child, 12,* 47–72.

Haley, J. (1973) *Uncommon therapy: The psychiatric techniques of Milton H. Erickson, M.D.* New York: W. W. Norton.

Harlow, H. K., & Harlow, M. H. (1966). Learning to love. *American Scientist, 54,* 244–272.

Hartmann, H. (1964). *Essays on ego psychology.* New York: International Universities Press.

Hartmann, H. (1958). *Ego psychology and the problem of adaptation.* New York: International Universities Press.

Hillman, J. (1983). *Inter-views.* New York: Harper & Row.

Hilton, R. (1980). General dynamics of character structure development and the therapeutic process. In Cassius, J. (ed.) *Horizons in bioenergetics: New dimensions in mind-body psychotherapy.* Memphis: Promethean Publications, pp. 178–197.

Horner, A. S. (1979). *Object relations and the developing ego in therapy.* New York: Aronson.

Jacobson, E. (1964). *The self and the object world.* New York: International Universities Press.

James, M., and Jongeward, D. (1971). *Born to win: Transactional analysis with Gestalt experiments.* Reading, Mass: Addison-Wesley.

Johnson, S. M. (1977). *First person singular: Living the good life alone.* New York: Lippincott.

Jones, E. (1919). Ueber analerotische Charakterzuege. *Internationiale Zeistschrift fuer Psychoanalyse.*

Judd, L., & Mandell, A. (1968). Chromosome studies in early infantile autism. *Archives of General Psychiatry, 18,* 450–456.

Karpman, S. B. (1968). Fairy tales and script drama analysis. *Transactional Analysis Bulletin, 7, 26,* 39–43.

Keleman, S. (1981). *Your body speaks its mind.* New York: Simon and Schuster.

Kernberg, O. (1976). *Object relations theory and clinical psychoanalysis.* New York: Jason Aronson.

Kernberg, O. (1975). *Borderline conditions and pathological narcissism.* New York: Jason Aronson.

Kohut, H. (1971). *The analysis of the self.* New York: International Universities Press.

Kurtz, R., & Prestera, H. (1976). *The body reveals.* New York: Harper & Row.

Lakein, A. (1974). *How to get control of your time and your life.* New York: NAL.

Langs, R. (1976). *The bipersonal field.* New York: Aronson.

Langs, R. (1973). *The techniques of psychoanalytic psychotherapy, Volume I.* New York: Aronson.

Liberman, R. P., King, L. W., DeRisi, W. J., & McCann, M. (1975). *Personal effectiveness: Guiding people to assert themselves and improve their social skills.* Champaign, IL: Research Press.

Lowen, A. (1958). *The language of the body.* New York: Collier.

Lowen, A. (1967). *The betrayal of the body.* New York: Collier.

Lowen, A. (1983). *Narcissism: Denial of the true self.* New York: Macmillan, 1983.

Lowen, A., & Lowen, L. (1977). *The way to vibrant health.* New York: Harper & Row.

Mahler, M. S. (1968). *On human symbiosis and the vicissitudes of individuation*. New York: International Universities Press.

Mahler, M. S. (1972). Rapprochement subphase of the separation-individuation process. *Psychoanalytic Quarterly, 41*, 487–506.

Mahler, M. S., Pine, R., and Bergman, A. (1975). *The psychological birth of the human infant*. New York: Basic Books.

Malan, D. H. (1979). *Individual psychotherapy and the science of psychodynamics*. London: Butterworths.

Malcolm, J. (1981). *Psychoanalysis: The impossible profession*. New York: Knopf.

Masterson, J. (1976). *Psychotherapy of the borderline adult*. New York: Brunner/ Mazel.

Masterson, J. (1981). *The narcissistic and borderline disorders*. New York: Brunner/Mazel.

Muller, E. (1982). L'Analyse du caracter à la Rumere de la psychologie de l'ego. *Analyse du corps*, Vol. I, 1.

Murphy, L., and Moriarty, A. (1976). *Vulnerability, coping and growth*. New Haven: Yale University Press.

Orme-Johnson, D. W., & Farrow, J. T. (1977). Scientific research on the transcendental meditation program. *Collected Papers, Vol. I*. New York: Maharishi European Research University Press.

Paul, J., & Paul, M. (1983). *Do I have to give up me to be loved by you?* Minneapolis: Compcare.

Pearce, J. (1977). *Magical child*. New York: Bantam.

Perry, J. C., & Klerman, G. L. (1978). The borderline patient. A comparative analysis of four sets of diagnostic criteria. *Archives of General Psychiatry, 35*, 141–150.

Prather, H. (1980). *There is a place where you are not alone*. Garden City, NY: Doubleday.

Premack, D. (1965). Reinforcement theory. In D. Levine (ed.) *Nebraska symposium on motivation: 1965*. Lincoln: U. of Nebraska Press, pp. 123–180.

Reich, W. (1949). *Character analysis*, 3rd. ed. New York: Orgone Institute Press.

Schiffman, M. (1967). *Self therapy: Techniques for personal growth*. Menlo Park, CA: Self Therapy Press.

Scott, G. T. (1976). Bioenergetics: Theory and Practice. Unpublished ms.

Spitz, R. (1965). *The first year of life*. New York: International Universities Press.

Winnicott, D. W. (1953). Transitional objects and transitional phenomena. *The International Journal of Psychoanalysis, 34*, 89–97.

Winnicott, D. W. (1965). *Maturational processes and the facilitating environment*. New York: International Universities Press.

INDEX

303